The provocative notion of a contemporary cross-cultural exchange within the medium of theatre is here imposed upon a dozen contemporary Anglo–American dramatists: Alan Ayckbourn and Neil Simon, Edward Bond and Sam Shepard, David Mamet and Harold Pinter, Caryl Churchill and Maria Irene Fornes, David Hare and David Rabe, Christopher Hampton and Richard Nelson. In each pairing, Ruby Cohn unites a British with an American playwright, exploring similarities both apparent and embedded – similarities that serve as a springboard for the exposure of a more profound, culturally based difference.

Cohn brings a critical eye of unusual versatility and experience to the reading of these paired playwrights. In Pinter and Mamet, for example, she notes the shared sense of linguistic play. In the plays of Bond and Shepard, on the other hand, she explores the plight of the artist in society; in those of Simon and Ayckbourn, the comic exposition of middle-class mores. Without engaging in cultural reductivism or misleading stereotypes, Cohn demonstrates how such themes lend themselves to differing interpretations in Great Britain and in the United States. A certain transatlantic double focus thus illuminates both the composition and the interpretation of dramatic works in an increasingly globally minded age.

Anglo–American Interplay
in Recent Drama

Dr. Ruby Cohn.

Anglo–American Interplay in Recent Drama

RUBY COHN

*Professor Emerita,
University of California, Davis*

CAMBRIDGE
UNIVERSITY PRESS

Published by the Press Syndicate of the University of Cambridge
The Pitt Building, Trumpington Street, Cambridge CB2 1RP
40 West 20th Street, New York, NY 10011-4211, USA
10 Stamford Road, Oakleigh, Melbourne 3166, Australia

First published 1995

Printed in the United States of America

Library of Congress Cataloging-in-Publication Data
Cohn, Ruby, 1922–
Anglo–American interplay in recent drama / Ruby Cohn
p. cm.
ISBN 0-521-47267-9
1. English drama – 20th century – History and criticism.
2. American drama – 20th century – History and criticism.
3. English drama – American influences.
4. American drama – English influences. I. Title
PR736.C54   1995
822′.91409 – dc20   94–22944
CIP

A catalog record for this book is available from the British Library

ISBN 0-521-47267-9 hardback

Some of the material on David Hare, David Mamet, and Harold Pinter was first
published in the Garland volumes on these playwrights. The Bond–Shepard
chapter was written for Longman's *Forked Tongues.* I duly thank these publishers
for permission to republish my own work.

Thanks also to the deliberately anonymous artist who presented me with the
frontispiece caricature at a rehearsal at the National Theatre of Britain.

For American Bill, English Bill, and Susie

Contents

Anglo–American Interplay
in Recent Drama

Introduction

The history of drama abounds in change, exchange, and paradox, but my present concern is a segment of contemporary theatre history. Shaw's quip still has point – that Britain and America are two countries separated by a common culture – but several dramatists of these countries also *share* a common theatre culture. Unlike interpersonal characters, dramatists speak each to each through their dramas, and, unlike the mermaids of Eliot's Prufrock, I think that they also speak to me, and, I hope, to you. This book records my impression of a transatlantic dramatists' exchange through the languages of the stage, mainly but not entirely expressed in words heard. Shifting my metaphor from the ear to the eye, I scrutinize plays of several American and English dramatists who offer mutual illumination through a double focus. I should say "double focus*es*," since I discern different points of tangency within each Anglo–American pair.

The half-dozen playwright couples worried their way into my mind, in empirical response to theatre productions. Empiricism used to have right of domain in Anglophone culture, but Latinate theory is colonizing its ground. Ignoring theory, I grapple with living and lively dramatists who are skilled in the languages of the stage. Uneasy with superlatives, I do not claim that these "twins" are the most durable dramatists of our time – well, not all of them. Nor did I seek out those who are the most representative of their countries. All artists are nurtured by a specific time and place, and although I cite printed texts, I try to situate each play in the specific time and place of first performance. As background, however, I offer a few paragraphs on the historical time and place in which these modern English and American dramatists function.

1

Time first. The earliest play within the body of my book is Harold Pinter's *The Room*, written during four afternoons in 1957, as a favor to a fellow actor at a university. Although the quasi-hermetic room later became a synonym of the Pinteresque, it remained unnoticed at a time of international crisis. In that year the Soviet Union shot a satellite into space, and there was no joy in the West at this scientific feat of the cold-war enemy.

Two places of "the West": England and the United States. Following World War II the United States emerged as the strongest power on a shrinking globe. The British Empire, upon which the sun proverbially shone, had been eroded in that same war, but a decade passed before British self-esteem withered, after the misguided invasion of Suez in 1956. A headline screamed: "EDEN GETS TOUGH. SAYS 'HANDS OFF OUR CANAL'. IT'S *GREAT* BRITAIN AGAIN!" (Quoted in Maschler, *Declaration*, p. 156). Such boasts had to be swallowed when Britain (and a token French force) was ignominiously forced to withdraw. Moreover, the cold-war enemies collaborated toward the final humiliating armistice. A superseded Winston Churchill wrote in vain to President Eisenhower: "I do believe with unfaltering conviction that the theme of the Anglo–American alliance is more important today than at any time since the war. . . . If [misunderstanding] be allowed to develop, the skies will darken indeed and it is the Soviet Union that will ride the storm" (Hitchens, *Blood, Class and Nostalgia*, p. 283). Churchill as a false prophet would be savagely lampooned by his countrymen Charles Wood (*Dingo*, 1967), Joe Orton (*What the Butler Saw*, 1969), and Howard Brenton (*The Churchill Play*, 1974), but the cold war of Churchill (along with his many collaborators) is nevertheless the most persistent background for the theatre of both Anglophone countries, until the implosion of the Soviet Union in 1991.

Since the cold war lasted nearly half a century, both Western countries became inured to its skirmishes, and each nation gnawed at its own problems, upon which I touch with a few dates. The year 1958 marked the birth of a British movement for nuclear disarmament, in which women assumed leadership. In the United States during the 1960s the Civil Rights movement magnetized young idealists, with blacks assuming political leadership for the first time since Reconstruction. American involvement in Vietnam expanded in 1964, and student protests flared in 1968, more inflammatory in the bellicose United States than in a shrunken Britain. By the end of the 1970s, both nations retreated into parallel conservatisms. Margaret Thatcher's first term dates from 1979, and Ronald Reagan was elected president in 1980; four years later, each of them was reelected. More than ever before, such news was viewed instantaneously in the television culture of both countries.

For the most part the theatre reflected such events slowly, obliquely, or not at all. In England David Mercer is virtually alone to frame several plays in an explicit cold-war context, but historic events do figure in other dramatic fictions. The Suez debacle of 1956 frames John Osborne's *The Entertainer* (1957), as it does Christopher Hampton's *White Chameleon* (1991). The space rivalry of the Soviet Union and the United States contributes to Tom Stoppard's moon plays *M is for Moon among Other Things* (1964) and *Jumpers* (1972). Three decades of the cold war are traced in David Edgar's *May Days* (1983). Lanford Wilson's *Angels Fall* (1982), Caryl Churchill's *Serious Money* (1987), and Tony Kushner's *Angels in America* (1991) react to their countries' conservatism in radically different theatrical languages. None of these plays figures in my study, but the frequent chronological gap between event and play illustrates the political obliquity of formal theatre. What was clear in the text, subtext, and context of drama was the spoilage of the American dream, paralleled across the Atlantic by the spoilage of British national pride.

From this scattershot of historical dates, I turn to the stages of both countries, alike in spanning formal theatres as well as churches and attics. In the first half of the twentieth century theatre history and history of drama were virtually synonymous, but they separated in the second half-century. A history of twentieth-century British drama characterizes it as "a rational drama dealing with social issues" (Innes, *Modern British Drama*, p. 2), and, not dissimilarly, a history of twentieth-century American drama characterizes it as "realistic contemporary middle-class domestic melodrama" (Berkowitz, *American Drama*, p. 3). These descriptions are more accurate before midcentury than after, but even in the earlier period new forms materialized, from the music hall made literate (Auden and Isherwood) to religious verse drama (Eliot and his disciples). In the United States, too, there were dramatic escapes from the middle-class living room; current problems were raised in the Living Newspaper, and into domestic melodrama intruded factory workers, sharecroppers, and immigrants, who were unfamiliar to middle-class audiences.

Of individual Anglophone playwrights before midcentury, only Shaw and O'Neill could tower with such earlier European giants as Ibsen, Strindberg, Chekhov, or Pirandello. Although Shaw died in 1950 and O'Neill in 1953, their legacies were felt for decades afterward. Both transplanted Irishmen essayed several dramatic styles over their long careers, but it is their divergently realistic plays that garnered the largest audiences. Of polar temperaments, Shaw is a writer of social comedy, O'Neill of mythic tragedy. Perhaps corollary to the generic cleavage, Shaw's dramas are embedded in the class-based British society of his time, even when the setting is nominally ancient Egypt or Rome. O'Neill's dramas traverse a century of American history, and however conscientiously he seeks social differentiation in a play like *The Iceman Cometh*, he paints lonely individuals who interact painfully across chasms deeper than class. In plumbing the stage for tragedy Miller, Williams, Albee, and Shepard are all his sons. In contrast, Shaw's English sons – and daughters – wield a deft wit in his tradition of socially critical comedy; the plays of Bond, Brenton, Frayn, Gray, Hare, Churchill, Gems, and even Pinter and Stoppard, thrust and parry with sharp phrases in a socially nuanced world.

A few dates reveal startling transatlantic theatre juxtapositions that did not startle at the time. The year 1956 is usually cited as the birthdate of contemporary British drama, because of the opening of John Osborne's *Look Back in Anger* at the newly refurbished Royal Court Theatre. That same year O'Neill's *Long Day's Journey into Night* opened in New York, not only bringing posthumous acclaim to its author, but astonishing audiences with a sympathetic portrait of a drug addict. Hindsight reveals that O'Neill is less traditional than Osborne, not only in his muted climaxes, but also in the existential isolation of his tortured, self-deluding characters. Jimmy Porter's mellifluous tirades prove to be less eloquent than the hesitant stammering of Edmund Tyrone.

In 1964, with the Broadway opening of *Hughie*, O'Neill emerged as a prophetic absurdist, while Off-Off Broadway 20-year-old Sam Shepard stomped onto a church stage with his mythoabsurdist *Cowboys*. In London that year Pinter was inhabitually silent, but mannered comedy was spawned afresh by Joe Orton's *Entertaining Mr. Sloane*, conceived in unlimited lust. Not only were sexual frontiers penetrated in that year but so were linguistic boundaries with the invented Scots of John Arden's *Armstrong's Last Goodnight*. Peter Shaffer's *Royal Hunt of the Sun* emblazoned resplendent design in Michael Annals's kaleidoscope of colors on the Chichester Theatre's stage. With the loss of empire, Britain was also losing her decorous theatrical insularity.

Critical histories exist of the past century of British and American drama respectively, and I do not propose to blend them. What I do wish to stress is that the playwrights of both countries are dedicated to what has become a minority art – the theatre – and that theatre has often turned against drama during this period. Actor-managers of both countries had virtually disappeared by midcentury, but they were replaced by dictatorial directors with distinctive signatures. Elia Kazan worked with (and sometimes against) new playwrights in New York, and John Barton, Peter Brook, or Peter Hall subdued Shakespeare in Stratford. More in the United States than in England, actors' physical feats took precedence over vocal control. Commercial temptation – film and television – on the one hand, and antiverbal, site-specific experimentation on the other siphoned practitioners away from drama in both countries. By the end of the twentieth century, it takes an act of aesthetic courage to commit to the palpable presence of actors projecting through the several languages of theatre, especially speech. (I vividly recall a Grotowski-trained actor pleading with him: "I want to pronounce words, words, words!")

Glancing back at this date-marked zigzag through theatre history on each side of the Atlantic, I perceive that I haven't mentioned what I cannot quite document – contrasting histrionic expectations. Most germane to this study is England's *literary* bent versus the American "Method." On the face of it, there would seem to be no obstacle to improvising in a literary context, or to cloaking a script in seeming spontaneity. In theatrical fact, however, the inward-probing actor was invariably contrasted with the technical actor: say, Marlon Brando or Geraldine Page versus Laurence Olivier or Maggie Smith. Again, I cannot document it, but I think that the Method orientation of personal psychology helped create a climate of experimental indulgence for physicalizations, gallery performances, and happenings of the 1960s and 1970s. In contrast, even salacious English subjects were garbed in elegant phrases, usually heard in formal theatres.

Then there is the fact of geography: Willy-nilly, Britain is located in Europe. Even in the aeronautical age of swift flights, theatre travel is cumbersome, what with sets, properties, costumes, and the demands of different theatre spaces. Given the geographical proximity, even inexpensive European productions arrived sooner in London than in New York: Peter Hall's domestic *Godot* played in London in 1955, but only in 1958 did Herbert Blau's San Francisco *Godot* arrive in New York; absurdist seepage into mainstream theatre was thus delayed. The impact of Brecht was not only earlier but more direct in Britain than in the United States; epic staging followed almost immediately upon the 1956 visit to London of the Berliner Ensemble. Quasi-Brechtian dramaturgy – Bolt, Shaffer, Arden, even Bond – took a little longer. (Christopher Hampton converted Brecht into a character in *Tales from Hollywood* in 1983.) Brecht himself spent much of World War II in Santa Monica, California, but his teachings were fragmented in the United States: His social commitment was espoused by the Living Theatre, his exploitation of popular arts by the Bread and Puppet Company, his sociocritical approach to acting by the Open Theatre, and his narrative performance by the Mabou Mines.

To this day contemporary British drama will occasionally risk a socioepic sweep, whereas American drama is comfortably confined in the stage living room; that thumbnail contrast pits sociological versus psychological theatre. But however inventively deployed, the stages of both countries continue to harbor individuals; and however hemmed in by flats, the stages of both countries are set in a global context. Nationalistic critics of both countries tend to plead the virtues of home-grown products as against transoceanic rivals.[1] Such contests are, however, fomented by news-greedy journalists, and not by audiences who revel in the infinite riches of the several little rooms of theatre. Dramas speed across the Atlantic in both directions. In Britain some American classics have acquired a new resonance, for example, Keith Hacks's comic inflection of O'Neill's *Strange Interlude* and Michael Blakemore's racial inflection of Miller's *After the Fall*. In regional American theatres rather than on Broadway, English classics can be meaningfully naturalized, as in the case of Tony Taccone's Bay Area *Volpone* and Carey Perloff's New York Pinter. Unspeakable Shakespeare Festivals spot the American landscape, even more markedly than in Britain.

6

My turf is new drama. An embattled new drama achieves production over the opposition of safe classics, on the one hand, and
of antiverbal experiments, on the other. Having enjoyed new drama in each country for some forty years, I at long last have arrived
at a half-dozen Anglo–American juxtapositions that seem to me,
quite frankly, fascinating. In spite of the somewhat different social
forces in each nation; in spite of the wide differences in histrionic expectation, to which I earlier alluded; in spite of the different
theatre heritage of each country; I find astonishingly comparable
points and plays.

In my own reading I am irritated by introductions that summarize the still unread book, so it would ill behoove me to do so, but
I nevertheless hazard a few generalizations about the following
pages. My dozen dramatists have mastered the several languages
of the stage to different degrees, whether it be plot and character
presentation through dialogue, molding of stage space with or
without sets, but obligatorily with lights, a panoply of nonverbal
sounds, and a kaleidoscope of stage properties. Ayckbourn's ma-
nipulations of stage space, Fornes's[2] transformations of stage characters, Shepard's several songs, and Bond's scenes of split focus are
some of the inventive strategies I consider, but I recognize that I
am partial to fresh air rising from what we still call the *English*
language. At a time of critical jargon, of pious multiculturalism, of
lofty theories, I stand my ground on the playwrights' concrete de-
motic language sounded in the voices of trained actors. I hope that
my account of the exchange between English and American playwrights will incidentally communicate my own pleasure in the
seeing, reading, and writing about these plays.

I do not approach the dramatists systematically or mechanically.
In the case of Neil Simon and Alan Ayckbourn I try to present the
stage worlds that emerge from their respective stage skills. In the
less evident comparison of Edward Bond and Sam Shepard I confine myself to a single facet of their rich dramaturgy: the stage artist
and how he or she reflects the playwright's art. Stage speech is
anatomized in the plays of Harold Pinter and David Mamet. Theatrical forms of instruction are scrutinized in the plays of María
Irene Fornes and Caryl Churchill, whereas I listen closely to the
speech of women *characters* in the plays of David Rabe and David
Hare. I back off for a larger view of structure and syntax in the
stage speech of the drama of Christopher Hampton and Richard

Nelson. Through the points of tangency runs the thread of stage languages, especially speech.

Tough critic that I am, it may not be apparent that, in one way and often in more than one, I admire all twelve playwrights, so I hereby state it categorically.

Funny money in New York and Pendon
Neil Simon and Alan Ayckbourn

The American Neil Simon and the Englishman Alan Ayckbourn are magnets to the theatre in an age of mass media. Both playwrights are energetically productive, what with Simon's twenty-seven plays and Ayckbourn's thirty-nine, although the numbers may be mounting as I write. Both men are devoted to comedy, but they have at times voiced a yearning for a Chekhovian blend of the comic and the tragic. Ayckbourn calls his plays "black farce" (Innes, *Modern British Drama*, p. 317). Black or white, their plays have been translated into many languages, yet each playwright has had only limited appeal in the country of the other. Grounded in the middle-class mores of their respective countries – Simon urban and Ayckbourn suburban – the two playwrights are routinely paired, almost as though they were a comedy team, but no one has lingered over their likenesses as they craftily delineate family strains.[1]

Ayckbourn himself distinguished half-humorously between them: "If you dropped a play of [Simon's] in the street and the pages fell out in any old order, you'd still be laughing as you picked them up. If you dropped a play of mine, too bad. As a writer, he's highly verbal whereas I'm situational" (Kalson, *Laughter in the Dark*, p. 44). My quotation from Simon is more general, differentiating two cultures rather than two writers: "American humor is rooted in people's neuroses, while English humor is more slapstick" ("Make 'em Laugh," p. 14). There is some truth in both insights, each playwright surreptitiously defending his own practice. However, I am going to argue that the two dramatists create similar worlds, through quite different manipulation of the languages of the stage – verbal or situational, slapstick or neurotic.

9

I therefore disagree with the redoubtable British critic, Michael Billington, who has taken exception to coupling Simon and Ayckbourn: "The two dramatists have little in common other than that they write deceptively serious comedies, make a lot of money and get their work performed in their own theatres" (*Alan Ayckbourn*, pp. 50–1). I suppose it is true that they both "make a lot of money," but Simon has never had his own theatre, even though a Broadway theatre has been named for him. No theatre bears Ayckbourn's name, which does, however, grace a New York alley. More important, Ayckbourn has since 1976 been the artistic director of, and a very active director in, the Stephen Joseph Theatre at Scarborough, a resort town on England's northeast coast. Simon has opened some two dozen plays outside of New York before displaying them on Broadway, and this is comparable to Ayckbourn's Scarborough premieres before he ventures into London's West End, usually with a different cast. Since such "out-of-town" tryouts, and subsequent revision, account in part for their "lot of money," it is a salient similarity between the two writers, but it neglects the specifics of the plays themselves.

For that, we may begin with Billington's puzzling genre designation – "deceptively serious comedies." What the British critic probably means by his condensed phrase is drama with serious purpose beneath a deceptively comic surface. Since neither Simon nor Ayckbourn is monolithically farcical in the manner of English Ben Travers (to whom Ayckbourn dedicated his *Taking Steps*), or American Kaufman and Hart, some degree of seriousness may be discerned within the comic canon of each of these writers. By and very large, one might say that both dramatists have gradually groped their way through comic structures toward serious themes. In Ayckbourn's words: "Let's see how clever we can be at saying unpalatable things in a palatable manner" (Billington, *Alan Ayckbourn*, p. 165). What both playwrights *are* clever at is offering tasty lines to actors; those of Simon are snappy, whereas Ayckbourn's people tend to bumble.

After a quick tour through their respective careers, I will pair a few of their plays. Before molting into a dramatist, Neil Simon (b. 1927) wrote scripts for comic personalities on radio and television – Sid Caesar, Phil Foster, Jackie Gleason, Jerry Lester, Garry Moore, Phil Silvers. Alan Ayckbourn (b. 1939) came to drama by way of stage management and then acting in the theatre.[2] Their plays display the residue of this training. From *Come Blow Your Horn* (1961) to *Laughter on the 23rd Floor* (1993) Simon is king of the one-line quip, which he dispenses prodigally among his characters. In Simon's first published play, for example, two brothers bicker, and their sallies bounce indiscriminately off either one; one brother complains, "I thought we were splitting everything fifty-fifty," and the other brother retorts: "We were until you got all the fifties."

In contrast, a *mute* protagonist energizes Ayckbourn's first published play (and the first of many that he himself directed). His eponymous Mr. Whatnot (1963) leaps, trips, falls, drives an automobile, climbs up a piano, treads on its keyboard, plays cricket with a tennis racket, bounces on a bed, and devours a banquet while concealed beneath a table. A frantic stage manager has to accompany these acrobatics with taped sounds. Ayckbourn's mentor Stephen Joseph summarizes the farcical mayhem: "Real properties, phoney properties and mime properties all enriched the scene, ranging from a genuine steering wheel to represent a car, to an entirely imagined piano that was played furiously" (*Theatre in the Round*, p. 57).

It is tempting to dive into Ayckbourn's various properties and Simon's several sallies, but that would contrast apples and oranges, whereas the two playwrights *are* comparable in their dramatic situations, stemming from Greek New Comedy. In that genre the plot turns on the elimination of an obstacle that separates a nubile woman from her ardent young suitor. Simon and Ayckbourn may age the problematic couple, and by the end of their comedies the obstacle might still cast its shadow, but the two playwrights nevertheless address audiences who possess some residual nostalgia for the New Comedy form. Contemporary content often inflects that form in Simon's plays, but its residue may disappear in Ayckbourn's most serious plays.

As in sitcoms of the media, the plays of both Ayckbourn and Simon prowl around endemic predicaments – mismatched couples, disjointed generations, dissimilar siblings, bad neighbors, frail friends, and hilariously hostile modern environments. Both Simon and Ayckbourn skewer their characters so that they wriggle helplessly – and laughably – often within the family. Simon's unprepossessing characters yearn to be a little bigger than they are, or to reach a little further than they can, within low and limited horizons. Most of Ayckbourn's people are resigned to the traditional British suburban milieu, which repays them ungratefully. The plays of both writers tend to ignore wider issues; not only laws, wars, and poverty, but also racial and religious conflicts, drug abuse, energy depletion, global crises; in short, the world at large. Within their dramas, neither writer is irreparably addicted to the conventional happy ending, but Ayckbourn's finales are increasingly problematic, whereas Simon usually offers his characters an escape route, if only to another temporary clearing in the urban jungle – a quip on their parched lips.

Many Simon plays of the 1960s and 1970s string jokes on a thin thread of plot, but in his main work of the 1980s he filters jokes through time-bound plays that draw upon his own life – *Brighton Beach Memoirs* (1982), *Biloxi Blues* (1985), and *Broadway Bound* (1986). Simon's alter ego, a would-be writer named Eugene Morris Jerome, is 15 years old in 1937, when war clouds threaten Europe (and especially European Jews) while the Jewish-American Jerome family is mired in the economic Depression. *Biloxi Blues* departs from Simon's native New York to Biloxi, Mississippi, during World War II, where Gene undergoes military training, sexual initiation, and romantic yearning. *Broadway Bound* remains a promise in 1949, the year of the third play, when the senior Jeromes separate, but their two sons start a career as radio gag writers. Paradoxically named for the tragic O'Neill, Simon's comedic Eugene is at once the protagonist and the memorialist of his trilogy, in the manner of Tennessee Williams's Tom of *The Glass Menagerie*. Simon's more recent *Jake's Women* (1990)[3] is even more ambitious in its model; like Arthur Miller in *Death of a Salesman*, Simon sets scenes in the mind of his protagonist.

Ayckbourn has been candid about his own debts – to Oscar Wilde for misprision, to Ben Travers for manic farce, to Noël Coward for an occasional scene, to Harold Pinter for a fine-tuned lexicon (Kalson, *Laughter in the Dark,* passim). He shrugged these mentors off by the 1970s, when he confounded audience expectation by a cunning blend of onstage neurosis, offstage action, and the most blatant manipulation of settings ever seen on the English (or any other) stage. His serious notes – especially in the whimper of his women characters – are sounded a decade earlier than those of Simon. Coincidentally, too, it is a trilogy, *The Norman Conquests* (1973), that established Ayckbourn as a dramatist of serious purpose, however he would mock that academic phrase. Unlike the plays of Simon's trilogy, which advance chronologically, those of Ayckbourn occur simultaneously, in a dizzying round of on-stage and offstage action. Then, flaunting his control over plot mechanisms, Ayckbourn produced alternative endings for *Sisterly Feelings* (1978) and sixteen variants for four scenes in *Intimate Exchanges* (1982), which was filmed by Alain Resnais as *Smoking and No Smoking*. A few years later *A Small Family Business* (1987) and *The Revengers' Comedies* (1989) virtually writhe through their convoluted plots.

Simon writes as though the subplot had not been invented, but he displays concern for character. He told Edythe McGovern: "The playwright has obligations to fulfill, such as exposition and character building" (*Neil Simon*, p. 4). Subscribing to the worth of the traditional nuclear family, Simon's characters, particularly his married characters, are sometimes frustrated by their tradition. As his policeman remarks in *The Odd Couple*: "Twelve years doesn't mean you're a *happy* couple. It just means you're a *long* couple." Wittily complaining, Simon's families tend to endure, although the balance of power may shift.

Ayckbourn is an insidious subverter of family harmony, and more and more he undermines the festive final coupling of comedy. Even in the happy ending of *Relatively Speaking* "a disastrous marriage" is prophesied, especially since we never learn whose slippers have wandered into Ginny's bedroom. A modicum of happiness results from *uncouplings* in *Time and Time Again, The Norman Conquests, Taking Steps, Time of My Life*. It is in Ayckbourn's cruelest plays that marriage endures – *Absurd Person Singular, Absent Friends, Just Between Ourselves, Joking Apart, Season's Greetings, Woman in Mind, A Small Family Business*. In many of these plays a dense but well-meaning husband can drive a wife to quite literal distraction.

Although Ayckbourn's ingenious plots have been admired more than Simon's conventional minitriumphs over mini-obstacles, it is for their characters that both playwrights have reaped praise – and particularly for their sympathy with women. Simon and Ayckbourn are similar in creating women whose ideal of happiness, or even of mental stability, rests upon a man. Simon's Jennie Malone of *Chapter Two* exults: "I'm wonderful! I'm nuts about me!" But in the next breath she nervously asks her recalcitrant husband: "If you don't call me, can I call you?" Almost always Simon allows one or the other of his romantic leads to "call."

Ayckbourn's sympathy for women grows slowly. Eva's suicide attempts in *Absurd Person Singular* (1973) – gas, stabbing, defenestration, electrocution, hanging, and simple pills – are fodder for Ayckbourn's farce, but farce turns dark with the catatonic wife Vera in *Just Between Ourselves* (1977), and with the finally insane wife Susan in *Woman in Mind* (1985). Along the way Ayckbourn paints somewhat sympathetic portraits of Norman's three conquests, of two sisters and their unappreciated sister-in-law in *Sisterly Feelings*, and of wife, woman employee, and especially of female robots in *Henceforward*.

Both playwrights thrust farcically against women who are no longer erotically viable. Simon peoples his sidelines with avatars of the Jewish mother of gagdom. Mrs. Baker of *Come Blow Your Horn* anticipates her husband's blame: "He'll say 'Because of you my sister Gussie has two grandchildren and all I've got is a *bum* and a *letter*.'" Ethel Banks of *Barefoot in the Park* interferes in her daughter's marriage: "I worry about you two." Mrs. Hubley of *Plaza Suite* cannot admit that her daughter cringes at resembling her. Although the Jewish mother of Simon's autobiographical trilogy loses her husband, the last line accommodates her to a running gag: "After all, she did once dance with George Raft."

Ayckbourn's English casts lack the ethnic diversity of a Jewish mother, but he exposes the poison beneath the proprieties of son-adoring mothers – *Just Between Ourselves, Woman in Mind, Bedroom Farce, Time of My Life* – or busybody sisters – *Time and Time Again, The Norman Conquests, Sisterly Feelings, Taking Steps, Season's Greetings, Woman in Mind, A Small Family Business, The Revengers' Comedies*. Tedious as it is to read a series of titles, their plenitude testifies to the stereotype that nurtures farce.

For all their vaunted sympathy with women, both playwrights give more scope to men. Simon's protagonists are usually male, whether it be the romantic lead, who always *leads*, or the older frustrated comic. Simon's older men are either puritanical or philandering; Mr. Baker of *Come Blow Your Horn* imposes monogamy on his sons, but aging Barney Cashman of *The Last of the Red Hot Lovers* grasps forlornly at illicit sex. No one in Simon's plays is evil, and his philanderers inevitably reform. Alan Baker of *Come Blow Your Horn* turns into a duplicate of his monogamous father. Victor Velasco of *Barefoot in the Park* finally accepts the sexual and digestive limits of his age. Barney Cashman, the last of the red hot lovers, makes his final assignation with his wife. Only Lou Tanner of *The Gingerbread Lady* remains unregenerately profligate, and even he is vulnerable and insecure: "Together, Evy, we don't add up to one strong person."

Not until Simon's fourth play did he hit upon the title *The Odd Couple* (1965), but it is apposite also to plays written earlier and later. This is hardly surprising, since the technique of a comically contrasting pair is at least as old as Plautus, with his Menachmus brothers, and that device was undoubtedly reinforced by the two-brother structure of Simon's own family. In Simon's first play, *Come Blow Your Horn* (1961), two brothers change and exchange their temperaments, and two dissimilar brothers recur in *The Prisoner of Second Avenue, Chapter Two*, the autobiographical trilogy, and *Lost in Yonkers*.

Traditional dramatic conflict is reduced by Simon to contrasting personalities. In *Barefoot in the Park* (1963) Paul, a conservative attorney, is newly married to Corie, who enjoys walking barefoot in the park, like a free-spirited Bohemian. *The Odd Couple* are middle-aged men who are rejected by their respective wives and who cannot dovetail in a common household.[3] *Last of the Red Hot Lovers* (1969) returns to compromise in marriage, after Barney Cashman has figured in odd couples with each of the three women he vainly tries to seduce. *The Sunshine Boys* (1972) pairs mutually loathing comedians. Although only one victim is designated by the title *The Prisoner of Second Avenue* (1972), a nagging married couple is trapped in its expensive cell, and they alternate in bemoaning its inconveniences. Even in the sunshine couples storm at one another through the four scenes of *California Suite*. Throughout his work Simon infects his rival siblings, odd couples, or longtime friend/enemies with small or large neuroses, which he sees as the basis of American humor.

Given the box-office success of the two prolific playwrights, it is somewhat ironic that they are rarely sympathetic to successful males. Simon pokes fun at the wax-fruiterer Mr. Baker, the adulterous executive Sam Nash, the vain movie star Jesse Kiplinger, the self-pitying writer George Schneider. Ayckbourn's successful men – philandering Phillip of *Relatively Speaking*, benighted Frank Foster of *How the Other Half Loves*, furtive Graham of

Time and Time Again, and pompous Keith of *Way Upstream* – are merely foolish, but Sidney Hopcraft of *Absurd Person Singular* grows vicious as he slithers up the socioeconomic ladder. Gerry Stratton of *Time of My Life* is ruthless against business associates and competitors, but dictatorial Vince of *Way Upstream* and criminal Vic Parks of *Man of the Moment* are melodramatic villains. When smug Paul's distraught wife pours cream on his head in *Absent Friends,* Ayckbourn turns farce against his successful businessman. Rarely does Ayckbourn permit sympathy for this stereotype of the hard-driving male; the vulnerable solicitor husband of *Sisterly Feelings* is exceptional.

Unlike his successful males, Ayckbourn's bungling husbands drive their wives to madness, but still other ineffectual wimps are meant to be lovable.[4] Len of *Time and Time Again* consoles his rival: "We just seem to have mislaid the trophy," where the trophy is the girl, who rejects both suitors. Len sets the pattern for Norman of the failed conquests and for the briefly approved Guy of *A Chorus of Disapproval.* Equally pleasant are a few Ayckbourn clodhoppers who do get their girls – Stafford of *Sisterly Feelings,* Tristram of *Taking Steps,* and Douglas of *The Revengers' Comedies.* Beneath cosmetic variants stumbles the stereotype of the clumsy male wooer. Despite Ayckbourn's designation of himself as situational and Simon as verbal, both playwrights exploit familiar situations, and both playwrights rely on gender and family stereotypes within those situations.

Even before we make the acquaintance of their comparable characters, we can distinguish Simon and Ayckbourn by their approaches to stage space and fictional time. Simon is a voluntary prisoner not of Second Avenue alone, but of many a Manhattan realistic living room. Granted that limitation, however, Simon furnishes his rooms with the inconveniences that elicit laughter – from the bare attic of *Barefoot in the Park* to the messy poker room of *The Odd Couple;* from the neat pied-à-terre of *The Last of the Red Hot Lovers* to the burglary residue of *The Prisoner of Second Avenue. The Sunshine Boys* presents a miniscule Broadway apartment that baffles its ancient occupant. *Chapter Two* (1978) is slightly more daring in its simultaneous staging of two dissimilar living rooms, on the East and West sides of Manhattan. East Side, West Side, all around the town, Simon's stage rooms are burdened with malfunctioning doorbells, telephones, and sundry appliances, which nevertheless function unerringly in farce.

Although Ayckbourn's props are equally familiar, his sets are far more various. His early *Mr. Whatnot* imposes cinematic scenes upon the theatre – games, chases, musicals, weddings, dinners, and a deathbed – all snuffed out by a flick of a light switch. Nearly a decade later, Ayckbourn in *How the Other Half Loves* stages *"two [living] rooms contained and overlapping in the same area,"* the one tasteful and orderly and the other trendy but sloppy. This is not mere contrast, as in Simon's *Chapter Two*, but actual overlap; the couch has cushions for each décor, and the characters are sometimes close enough to touch while being separated by invisible walls. At a dinner party a married couple are guests in two homes simultaneously; they swivel back and forth on the split set, at accelerating pace. Their dialogue resonates hilariously through the artifice of the stage.

One can hear the stage manager (albeit with tongue in cheek) when Ayckbourn affirms: *"Time and Time Again* I principally remember as the play in which I used water for the first time on stage"* (Page, *File on Ayckbourn*, p. 25). The use is innocuous enough – *"a murky pond, over which presides a battered stone gnome,"* who is the favorite companion of the feckless protagonist. This tiny pond is a (nearly) dry run for Ayckbourn's more ambitious use of stage water – in *Way Upstream* and *Man of the Moment*. The very title of the former points to water, specifically (and somewhat pretentiously) the River Orb, up which a four-berth cabin cruiser sails – when it is not run aground. (At the National Theatre in London, this aqueous set delayed the play's opening by six weeks.) Ayckbourn's stage managers are not alone in fearing water, since it also threatens his characters in the form of rain in *Sisterly Feelings* and a swimming pool in *Man of the Moment*. *The Revengers' Comedies* open and close on London's Albert Bridge; although we cannot see the Thames below, we do hear the final suicidal splash of the revenger – sound effects in Ayckbourn's repertory of stage languages.

Water is a stage manager's nightmare, but Ayckbourn's land is also fraught with peril in his "stagescapes" (Watson's apt word, *Conversations with Ayckbourn*, p. 88). *Absurd Person Singular* dramatizes distress in three different kitchens on three different

Christmases, and *Bedroom Farce* erupts in three simultaneously visible bedrooms. *Season's Greetings* are exchanged and subverted in five different acting areas in a single comfortable, miserable household, and *The Norman Conquests* anatomizes a family in three areas of the home of their invisible mother. *Sisterly Feelings* begins on Pendon Common after a funeral, and ends with a wedding in the same bucolic setting. *Woman in Mind* opens a small suburban garden into an estate imagined in madness. *Taking Steps* virtually stages an architect's blueprint, as the characters huff and puff on stage-level staircases. *A Small Family Business*, a business of ready-made furniture, sports *"various areas [that] will serve as rooms in the different houses of the family,"* who live with identical furniture. *Henceforward* inhabits a science-fiction nightmare somewhere on London's Northern Line, replete with videophone and sophisticated audio equipment. *The Revengers' Comedies* zig-zag swiftly and frequently between a London skyscraper and pastoral Dorchester, but the double play begins and ends with imperturbable symmetry on the Albert Bridge as a suicide site. For theatre cognoscenti Ayckbourn's versatile sets offer the pleasure of new configurations in old stage space, and those sets have proved pliable to transfer from the circular stage of Scarborough to rectangular stages in London.

Simon conveys the atmosphere of greater New York mainly through dialogue, and, comparably, Ayckbourn treats his faithful audiences to sporadic verbal references to an imaginary village, Pendon, that rhymes (roughly) with London, but puns on "penned on."[5] Pendon first emerges in *Relatively Speaking* (1965), since the heroine's lover and his wife live in Willows, Lower Pendon, Bucks. Ayckbourn's village acquires a cricket team, the East Pendon Occasionals, in *Time and Time Again* (1971). In *Ten Times Table* (1977) a pageant honors the Pendon Twelve, agricultural laborers who were massacred two centuries ago. *Sisterly Feelings* (1979) bristle on Pendon Common in Berkshire, and the cabin cruiser of *Way Upstream* (1981) passes under Pendon Bridge. Pendon then skips to Wales, where Gay's *Beggar's Opera* is rehearsed by the Pendon Amateur Light Opera Society in *A Chorus of Disapproval* (1984). (The National Theatre Program for this last play also lists the Pendon Police Auxiliary Silver Band, the Pendon Magic Society, the Pendon Amateur Dramatic Society, and the Pendon Women's Institute – none receiving financial assistance from the

Arts Council of Great Britain.) To Ayckbourn's surprise, he recently learned of the existence of an actual model village of Pendon
(Dukore, *Alan Ayckbourn,* p. 7).

Like New York and Pendon, time is conveyed verbally by both
playwrights. The fictional duration of the American's plays may
vary from the actual playing time of his brief scenes in his two
*Suite*s to the twelve-year span of the three plays of his trilogy.[6] In
contrast, Alan Ayckbourn plays a diapason of stage times as he in-
ventories the foibles and follies of contemporary middle-class Britain.[7] In the program note to his *Time of My Life* Ayckbourn registers his awareness of time as a dramatic tool: "I am hardly the first
dramatist to be fascinated by time. Time, I mean, as an aid to dramatic story telling. . . . For I do suspect that the choice of time scale
in a dramatic structure is often one of the most important basic
decisions a dramatist needs to make about their [*sic*] play." Three
Ayckbourn plays even contain the word "time" in the title. *Time
and Time Again* (1971) unfolds a love story that opens in spring
and closes in autumn (whereas Simon's love story in *Chapter Two*
opens in February and closes more traditionally in spring). Ayckbourn's *Ten Times Table* (1977) digs at *repetitious* committee meet-
ings but calls no attention to the passing of several weeks. *Time of
My Life* (1992) deals more inventively with time. The first person
possessive pronoun hints at a cliché of joy, as in: "I had the time of
my life." No one utters this phrase in a play that moves backward
and forward from a central event, a woman's birthday dinner in a
restaurant.

Ayckbourn's favorite time period is the weekend, with its lei-
sure for parties and picnics – *Taking Steps* (1979), *Season's Greetings* (1980), *Woman in Mind* (1985). As already mentioned, the
long weekend of *How the Other Half Loves* (1971) contains two
simultaneous dinner parties putatively occurring on *successive*
nights. Three plays happen simultaneously during a weekend in
The Norman Conquests (1973), but they are staged sequentially.
Several weekends fill *Sisterly Feelings* (1978), with alternative plots
triggered by the sisters of the title. However, Ayckbourn is not wed-
ded to the weekend; he can shrink stage time to actual time in *Absent Friends* (1974), and he can expand to a long night's series of
journeys in *Bedroom Farce* (1975). As early as *Relatively Speaking*
(1965) Ayckbourn confined his action to a few hours in a single
day, and he repeats that time limit in *Man of the Moment* (1988),

but the action of the latter insistently recalls a minute of armed robbery seventeen years earlier. Three successive Christmases sour through *Absurd Person Singular* (1972), and an avalanche of birthdays descends on the calendar year of *Just Between Ourselves* (1976). *Joking Apart* (1978) encompasses Ayckbourn's longest time lapse – twelve years. The allegorical *Way Upstream* (1981) exploits the biblical resonance of seven days, whereas *A Small Family Business* (1987) simply lasts "one autumn week." *A Chorus of Disapproval* (1984) is vague about the period "between the first rehearsal and first performance of an amateur production," which is staged as a flashback. The vagueness is more menacing for the few days "sometime quite soon" of the futuristic *Henceforward* (1987). *The Revengers' Comedies* (1989) are particularly piquant as to time, for the forty-two scenes of the two comedies are meticulously clocked from the opening midnight to the closing midnight, but the intervening duration is deliberately vague – "six months ago – seven months – I don't know." The character may not know, but Ayckbourn has the knowledge of a metronome as he clocks his ingenious plots.

Ayckbourn has usurped more of my space than Simon in the last few pages because he is a more inventive stage linguist. Although both craftsmen are situational *and* verbal, as well as stereotypical of character, Ayckbourn alone deploys stage space and fictional time in new configurations that enhance the comic quality, and he is fascinated by the possibilities of taped sound and a spectrum of lights. Despite these differences, it is similarly with their humor that both playwrights draw audiences. Yet Ayckbourn in 1984 claimed: "I spend most of the time now taking out the jokes not putting them in" (Page, *File on Ayckbourn*, p. 91), and although I cannot find the right quote for Simon, he has made comparable statements. Nevertheless the old burlesque phrase – "Funny is money" – accounts for their continued audience appeal.

Into variants of New Comedy plots both playwrights usher stereotypical characters who utter funny phrases – Simon's consciously, Ayckbourn's unconsciously. These phrases bounce off that old comic staple – the running gag. Simon harps on the waxed fruit of *Come Blow Your Horn*, the five flights of stairs of *Barefoot in the Park*, Oscar's genial sloppiness and Felix's maniacal neatness of *The Odd Couple*, Barney's bungled lies of *Last of the Red Hot Lovers*, the Edisons' treacherous apartment of *The Prisoner of Sec-*

ond Avenue. The alcoholic drinks of *The Gingerbread Lady* and the failing memories of *The Sunshine Boys* function thematically as well as comically.

Ayckbourn displays growing skill in enfolding running gags into his plots or characterizations: the lubricious telephone calls in proper households of *How the Other Half Loves*, the unappetizing food at the several meals of *The Norman Conquests*, John's onstage jiggling and Gordon's offstage illnesses in the mismatched marriages of *Absent Friends*, a soliloquizing wife and a split-phrased husband in *Bedroom Farce*, a temperamental garage door and an immobile automobile in *Just Between Ourselves*, Brian's interchangeable girls (played by the same actress) in *Joking Apart*, and a restaurant's interchangeable waiters (played by the same actor) in *Time of My Life* – all help accumulate funny money. In *A Small Family Business*, Ayckbourn's running gags are thematically significant – the senility of the founder of the furniture business, one son's penchant for new machines and the other's for exotic cuisine, the clothes and lovers of one son's wife and the fixation on her dog of the other son's wife; most sinister are the self-righteous claims to his honor by the gradually criminalized protagonist.

Running gags are security blankets for these two playwrights, with Simon the more verbal. Yet both playwrights also write funny dialogue for their individual characters. Simon's one-liners, often couched in Yiddish rhythms, are wittily depreciative – of the climate, the environment, the actions and reactions of the characters, and the familiar inconveniences of life in greater New York. In contrast, Ayckbourn amuses by the innocent blunders of his imperceptive characters, especially in the confusion of festive occasions, into which Michael Billington reads an important social statement: "Look at Ayckbourn's work *in toto* and you see that it is about the way we preserve a whole set of rituals – Christmas, family weekends, wedding anniversaries, birthdays, cocktail parties, monogamy even – which bear less and less relation to our actual needs" (*Alan Ayckbourn*, pp. 51–2). Yet the celebrations misfire hilariously, while the needs remain vague. By and large, Ayckbourn's comedy differs from Simon's as the stage manager differs from the TV gag writer.

Like Billington, I have commented mainly on differences between Simon and Ayckbourn in their several stage techniques –

plot but not situation, sets but not props, and the varied paces of their dialogue. I nevertheless argue for their basically similar worlds – of more or less comfortable Western abodes peopled by white middle-class characters who speak without eloquence, act without violence, and rarely rise above trivia or ephemera. In shifting now to a closer look at specific plays, I underline the very fact that certain of their plays *are* comparable, as to structure, sub-genre, protagonist, or seriocomic tone.

In their early plays, Simon's *Barefoot in the Park* (1963) and Ayckbourn's *Relatively Speaking* (1965), both playwrights aim small – four-character, three-scene spinoffs of New Comedy, with climactic curtains and neat resolutions. Simon's comedy bubbles up primarily from petty crises of the temperamentally opposed newlyweds and, secondarily, from different life styles of an older couple. During the Act I exposition most of the humor arises from the small, unfurnished fifth-floor walkup apartment. In Act II the four characters on a double date pop exotic knichi into their mouths – with diverse degrees of dexterity and pleasure. When the foursome return from an Albanian restaurant on Staten Island, alcohol has fertilized their wits. Simon then interweaves the quarrel of the newlyweds with their anxiety about the bride's mother, before the comedy's final high note, when the once proper young husband drunkenly sings an Albanian folk song while precariously balanced on a skylight. He can be as Bohemian as his wife, who walks "barefoot in the park."

Ayckbourn's comparable family farce, *Relatively Speaking*, was originally entitled *Meet My Father*. It turns on a gullible young man's acceptance of his girlfriend's lying explanation that her middle-aged ex-lover is her father. Before the young swain meets the putative parents of his beloved, however, Ayckbourn swathes Greg in the accoutrements of farce. We see him in a sheet draped as a loincloth, slippers too large for him, festooned with dripping flowers. After struggling with a jammed drawer, he opens another drawer with such force that he scatters its contents. Finally, he gathers up a stranger's slippers and the cigarette packet with its telltale address of the action to follow. Through Greg's visible discomfort, Ayckbourn lightens his several reminders of the well-made play – a woman with a past, incriminating letters, chance confrontations, suspenseful curtains. The Act I sight gags prepare for and dissolve into an Act II dialogue of mistaken identity. Although the plots of these early plays are pat, and the characters undeveloped, the profusion of comic detail is cornucopian, strategically paced by Simon and carefully sustained by Ayckbourn.

As both playwrights sharpened their skills, they learned to exploit their sets and to juggle several characters in *The Odd Couple* (1965) and *How the Other Half Loves* (1971). Coincidentally, the focus is on six characters in both plays. Each of Simon's three acts opens on a six-man poker game in Oscar's living room. The room is slovenly in Act I, but "spotless and sterile" in Acts II and III, after the divorced Oscar invites a suicidal Felix to share his eight-room apartment. Although Simon's "odd couple" substitutes contrasting characters for conflict, he does explore set and properties as background for the one-liners of his poker players. We had to take it on faith that the apartment of *Barefoot in the Park* was located on the fifth floor, whereas we actually *see* the transformation suffered by Oscar's living room. The frenzied housekeeping of Felix, along with his self-pity, provokes Oscar to rue his generosity. In Act III as in Act I the poker players worry about Felix's threats of suicide, but in Act III as in Act I Felix happily lands on his well-shod feet when neighborly sisters invite him to share their apartment. Oscar taunts his erstwhile roommate with one of the play's many quips: "Aren't you going to thank me? . . . for the two greatest things I ever did for you. Taking you in and throwing you out." One of the greatest things that was done for Simon in *The Odd Couple* was the casting as Oscar of Walter Matthau, the dour-faced actor who slouches impeccably into major Simon roles.

In contrast, the presence of Robert Morley in *How the Other Half Loves* almost scuttled Ayckbourn's West End career. The veteran actor told the neophyte author: "Look, nobody wants to come to the theatre and see people squabbling . . . . We don't want all these nasty cross people, and people shouting at each other" (Watson, *Conversations with Ayckbourn*, p. 77). He then edited Ayckbourn's lines accordingly. Little did Morley dream that these "nasty cross people" would delight audiences because the nastiness is funny. Inept Frank Foster, the Morley character, is the most affable of Ayckbourn's sextet, oblivious of his wife's adultery with his subordinate Bob Phillips, who thus escapes his disorganized wife and their offstage infant. Socially lowest are the Featherstones, the unwitting alibi of both members of the adulterous affair. The bravura dinner scene leads to fisticuffs between Bob and his putative rival, which leads in turn to a distraught Mary Featherstone fleeing the one household to fall in a faint on the threshold of the other – a stage footstep away.

Although all three marriages gather cracks – the other halves love with similar nastiness – William Featherstone is the most loathsome spouse, wrist-slapping his wife to display disapproval. Informed of his wife Mary's supposed adultery, he responds: "Do you realize ... the hours I've put into that woman? When I met her, you know, she was nothing. Nothing at all. With my own hands I have built her up." His egotistical mumblings are funny, and he finally undergoes audience-satisfying humiliations. Although *How the Other Half Loves* begins and (almost) ends with the hackneyed ring of a telephone, Ayckbourn ingeniously exploits the offstage cries and the onstage debris of an invisible baby. Above all, he builds Featherstone's discomfort in the overlapping dining room. Contrary to Morley's prediction, the play ran for two years in the West End, although it closed after a few weeks in New York.

As both playwrights edged toward serious themes, they enfolded jokes into the delineation of character, particularly that of women – Simon's *The Gingerbread Lady* (1970) and Ayckbourn's *Just Between Ourselves* (1976). Simon's plot turns on a single question: Will the ex-alcoholic Evy Meara be able to remain "dry"? Immediately after her return from a rehabilitation center, Evy Meara is deserted by her married friend Toby and her gay actor friend Jimmy. Just as Evy begins to panic at being alone, her 17-year-old daughter Polly arrives, and she nostalgically recalls her Christmas gift at age 9: "Don't you remember the gingerbread house with the little gingerbread lady in the window? ... I always kept it to remind me of you. Of course, today I have the biggest box of crumbs in the neighborhood." (Is it churlish to object that crumbs will not last eight years?)

Although Evy cites her inadequacies as a mother, Polly is adamant about moving in with her, and this fortifies Evy to reject her abusive lover: "What I need now is a relative, not a relationship. And I have one in there unpacking." Three weeks later Evy pours champagne for her friend Toby's birthday, but she herself drinks it at the news of catastrophe; Jimmy has been replaced in his stage role, and Toby's husband wants to divorce her. Disappointed at her mother's lapse, Polly locks herself into her bedroom, and a lonely

Evy telephones her abusive lover: "Guess who wants to come over to your place?" The next morning Evy has a black eye and a hangover, but her daughter Polly, who has herself sought solace in alcohol, insists that she keep an appointment to discuss her future. The original version of *The Gingerbread Lady* ended with "Evy getting drunk in the dark . . . interrupted by a Puerto Rican grocery boy. Clearly, he would make a successful pass at her" (Meryman, "America's Funniest Writer," p. 60D). Originally, Evy was to send Polly out of her apartment and out of her life, while she herself was to sink to the level of a Puerto Rican lover (blatantly racist on Simon's part). However, negative reviews during Boston tryouts persuaded Simon to change the ending.[8] In the published version Polly cajoles Evy to attend the crucial meeting, and the uncrumbled Gingerbread Lady vows to her daughter: "When I grow up, I want to be just like you." The weak woman, using the weaknesses of her friends as an excuse to slip back into alcoholic oblivion, is not likely to grow up "just like" her purposeful daughter, but the wish ends Simon's play on a funny, reassuring line.

In Act I Evy's lover compliments her: "If nothing else, Evy, you have a way with a phrase. . . . whenever I needed a good honest laugh, I had to quote you, Ev." This is not mere self-praise on Simon's part. Since Evy is as bright as she is weak, her one-liners are in character, arousing "honest" laughter, mainly at her own expense. What is dishonest is the miraculous sitcom dissolution of Evy's critical self-appraisal, so that she is putty not only in her daughter's hands, but in those of Simon. Up to the revised ending, Evy Meara is the most fully formed woman in Simon's theatre, and if her horizon is limited to her immediate plight, that is not improbable for someone who has just emerged from ten weeks in a sanitarium. Evy's two insecure friends chant in running gags – Jimmy's acting and Toby's makeup – which spark Evy's witty deprecations. Occasionally, one of the friends steals Evy's wit, as when Jimmy replies to her joking proposal of marriage: ". . . you're a drunken nymphomaniac and I'm a homosexual. We'd have trouble getting our kids into a good school." At one juncture, too, Evy's friend Toby waxes tiresomely didactic: "We all hold each other up because none of us has the strength to do it alone. . . . The way I see it, you've got two choices. Either get a book on how to be a mature, responsible person . . . or get [Polly] out of here before you destroy her chance to become one." Toby underlines Evy's choice; as a mother, she must either relinquish Polly or contribute to her ruin. In the original version of *The Gingerbread Lady* Evy made the first choice, but in the revised version she undergoes an improbable conversion. In either case Simon grounds a play in a credible problem, alcoholism, spurring him to advance to the problem of unemployment in *The Prisoner of Second Avenue,* and that of aging in *The Sunshine Boys.* This is not to say that a contemporary play must focus on a problem, but unless Simon does so, his slender plot threads are overburdened by his jokes.

Although Ayckbourn has also devised alcoholic women, none of them is a protagonist. *Just Between Ourselves* resembles the original *Gingerbread Lady* in its tight plot, single setting, and, above all, in an action that traces the progressive deterioration of a woman. Ayckbourn himself called *Just Between Ourselves* "the first of my 'winter' plays," and although he amusingly explains that he wrote it in December for performance in January, winter also has the resonance of an unhappy ending – what Simon avoids in *The Gingerbread Lady.*

"Just between ourselves" is a colloquial cliché, and we hear it five times in Ayckbourn's play, always uttered by Dennis, three times *about* but never *to* his wife Vera. Dennis spends his weekends ineffectually tinkering in his garage, while his mother and wife vie for control of the offstage house. In *Just Between Ourselves* the running gags are indices of character: Over the course of a year Dennis keeps threatening to fix the garage door; over the course of a year Dennis, unable to sell his wife Vera's car, cannot even give it away. While the amiable Dennis laughs and lauds laughter, his wife's sanity crumbles away – an attrition that Ayckbourn traces through visible birthday "celebrations" – also the occasion of the breakdown of Simon's Gingerbread Lady.

Ayckbourn's first birthday is that of Pam, married to Neil, who arrives at Dennis's garage to look at the car that Vera no longer drives. Although both couples are on their best behavior, Vera is buffeted between her mother-in-law's interference in her kitchen and her husband's repetitive mockery of her clumsiness, so that she drops a stack of dishes to end the scene. The second scene pivots on Dennis's birthday, with his mother chanting that Vera has not baked a cake for her husband, and with Dennis still laughing at Vera's clumsiness. By the third scene, when Dennis's mother and Neil happen to share a birthday, mother and daughter-in-law are no longer speaking, but Dennis refuses to worry. "They rub along," he reassures Pam, who has taken to drink in frustration at her own marriage. At the scene's end Pam is slumped over a braying automobile horn, Vera attacks her mother-in-law with Dennis's electric drill, and Dennis's birthday surprise comes to fruition: *"Neil enters from the kitchen bearing the illuminated cake. As he enters the garage, he switches on the lights, bathing the scene in a glorious technicolour."* By scene 4 it is Vera's winter birthday – an appropriate if obvious symbolism. In the earlier scenes Vera has broken crockery, but in this scene it is she who is broken. Her mother-in-law rules the roost, and Dennis believes that his wife is "disorientated" because she prefers the cold garage to being "tucked up at home." The four "orientated" characters serenade Vera with "Happy Birthday." Silent throughout the scene, *"Vera's lips move silently with them."* Although the maudlin tune has been heard twice before, this is the first time it is sung *in chorus* – an ironic counterpoint to the vacuum between the several selves of *Just Between Ourselves*.[9]

Dennis is unaware of his own responsibility for his wife's breakdown, but Ayckbourn gives Neil a quip of self-reproach: "Women need a rock, you see. A rock. Trouble is, I'm a bloody marshmallow." Neil strains credibility in achieving such insight, where Ayckbourn has succumbed to a Simonian gag, for Neil is a distorted image of genial Dennis; both husbands annihilate their wives with good intentions.

In contrast to Simon's bright, boozy Evy, Vera is decorously submissive. Finally, Simon lacked the courage of his characterization, whereas Ayckbourn braves a woman's breakdown, and resists ending his play on a joke. One-set plays, *The Gingerbread Lady* and *Just Between Ourselves* are seriocomic as they trace the deterioration of a woman character. Except for drinks and doorbells, however, Simon ignores his set, whereas Ayckbourn anchors his dialogue in a garage door with a mind of its own, a stationary automobile that roars and rumbles, an ineffectual electric drill, crashing dishes, and "glorious technicolour." Even realistic plays challenge Ayckbourn to ingenuity.

For all Ayckbourn's inventive birthdays in *Just Between Ourselves*, the play is realistic in execution, like most of Simon's plays. Yet each playwright has launched into the baroque form of the play within the play – Simon's *The Sunshine Boys* (1972) and, over a decade later, Ayckbourn's *A Chorus of Disapproval* (1985).[10] The latter is more thickly populated, for Simon focuses on a comedy act, Lewis and Clark, analagous to Laurel and Hardy, or Abbott and Costello. Far from the intrepid explorers, Lewis and Clark, the comedians have depended on well-rehearsed routines in their decades of vaudeville as the Sunshine Boys. Simon dramatizes them in a period long past their prime; both in their 70s, no longer on speaking terms, Lewis lives with his daughter in New Jersey, but Clark clings to his miniscule apartment on upper Broadway, where, health and memory failing, he deludes himself about a career. Less tightly plotted than *The Gingerbread Lady, The Sunshine Boys* also turns on a single question: Can the acerbic old men manage to reenact one of their successful sketches for big money on television?

Since Lewis and Clark are comedians, the play fittingly contains Simon's highest quantity of one-liners. Clark is the crustier member of the twosome, taking umbrage at any affront to his dignity, and lashing back in vituperative epithets. About his erstwhile partner Lewis, Clark snarls: "As an actor, no one could touch him. As a human being, no one *wanted* to touch him." Clark is sharp-tongued, too, about his loyal nephew, Ben the talent agent, who announces that CBS is doing a special program on the history of comedy, including the Sunshine Boys. Neither old man will admit to needing money, but Ben cajoles them into a rehearsal of their most celebrated skit, "The Doctor and the Tax Examination." The rehearsal bogs down at its opening line: Will it be the tried and true "Come in," or the freshening factor "Enter?" At the rehearsal studio, the two ancient comedians continue to bicker, and yet Simon adroitly slips an old-time burlesque skit into their repartee, before Clark suffers a heart attack. In the next scene tough old Clark is as sharp as ever, spurning his nephew's home for an actors' asylum as his last abode. Unapologetic though chastened, Lewis informs Clark that he will soon be leaving his daughter's home: "If you're not too busy, maybe you'll come over one day to the Actors' Home and visit me." Clark smirks: "You can count on it," but he does not reveal that he too will be living there. *The Sunshine Boys* closes as the two garrulous old men ramble on about the identity of familiar names in the Broadway weekly, *Variety* – a preview of twilight in the Actors' Home.

In this exceptionally unsentimental play Simon resists endowing his comedians either with warm hearts or new stage triumphs. He wisely limits the play within the play to the brief, rhythmic, visually dynamic skit performed by professionals. Out of the public eye, old age is dramatized as dirty, demeaning, confusing, and utterly lonely. Yet Simon also makes it funny, so that we laugh with a sympathy that the selfish old souls scarcely deserve.

Simon chooses an American burlesque sketch for his inner play, but Ayckbourn chooses an English classic, *The Beggar's Opera*, for his play-long inner play. The solicitor director Dafydd cajoles his recalcitrant amateur cast toward performance, even though he is aware: "Here we are, playing around with pretty lights and costumes held together with safety pins. Out there it's all happening." The "all" that is happening is hardly cataclysmic, and Dafydd is unaware of most of it. Guy Jones, an English stranger in Welsh Pendon, is speedily involved in intrigues amatory, monetary, and intricately Ayckbournian, while he ascends the cast ladder to the lead role of Gay's Macheath.

Ayckbourn's main running gag is Gay's opera. Opening on Gay's finale, with Jones as Macheath surrounded by an adoring cast, comic reversal follows after the curtain falls, for the cast shuns Jones in a silent "chorus of disapproval." Ayckbourn's play then backtracks to trace Guy's adventures among the nonprofessional contemporary thieves, who also seek profit from bribery, speculation, and sexual blackmail. Ayckbourn implies through Gay that comedy and chicanery are alive and well in the twentieth as in the eighteenth century. Thus, the cast in the contemporary pub sing Gay's drinking song. After the lawyer Dafydd sounds Guy out about property of the company where he is a lowly employee, a cast member sings Gay's song about lawyers stealing your whole estate. Two different Macheaths bask in the rivalry of their respective women: Lucy and Bridget vie for Crispin, as do Hannah and Faye for Guy. Finally, Ayckbourn follows Gay in the artifice of a happy ending, to the extent of the success of the play within the play.

Aside from the baroque subgenre, *A Chorus of Disapproval* is a familiar Ayckbourn farce interweaving adultery, inept deception, and general mayhem. As in earlier Ayckbourn plays, the clumsy bumbler finally departs without the girl, but Guy is nevertheless more fortunate than Norman of the conquests, since he *has* shuttled between the beds of two wives, without the annoyance of marriage to either one. Guy's victim Dafydd is as clumsy a husband as he is a director, and, as Dennis of *Just Between Ourselves* tinkers with his tools, Dafydd tinkers with his cast. In this play about a play, Ayckbourn the former stage manager relishes the trappings of theatre – curtain calls, makeshift properties and costumes, graceless stagehands, missed cues and unlearned lines, foreign-is-funny un-English accents, and the misplay of lights at the technical rehearsal. Ayckbourn's reputed sympathy with women is markedly absent from this play, where the women are sexually greedy – in parallel with the financially greedy males. In a conversation with Ian Watson, Ayckbourn comments: "I was chasing the theme of inner corruption inside a society, and how an honest man in a dishonest society looks like the biggest rogue of all" (*Conversations with Ayckbourn*, p. 111). Although Ayckbourn's society *is* dishonest, his Guy Jones is not so much honest as naïve. Perhaps Ayckbourn's mind was already on *A Small Family Business*.

A Chorus of Disapproval is enjoyable as an adultery farce, but its parallels with *The Beggar's Opera* are somewhat forced, and they were elided in the original production (even more so in the naturalistic movie, set in Scarborough). Simon, in contrast, chooses a diminutive inner play to enhance the anachronism of his irascible protagonists, the erstwhile Sunshine Boys. An old hand at radio and television, Simon is comfortable – as Ayckbourn is not – in this metatheatrical venture.

In more recent plays, both playwrights reach for wider social commentary – Alan Ayckbourn's *A Small Family Business* (1987) and Neil Simon's *Lost in Yonkers* (1990). The latter play might well be called "a small family business," since the setting is an apartment in Yonkers, above "Kurnitz's Kandy Store."[11] By means of that business and her rigid discipline, a German Jewish widow has raised her four living children, whom she continues to dominate in adulthood. Unusually for Simon, the structure of the play has an Ayckbournian symmetry, with four scenes in each of its two acts. Even more unusually for Simon, the play has a group protagonist, for all members of the Kurnitz family are "lost in Yonkers" – most literally Bella, the 35-year-old child who gets lost when she occasionally forgets where she lives: "She missed the first year [of high school] because she couldn't find it." Metaphorically lost are Bella's stern friendless mother, her lung-damaged sister Gert, her gangster brother Louie, her widower brother Eddie, and his two sons, Jay and Arty.

The time is 1942, and the illness of Eddie's recently deceased wife has plunged him into debt – "The doctors, the hospital, cost me everything I had ... And everything I didn't have." But since it is 1942 during World War II, jobs are suddenly available, and Eddie can sell scrap iron in the Southern states. He has come to Yonkers to plead with his mother to shelter his adolescent sons while he is away working off his debt. Although she refuses, her child-like daughter Bella coerces the old woman into accepting the presence of the boys: "You and me and Jay and Arty ... Won't that be fun, Momma?"

It is fun only for the audience, even though Simon reduces his one-liners while the strands of his plot unwind. Each scene opens with a voice-over – a new technique for Simon – usually a letter from absent Eddie to his sons. Grandma Kurnitz and her grandsons are at comic loggerheads. Her son, the gangster Louie, hides out in his old Yonkers home; her daughter, the brain-damaged Bella, falls in love with a mentally retarded movie usher. Unaware of these strains, Eddie writes to his sons: "The one thing that keeps me going is knowing you're with my family." When Bella enlists family support for money to marry, her mother dismisses the idea – "Dot's enough! ... I don't vant to hear dis anymore!" Here foreign is *not* funny. Bella runs away, but she returns to her Yonkers home when her swain cannot bring himself to leave his parents. Eddie returns to Yonkers to reclaim his sons, while lawless Louie enlists in the Pacific War. A final victory belongs to Bella, who calmly informs her mother that she would like to invite a girlfriend to dinner, and the friend has a brother.

Simon's characters resemble other American prototypes – the harsh matriarch of Hellman's *Little Foxes*, the loving brain-damaged women of Shepard's *A Lie of the Mind*, the good-hearted gangster of Grade-B movies, the vivacious boys of *Tom Sawyer* and *Huck Finn* – but Simon's material is invested with a feeling of lived experience. In spite of a clumsy exposition, contrived exits and entrances, and misplaced one-liners – such as Louie's "Sometimes bein' on the up and up just gets you down and down" – the characters bristle with independent energy. As in Simon's other plays, no one is evil; Grandma Kurnitz became tough to survive, and she undergoes no softening. An unreformed gangster Louie joins the army, and weak Eddie finds neither new strength nor a new wife. Although Bella triumphs twice, she remains a child mentally; even though her new friend has a brother, New Comedy seems far in the past. Grandma and Bella presumably carry on in the family business, but the boys have matured beyond the lure of its (invisible) ice cream sodas.

Loosely plotted, the play charms by its characters, whose jokes accord with their personalities. Eddie's subservience to Grandma is funny, as is that of criminal Louie. The latter calls himself a businessman, and adopts movie poses, but Jay cuts him down to size: "Well, you're no Humphrey Bogart." Sister Gert's wheezing is a minor running gag. Although Bella is often in a state of comic confusion, Simon displays rare delicacy in balancing the childlike mind and the woman's body – *"a mess at dressing."* The play's humor arises mainly from the discomforts of life in the family, but unlike Ayckbourn's irrepressible physicalizations, Simon's family troubles are verbally stressed.

Ayckbourn's *A SMALL Family Business* (my emphasis) is several steps up the capitalist ladder from Kurtnitz's Kandy Store; Ayres and Graces manufacture fitted furniture.[12] In *Lost in Yonkers* we had to take the downstairs candy store – and even its wares – on faith, but Ayckbourn never lets us forget the furniture business, since its products embellish the four visible stage households where the action takes place. Moreover, it may be a small business, but it is a large stage family, each of whose members dangles her or his subplot. Ken Ayres, who founded the firm, borders on senility – "the odd blank patch" – but not to the extent of designating his restaurant-craving son Desmond as his heir. Instead, he chooses his daughter Poppy's husband, honest Jack McCracken. Jack's brother Cliff already works for Ayres and Graces, as does Desmond's wife's sister and Jack's son-in-law Roy. The extended family is thus very much involved in the business – so involved, we soon learn, that they steal the firm's wares to be sold as Italian imports, with the connivance of the Rivetti brothers, whose own small business of a large family has connections with the Mafia. When honest Jack learns the extent of the chicanery, he furiously calls a family meeting: "We are going to sponge the shit off the family name, all right? . . . We are going to put the business together as it was. As a decent, honest, small family business."

Having already hired a private detective, however, Jack learns that this unsavory person will have to be paid off with a large sum, and the resident Rivetti brother assures him that the sum could "arrange something more permanent" to ensure the detective's silence. By the end of the play, that is exactly what happens. In Jack's absence his wife and elder daughter are threatened by the detective, who is then toppled into the bathtub by Jack's younger daughter, a drug addict. The Italian connection gets rid of the body, but the representative Rivetti demands payment: "I mean, their bill for the removal and disposal of our friend is costing an arm and a leg, if you'll pardon the expression" (and if you'll pardon the Simonized line). What it costs is distribution by the small family business of "urgent medical supplies," or drugs. Step by relentless step, Jack has yielded to corruption. Circling to another party – for the 75th birthday of senile Ken Ayres – the play closes with Jack McCracken's toast to the family business.

Although Ayckbourn's ending is predictable, the plot moves forward like a steamroller. Ayckbourn also enters Simon's terrain of generational conflict; Jack is out of touch with both his daughters, and old Ken confuses his son with his son-in-law. Private relationships are as crooked as the family business. The ubiquity of malefaction is implied by frequent generalities: "Everybody else works little fiddles. That's what the system's designed for." And yet the play seems confined by its social case history, without reaching out to indict a system – whether capitalism or Thatcherism.

Although the drama toys with dishonesty – from paper clips to drugs in a week – *A Small Family Business* thrives on devices of farce. The schematic characters are often reduced to running gags relevant to the plot – Ken's semisenility, his son Desmond's escapist cooking, his daughter-in-law's preference of a dog to a husband (her maiden name is Doggett), Jack's brother's penchant for expensive gadgets, his wife's penchant for expensive clothes and Italian lovers; foreign has become sinisterly funny. The play also sports the physicality of farce in the deft shifts from household to household, with identical furnishings; the five Rivetti brothers are played by the same actor (whose name is wittily scrambled in the cast list of the original production); money is stuffed into a suitcase (the twin of Uncle Louie's suitcase in *Lost in Yonkers*), and murder takes place in the bathroom. Ayckbourn's comic ingenuity makes it hard to be horrified.

Like other Ayckbourn plays *A Small Family Business* opens and closes on a party. The first is Poppy's surprise party for her husband Jack on his retirement from the fish(y?) business; since he thinks that he and his wife are alone, he wants to make love, and when his family spring out of the darkness to surprise him, he is literally caught with his pants down. The play closes on the birthday party for old Ken, the founder of the small family business. To that party Michael Gambon as Jack wore a wide-striped suit that might have been left over from *The Godfather.* Still considering himself honorable – "It still stands" – Jack is trapped with his ethical pants down.

In his mature plays Simon is still learning such basic dramaturgical techniques as exposition, relevance, climax, and the syllables of nonverbal languages of theatre. Ayckbourn is past master at intricate plot, economical exposition, acrid resolution, and the most ingenious scenescapes ever concocted. But clumsily as Simon draws them, Grandma Kurnitz and her daughter Bella evince a new level of complexity; whereas, deftly as Ayckbourn manipulates his large cast, the characters remain behavioral counters.

Over the course of their long careers, Neil Simon and Alan Ayckbourn have aroused laughter from many audiences in many theatres. In spite of the ethnic dissimilarity of their characters, however, they are white, middle-class, and Eurocentric. Notes of prejudice sound in Simon's plays. Do the anti-Hispanic remarks made in *The Gingerbread Lady* and *The Sunshine Boys* belong to Simon or his characters? Ayckbourn's characters are utterly unaware that Britain, like the United States, is a multicultural country. Is that the character's limitation or the playwright's?

Ayckbourn and Simon are amusing recorders of small experience, as displayed in small stage business. For all Simon's sentimentality and Ayckbourn's ingenuity, their stage countries are circumscribed in similar dimensions of irritating triviality, and I mean that in two senses:

1. Their characters worry about indecorous noises, incompetent cooking, overindulged pets, or sexual peccadilloes.
2. The playwrights themselves rarely situate such trivia on a large canvas.

Feydeau's farces, still spritely on stage, nevertheless indict *la belle époque;* the comedies of Simon and Ayckbourn indict the pace of contemporary life, or the characters bent on success, or the denseness of good intentions, but they rarely provide a context for the good or nasty humor on their stages. Their popularity is based on an appeal to social groups that account for a large percentage of dwindling theatre audiences on both sides of the Atlantic.

Reviewing Ayckbourn's *Way Upstream,* with its boating mishaps on the precarious River Orb, Sue Jameson noted: "Somehow my leaky roof at home didn't seem quite so bad" (*London Theatre Record,* 1982, p. 549). If we extend her remark to the abrasive relations in the plays of Simon and Ayckbourn, we can appreciate much of their magnetism. Sight gags and verbal gags not only elicit our sympathy for the feckless and irritated; but the humor also confirms our own superiority to the mediocrities on stage. Both playwrights, in their different ways, amuse us with recalcitrant objects and situations so problematic that our own don't "seem quite so bad" on either side of the Atlantic.

Artists' arias
Edward Bond and Sam Shepard

Comparing Neil Simon and Alan Ayckbourn, I hope I have shown how their family comedies are commonly strained through clichés and stereotypes, despite Ayckbourn's fluency in the physical language of the stage. From this comedic couple, I turn to an Anglo–American pair with a tragic bent. Edward Bond and Sam Shepard have experienced only partial success in their own countries – and never on the Broadway and West End that have cuddled Simon and Ayckbourn. Bond accrues more royalties abroad than home in Britain, while Shepard is acclaimed as an American film star rather than a dramatist. Ranging over a variety of styles – and not merely devices – Bond and Shepard do not readily lend themselves to juxtaposition. Shepard is hailed (or condemned) as quintessentially American more often than Bond is cited as typically British. I would argue that both are rooted in their native soil, Bond in Britain's social history and Shepard in American myth, but these roots are too various for comparison. Where the two dramatists *are* comparable is in their predilection for artist characters who comment obliquely – and theatrically – on the art of their creators.

Born a decade apart, Edward Bond (1934) and Sam Shepard (1943) are autodidacts of broad range and culture. Both men began playwriting in climates of theatre experiment of the 1960s, and both, having produced a sizable body of literature, continue to write into the 1990s. Edward Bond preaches a Rational Theatre, and Sam Shepard claims to explore an inner landscape. Bond is the most unremittingly socialist of British political playwrights, whereas Shepard's recent plays center on that archetypal American subject of the nuclear family. Both have written not only plays, but

36

other genres – Bond his verse, stories, librettos, and polemics; Shepard his song lyrics, film scripts, rock log, and autobiographical vignettes. Both authors have contributed dialogue to films of Antonioni – Bond for *Blow-Up* of 1967 and Shepard for *Zabriskie Point* of 1970. Shepard's early plays were labeled Theatre of Assault, and Bond coined the term Aggro-effect for his own belligerency. The protagonists of both dramatists tend to be men, but they have also created tender and brain-damaged women – Bond's Ismene of *The Woman* (1978) and Shepard's Beth of *A Lie of the Mind* (1985). Stubbornly pursuing their individual dramatic paths, both Bond and Shepard occasionally direct their own plays. They have never met, and I have found no cross-reference of one to the other.[1] Their artist characters nevertheless provide mutual illumination.

Edward Bond has divided his plays into three groups:

1. descriptions of his familiar world, ending with *The Sea* (completed 1972);
2. analyses of the problems in that world, ending with *The Woman* (completed 1977);
3. answers to some of those problems (all subsequent work).

However Bond may displace his settings to feudal Japan or Jacobean Stratford, his own Western contemporary world – and ours – is at stake. In some thirty plays – the majority set in his native England – Bond dramatizes ideas by means of complex fables that involve coherent characters speaking pithy dialogue in decentered scenes. Although Bond boasts of his Rational Theatre, he does not hesitate to introduce such irrational elements as ghosts, dreams, and fantasies.

Sam Shepard rarely looks back at his oeuvre of some fifty plays, but critics have grouped:

1. early collages through *The Holy Ghostly* (1969);
2. fantasies about art or power through *Suicide in B-Flat* (1976);
3. family plays of surface realism.

There is, however, seepage between the groups, and a few plays resist this classification – for example, *Tongues, War in Heaven,* and *States of Shock.* Almost always Shepard's plays are set in one of the regions of the contemporary United States.[2] He has confessed:

"I'm pulled toward images that shine in the middle of junk" (Chubb, "Fruitful Difficulties," p. 24), and he forages in an all-American refuse dump of drugs, sports, rock music, astrology, science fiction, old movies, Western lore, detective stories, and races of cars, dogs, horses. Long before the French culture critic Jean Baudrillard hymned American – and especially Western – junk, Shepard enfolded it into his stage vocabulary.

The self-styled English rationalist and the intuitive American irrationalist share a keen eye for stage images and a keen ear for quasi-regional idiom, which they gear to specific characters. Although Bond and Shepard are not the only contemporary playwrights to stage artists, they do so with some consistency, and the portraits reveal aspects of their respective countries, as well as their respective dramaturgies. Rather than zigzagging between playwrights, I will examine the artist characters of each in separate sequences.

"Musical artists" explode multiply in Shepard's *Melodrama Play* (1967), and my quotation marks signify a playful, as well as a literal sense of the phrase. On analogy with musical chairs, successive characters – Duke, Drake, Cisco, and even Peter – are composers of songs; Duke and Cisco are singers as well. As opposed to these fictional musicians, the actual singers Bob Dylan and Robert Goulet are represented by eyeless photographs in a nondescript recording studio. In *Melodrama Play* Duke has stolen the song composed by his brother Drake. Like Simon, Shepard contrasts brothers in this play, but unlike Simon, he does not reduce stage conflict to a contrast. The businessman Floyd is indifferent to the identity of the artist; what he wants is another commercially successful song, however it may be obtained. In a spoof of the violence of melodrama, Floyd's hired thug, Peter, shoots Duke's girlfriend, clubs Duke and Cisco unconscious, and menaces the main artist figure, Drake.

Five songs comment on the action of *Melodrama Play*, functioning both with the emotional flavor of melodrama *and* with a quasi-Brechtian commentary. Through songs the German Marxist conveyed to his audience the class basis of history, which his characters could not grasp, but Shepard's songs offer insights into states of feeling.[3] Rather than reveal class division, the songs of *Melodrama Play* indict the artist for complicity in his own commercial entrapment. The hit song urges repeatedly: "So prisoners, get up out a' your homemade heads, / Oh prisoners, get up out a' your homemade beds." Artists must resist threats both internal – "homemade heads" – and external – "homemade beds."[4]

Shepard's *Melodrama Play* bounces stock types of the rock scene through an action-packed play, while the virtuous hero of traditional melodrama shrivels into the figure of the beleaguered artist, whoever he may be. Revealing Shepard's facility for pastiche, *Melodrama Play* is a minor work thriving on its songs and visual images – the eyeless giant photographs, the ubiquitous dark glasses, the artist Drake on all fours. These images could be British, except that Dylan and Goulet (photographed but unheard) are in fact American. In spite of the playlong confusion about the identity of the artist, our final image of him is the songwriter Drake cowering under the club of the thug Peter, when *"there is a loud knock at the door."* We cannot know whether that knock announces friend or foe of the artist as victim, and we cannot know how seriously that final image is to be taken in this *play* on melodrama, replete with music, violence, and comic relief.

The songwriter Drake scarcely resists his own exploitation, but Shepard's subsequent stage musicians are more deeply entrapped in success-oriented America. Shepard himself was torn in the early 1970s between a commitment to music or to drama, and he translated his personal predicament into several musician plays during that decade.[5] The first of these, *Mad Dog Blues* (1971), was written while on drugs in a state of terror; Shepard transfers that terror to his main characters, the rock star Kosmo and his sidekick Yahoudi. Each locked into his own fantasy, they separately encounter legendary figures – Mae West, Marlene Dietrich, Captain Kidd, Jesse James, Paul Bunyan – with whom they wander on a bare stage over ocean and desert, on island and frontier, past one another while physically close enough to touch. Finally, the "adventure show" arrives at home sweet midwestern home, where the entire cast participates in song, dance, and celebration *"through the audience and out into the street."* Although the rock star Kosmo is sporadically aware of a mission – "But I'm a musician! I've got to create!" – he does not sing solo in any of the play's seven songs, but does join the final chorus of "Home." More diffusely than *Melodrama Play, Mad Dog Blues* dramatizes a case of composer's block, and also of artistic isolation on a populated stage.

The musician's predicament changes in *Cowboy Mouth*, also of

1971. Although Shepard has claimed that the play emerged when he and the rock singer Patti Smith passed a typewriter back and forth in their room at New York's Hotel Chelsea, *Cowboy Mouth* bears his distinctive insignia of tormented artist, startling imagery, imaginative enactment, and manic arias in rhythmic, colloquial language. The Bohemian Cavale has kidnapped Slim to be "like a rock-and-roll Jesus with a cowboy mouth." The picturesque phrase, blending martyrdom with American nostalgia, is borrowed from Bob Dylan.[6] If the cowboy is "the quintessential American masculine icon" (Savran, *Communists, Cowboys, and Queers*, p. 19), Slim cannot fill the role. Torn between Cavale's ambition for him (but not for herself!) and an equally strong desire to rejoin his wife and child, Slim is Cavale's victim, who plays at being her protector. Responding to Cavale's myriad changes and charges, Slim joins her in theatrical scenes and musical duets. Only when their song "Loose Ends" cracks the shell of the Lobster Man does Slim escape Cavale's Pygmalion grasp.

In *Cowboy Mouth* Shepard imposes the legend of the rock hero upon that of the film cowboy – both subversive and both gambling with early death. In Cavale Shepard (or possibly Smith) creates his only female musician, grown from an ugly duckling to a more purposeful artist than sulky Slim. Although Cavale and Slim are both musicians, the rock-and-roll savior proves to be the mute Lobster Man, who flirts with suicide. Emerging from Chinese take-out, he cannot be taken seriously. In spite of a brilliant evocation of 1960s sordid sensuality, teeming with "miscellaneous debris," rock songs, guitar and drums, cowboy pictures, French literary references, and a dead crow "old black tooth," the cowboy and the rock-star myths do not quite mesh in *Cowboy Mouth*.

Not until *The Tooth of Crime*, written while Shepard was living in England in 1972, does he become a masterful conflator of myths: "It wasn't until I came to England that I found out what it means to be an American" (Marranca, ed., *American Dreams*, p. 198). "What it means" is dramatized in a tense duel between two musical artists. The reigning rock star Hoss is challenged by an upstart Crow. Hoss is at once a blocked composer and the tool of the media, but the punk rocker Crow is new on Shepard's stage. Hoss and Crow vie for supremacy as musicians, but words are their weapons, both in and outside of song. Their virtuosic duel is staged as a prizefight, with resonances of the gunfight of Western movies.

Shepard's subtitle for *Tooth* is "A play with music in two acts," and music takes the form of eight songs composed by the playwright: "I wanted the music in *Tooth of Crime* so that you could step out of the play for a minute, every time a song comes, and be brought to an emotional comment on what's been taking place in the play" (Chubb, "Fruitful Difficulties," p. 18).[7] Five years earlier, in *Melodrama Play*, Shepard twisted Brechtian estranging songs to his own purpose, but not until *Tooth* do the songs offer emotional understanding of the contending artists (as well as of Becky, their faithless companion). The allotment of songs is three for the newcomer Crow, two for the old-timer Hoss, two for the victimized victimizer Becky, and one for a four-man chorus. Already in *Melodrama Play,* and even more in *Cowboy Mouth*, Shepard dramatizes the pressures on the rock musician, but not until *Tooth* do we witness the slippage between ruthless artistic ambition and more ruthless media pressure.

Tooth opens close to its crisis. Needing a "kill" in "the game," Hoss fondles an array of guns – "the gear" – proffered by Becky, his servant-mistress-tutor. Hoss consults astrologers, henchmen, and medical men about his intuition of doom. When he learns that a Gypsy has been "sussed," the loner Hoss seeks an alliance with Little Willard in the East, only to learn that he "Shot himself in the mouth." Alone on stage, Hoss bifurcates into a dialogue with his father, to whom he complains: "They're all countin' on me. The bookies, the agents, the Keepers. I'm a fucking industry." Once Hoss accepts his father's reply ("You're just a man, Hoss. Just a man."), the harried artist also accepts a style match with the young Gypsy Crow. Even before their confrontation Hoss is "Just a little tired," and he leaves the stage for a nap.

Before we see Crow in the cool, cruel flesh, we hear his song "Poison" (in one version of *Tooth*). Although Crow looks like Keith Richards with an eye patch, he sounds like no one ever heard on the stage. Hoss and his henchmen speak in synthetic colloquialisms, but Crow's phrases are opaque in their clipped and mocking hostility. Hoss tries to assert his supremacy by imitating *"a kind of Cowboy-Western image,"* and then shifts to *"1920s gangster style,"* couched in appropriate dictions. After Crow imitates

Hoss's walk perfectly, the two musical artists charge and counter-charge in the jargon of automobile racing. While Hoss summons a Referee to formalize their duel, Crow sings of his own self-sufficiency:

> But I believe in my mask – The man I made up is me
> And I believe in my dance – And my destiny.

The duel opens on a quick, vicious attack by Crow. He fills round 1 with a capsule biography of a coward and a loser (anathema to the American macho image), while Hoss protests his originality. The Referee names Crow the winner. In round 2 Hoss accuses Crow of denying his musical roots in the blues of black people – "You'd like a free ride on a black man's back" – but Crow retorts, "I got no guilt to conjure! Fence me with the present." The Referee declares a draw. In round 3 Crow sneers in rhyme that Hoss's music is obsolete, imitative, impotent. As Jeanette Malkin aptly summarizes: "It is the *effect* of Crow's attack, not its essence, which counts: and the effect is to force Hoss's deviation from the 'neutral field state'" (*Verbal Violence*, p. 217). When the Ref calls a TKO, he is shot by the decidedly unneutral Hoss.

By thus violating "the code," Hoss himself becomes a Gypsy, and he implores Crow to give him lessons in survival, but Crow exacts a high price: "I give you my style and I take your turf." Crow has something to crow about, but Hoss cannot adopt Crow's style: "Pitiless. Indifferent and riding a state of grace. It ain't me!" Hoss finally prefers death to dishonor: "It's my life and my death in one clean shot." Hoss brags about the *originality* of his last gesture, but in fact he echoes the offstage suicide of Little Willard exactly – gun to mouth, with its sexual resonance. Alone on stage Crow praises his erstwhile rival, but to the loyal chauffeur Cheyenne Crow derides Hoss. Crow cannot afford to express admiration publicly. Crow's reign begins, but his final song, "Rollin' Down," casts doubt on its durability.

The Tooth of Crime is Shepard's most tightly plotted play, inscribing his artist antagonists on an endgame set, and endowing them with contrasting idioms – in words, music, and especially physical stance. But Shepard's themes are familiar – the tenuous position of the artist, his heritage of sound and fury, his susceptibility to popular culture and media greed – "Somebody bankable." The manic machismo of the 1960s, which Shepard absorbed with his drugs, culminates onstage in violent death. *The Tooth of Crime* is at once a contest between rock stars, a histrionic match of performers, a bout between generations (to which Leonard Wilcox adds the cultural generations of modernism against postmodernism), and a class war between the haves and have-nots, between the recently rooted Westerner and the catch-as-catch-can Gypsy – a class war innocent of Marx. The bite of Shepard's *Tooth* is honed on a syncopation of the lexicons of drugs, sports, film, crime, street smarts, gambling, science fiction, astrology, and the rock music that is presented and represented. For all the diversity of the verbal lexicon, the polyvalent monosyllables "hit" and "kill" toll a threnody of American popular culture.

When Shepard returned to the West Coast after two years in England, where *Tooth* was composed, he seemed cured of professional aspiration as a musician, but musical artists depart only slowly from his plays. Both works of 1976, *Angel City* and *Suicide in B-Flat*, place musicians onstage. In the former a mute saxophone player contributes mood music, but the highly vocal drummer Tympani yields precedence to a writer, Rabbit Brown, who is summoned to Angel City to retrieve a disaster movie for which Tympani is seeking "the one, special, never-before-heard-before rhythm, which will drive men crazy." Reluctantly, Tympani helps Rabbit in his search for a disaster. Tympani's rhythm entrances Miss Scoons, a sexy secretary who yearns to be a film star. By Act II Tympani plays drums as though he were a short-order cook with a griddle, and he arrives at a startling insight: ". . . we're locked into the narrowest part of our dream machine" – an insight for which he is punched in the stomach. Both musicians, the verbal Tympani and the mute saxophonist, fade out of the play, although the former has voiced the keenest awareness of the hypnotic power of film.[8] Finally, all the characters are seen as actors in a movie. In the words of Leonard Wilcox: ". . . the play becomes a horror film and the characters themselves are inexorably absorbed into the pop schizo text of babbling media voices" (*"The Day of the Locust* and *Angel City*," in *Modern Drama* 36 [1993], p. 73).

Suicide in B-Flat is anchored in music rather than film, since the protagonist Niles is a jazz composer. The flat of the title puns multiply on a musical key, the upstage wall, and the apartment setting. The suggestion of the title's "Be flat" hovers over the outline of a corpse on the floor; yet the suicide of the title is questionable.

Someone has apparently had his face blown off, and it is the outline of his body that we see on the floor. Two detectives, Louis and Pablo, proceed on the assumption that the victim is the musician Niles. Separately, however, each of the detectives theorizes that Niles may have taken advantage of someone else's death in order to disappear from the public eye, so as to renew his music in privacy. Although we hear music intermittently throughout the play – piano, bass, and sax – none of it springs from Niles, who is at first invisible to the detectives. When Niles is shot onstage, it is the detectives who are wounded, but they nevertheless handcuff the hapless composer, as he demands punishment for the death of someone who "was alive to the very last moment." Perhaps it is Niles's music we hear as the lights finally fade, for there has been an intimation that Niles the composer is doubled by a speechless piano player. Subsuming the blocked creativity of *Melodrama Play* and *Mad Dog Blues*, as well as the public pressure of *Cowboy Mouth* and *The Tooth of Crime*, *Suicide in B-Flat* tries to fuse the musical artist into the detective story frame, where the "murdered" artist is again shackled instead of encouraged on his artistic way.

Although Shepard contributed music to the piece he wrote with Joe Chaikin – *Savage/Love* – a decade elapsed before Shepard again dramatized a musical artist: Bob Dylan in *True Dylan* (1987).[9] Shepard first met Dylan in 1975, when he was invited to write a movie about a Rolling Thunder tour, but *True Dylan* offers a portrait of the musical artist that eludes *The Rolling Thunder Logbook*. Against the *"distant rhythmic splashing of waves"* a Jimmy Yancey piano solo is heard intermittently in this dialogue between Dylan, the longtime rock star, and Shepard, an interviewer well known to him. Intermittent, too, are references to musicians and film stars, but Dylan's music is as pervasive as the ocean waves: *"He continually fingers the neck of the guitar and keeps picking out little repetitive melody lines, short blues progressions, gospel chords."* Rambling around their shared passion for musicians and for actors who died young, the two old acquaintances converse comfortably. Shepard poses three improbable interview questions, but it is through the associative chatter of the two men that we come to know Dylan as a natural musical force, from the polkas he hummed as a child to his bedside singing for a hospitalized Woody Guthrie to his 1966 motorcycle crash near Woodstock.

Thus summarized, Dylan's musical dedication sounds rudimentary and almost didactic, but Shepard dramatizes him vividly.

From the unlocalized recording studio of *Melodrama Play* to the Pacific patio of *True Dylan* some two decades later, Shepard endows his musicians with stage music. *Mad Dog Blues* is largely verbal and gestural, and *Cowboy Mouth* is more intensely so, but *Angel City* syncopates words, music, and horrific dreams into a fantasy film. *The Tooth of Crime* swallows the whole country in its mass-fed musical maw. These plays about musical artists extend Shepard's theatre imagination; collectively they convey an impression of peripatetic American artists, ill at ease within four walls and commercial pressures, but not free of their blandishments. As Deborah Geis writes: "Like his artist-protagonists Duke/Drake, Hoss/Crow, Rabbit/Wheeler, . . . Niles/Louis/Pablo, Shepard splits his dramatic texts between a reliance on the pop culture milieu for the images of his art and a problematization . . . of the milieu that his art has created" (*Postmodern Theatric[k]s*, p. 75).

In contrast to Shepard's moody musicians, Bond's artists are invariably writers, and sometimes they are actual authors within our cultural tradition. The first Bond artist is, however, somewhat exotic, and probably unfamiliar to most Western audiences. *Narrow Road to the Deep North* (1968) was triggered by the translation of a seventeenth-century Japanese poet: "I started to read a book by Basho, the Japanese poet. . . . The poet, Basho, sees this child abandoned by the river – and he goes on his way. . ." (Hay & Roberts, *Edward Bond: A Companion*, p. 15). "I just shut the book and I couldn't read it anymore. . . . I more or less forgot about it but from time to time it came up in my mind and when I had this play to produce I just went back to the book and I read it, and wrote a play" (Roberts, *Bond on File*, p. 22). In choosing a setting far from contemporary Britain, Bond the playwright was following Brecht's narrow road of dramatic estrangement. After the Britain of a fantastic Queen Victoria in his *Early Morning*, Bond moved his *Narrow Road* to "*Japan about the seventeenth, eighteenth or nineteenth centuries*," centuries of the rise of Western capitalism and especially of British imperialism.

On a bare stage Bond's Basho presents himself to the audience and recites his most famous haiku, but Bond alters the tone of the original. Basho's translator writes: "Breaking the silence / Of an ancient pond, / A frog jumped into water – / A deep resonance."

But Bond writes: "Silent old pool / Frog jumps / Kdang!" The comic onomatopoeia upsets the tranquillity of old pools. Further, Bond's play omits Basho's gift of food to a child; instead, it delineates the misery of the child's parents. Bond wants us to be critical of the artist Basho, who ascribes the child's suffering to "the irresistible will of heaven."

After the initial incident involving Basho and the child, Bond's intricate plot is his own invention, continually shifting focus between the poet Basho, the tyrant Shogo, and the priest Kiro. Bond's "comedy" implicitly condemns their different behaviors: Basho writes poems while Shogo establishes a cruel order in the city; Kiro seeks personal fulfillment first through the agency of Basho, then through Shogo, but he shrinks from their violence. When British "justice" overtakes Shogo, Bond splits the stage: On one side Kiro reads the delicate haiku of the artist Basho – actually poems by Bond – but on the other side Basho, having recognized in Shogo the child he once abandoned, declares: "If I had looked in its eyes I would have seen the devil, and I would have put it in the water and held it under with these poet's hands." Bond's poet believes that he can murder a child.

After Shogo is lynched (to the glee of Basho and his British allies), the priest Kiro knifes himself ritually but silently. From the river a man calls for help. Saving himself unaided, and unaware of Kiro's suicide, the nameless man berates the dead priest with the final words of the play: "I could have drowned." Kiro virtually drowns in his own blood, but the man, as though newly born, lives on in hopeful conclusion. Of the three principals, Shogo and Kiro behave irresponsibly because they were victimized as children, but the artist Basho emerges as a villain because he warbled in haiku while the city suffered its successive tyrants. As Christopher Innes notes: "He represents false culture; and as the only outright 'villain' in Bond's early plays, he reflects the strength of Bond's conviction that art must be politically committed" (*Modern British Drama*, p. 160). Unlike Shepard, whose "loner" artists are tainted but also homogenized by the temptation to succeed, Bond individualizes the artist and immerses him in a whole society – priest, general, prime minister, commodore, students, peasants, soldiers, tribesmen, children (represented by dolls). Except for the caricatured British, however, members of the several classes speak with similar formality in an ahistorical Japan.

Bond sharpened and differentiated the stage idioms when, almost a decade later, he revised *Narrow Road* to *The Bundle* (1977). Bond's own linguistic versatility is displayed in the escapist verses of Basho, the dignified subservience of the Ferryman, the pointed questions by the once abandoned child, and the explosive nouns of poverty-stricken beggars who turn first to crime, and then to a revolutionary underground. Starting with the same event as in *Narrow Road*, Bond conceived a new plot, with new characters. Perhaps influenced by *Fanshen* (adapted by David Hare for the Joint Stock company, whose work Bond followed closely), he moved the setting from Japan to prerevolutionary China. This time the abandoned child, the bundle of the title, is rescued by a poor Ferryman, then apprenticed to Basho, who is not only a poet but also a judge in a repressive regime. Learning about social injustice by observing Basho, Wang becomes a rebel. When he in turn is faced with an abandoned child, Wang flings it into the river in order not to be deflected from his revolutionary purpose. Although Wang echoes Basho's cruelty to a child, Bond exonerates the rebel through a striking theatrical gesture: *"As [Wang] hurls the child far out into the river he holds a corner of the white sheet in his hand and it unravels, catches the wind and falls to hang from his hand."* The baby-bundle unravels into a momentary banner, mitigating the cruelty of the act. In the ensuing action Wang organizes an underground network, while the artist Basho continues a dual dedication – to delicate poems and merciless judgments. After Basho condemns Wang's Ferryman foster father to death, he himself grows old and demented, stumbling into the audience to plead for information about the narrow road to the deep north. At the last Basho, shrunken under his walking stick, resembles the bundle he abandoned at the play's beginning, but Wang tells the audience a fable with a lesson: "That is the worse story. To carry the dead on your back."

Although Bond claims that the Asian settings facilitated a simple and direct approach, his plots are in fact complex and intricate, and several scenes are only tangential to what he later designates as a central discourse. Dramaturgically, Bond's scenes resemble those of Brecht in their self-contained quality, but the scenes occur in sequence rather than montage. It is probable, too, that Bond's corrosive portrait of the evil poet-judge Basho is the deliberate obverse of Brecht's canny scribe-judge Azdak, and Bond's good Ferryman resembles Brecht's good Grusha of *The Caucasian Chalk Circle*, since both are seduced by a helpless infant. More important, Bond's portrait of an artist, the Asian poet as villain, emboldened him to dramatize fallible English writers in his plays of the 1970s.

The first of these is a fictional writer in *The Sea* (1972). Sometimes called Bond's *The Tempest*, written after his *Lear*, *The Sea* is a harmonizing comedy after tragedy. The Prospero figure is an upper-class Mrs. Rafi in a turn-of-the-century town on England's East Coast. While contemporary critics were reading a dominant ideology into traditional British culture, Bond created an upper-class character who manipulates culture to dominate her subordinates; she writes, directs, and produces a pageant for the local Coastguard Fund. Her subject is the Orpheus–Eurydice myth, which we see only in rehearsal, in the funniest scene of this "comedy."[10] Bond etches the town's social hierarchy into the amateur endeavor, where Mrs. Rafi's pretentiousness unwittingly subverts her dialogue: "Eurydice, let me clasp your marble bosom to my panting breast and warm it with my heart." Unlike the Orpheus whose role she plays, Mrs. Rafi charms no one with her music, and she rescues no beloved from hell, which she enters to the tune of "Home Sweet Home." As Elizabeth Hale Winkler perceives: "Almost all of the songs in the drama belong to the high comedy world of Mrs. Rafi and are used to uncover the hollow pretensions and perverted values of upper-middle-class society" (*Function of Song*, p. 153). Elegant and fastidious, Mrs. Rafi resembles Basho in regarding art as escapist, while she callously oppresses her social inferiors. *The Sea* gains strength from Bond's renunciation of the political sermons of his Basho plays.

The untalented artist Mrs. Rafi is a comic protagonist who invites our ridicule, but a year later Bond grapples with England's greatest artist, setting Shakespeare centerstage in *Bingo* (1973). Bingo is a game of chance, played for money on numbered squares, and so it is in Bond's play, but the game is deadly, as underlined by his subtitle "Scenes of Money and Death." In Bond's oeuvre *The Sea* (1972) directly precedes *Bingo* (1973); in the earlier play a young man Willy turns his back on a moribund English town, in order to build a new life elsewhere. Conversely in *Bingo* a dramatist (also named Will) has returned from London to his native English town, where he finds life increasingly intolerable. Bond's *Bingo*, after his re-view of *King Lear* and *The Tempest*, boldly stages the Bard himself.

Bond's Introduction to the published text of *Bingo* mentions his modifications of historical fact "for dramatic convenience." Set in and around Shakespeare's still extant home at New Place, Stratford, in 1615–16, *Bingo* depicts an old man, his great works behind him, hoping to retire in obscurity and security. Bond eschews the national myth of a Merrie England bubbling with creative spirits, for autumn envelops Stratford, as it does the town's best-known citizen: "It's the last of the sun."

Bingo first presents Shakespeare with writing paper in hand. After a few moments we learn that the paper is host not to immortal words but to worldly numbers – Shakespeare's calculations toward his financial security. With that goal in mind, Bond's Shakespeare acquiesces to the land enclosures that starve out poor Stratford farmers and force them to migrate. The play's villain, Combe, guarantees Shakespeare's holdings at the price of his silence in the mounting protest against enclosure: "It pays to sit in a garden."

In six scenes the *public* plot about Shakespeare, money, and death is balanced by a *private* plot about Shakespeare, money, and death, for Shakespeare's wife and his daughter Judith are the money-greedy monsters he has made of them: "I loved you with money." Shakespeare's bourgeois family is contrasted with a lower-class one: Shakespeare's wise old servant, her mentally deficient husband, and their Puritan son. The two families speak different dialects – coldly correct English in the one household and warmly active East Anglian in the other. The Old Woman loves both her husband and her son, but the latter abhors the carnal appetites of his brain-damaged father: "He hev the mind of a twelve year ol' an' the needs on a man." Dispossessed by the land enclosure, rebellious against such dispossession, the Son accidentally shoots his father in a wintry confrontation of opposing forces.

Each half of the six-scene play pivots on an outsider's arrival in Stratford. In Part I it is a nameless, homeless Young Woman, soon sentenced to whipping "till the blood runs" and afterward to hanging. She graphically binds the plot threads: given money by Shakespeare and blame by his daughter, fornicating with the feeble-

49

minded Old Man, judged by the landowner Combe in his office as magistrate. Her gibbeted body is visible throughout scene 3.

In Part II the outsider is Ben Jonson, stopping in Stratford on his walk to Scotland. Vigorous with lived experience, Jonson confesses his long-standing hatred to his rival, but he is oblivious of the peasant-rebels at the next table. A climactic Bond scene of split focus presents at one table the two drunken writers, and at the other table fomenters of revolution. Richard Cave pinpoints the richness of that scene: "Shakespeare is in an altogether finer mould [than Jonson], yet his presence in this scene is disturbing as he submits to Jonson's pressure to drink till he is insensible. Through the device of the double focus Bond is asking us to adopt two perspectives on the action" (*New British Drama*, p. 282) – an understanding both of the brewing revolution and of the inaction of the artists. Almost incidentally, Jonson shows Shakespeare the poison that he bought "In a moment of strength."

Outsiders are gone from Stratford after scene 4, but Jonson's poison is in Shakespeare's possession throughout scenes 5 and 6. Bedridden, Shakespeare is beset by his (offstage) hysterical wife, his importunate daughter, and his housekeeper's Puritan son rationalizing away his guilt at his father's death. A self-blaming Shakespeare intones: "Was anything done? Was anything done?" When the land-rich Combe enters his sickroom, Shakespeare asks for the poison as though it were medicine: "Some tablets. There. On the table. Please." As Combe and the Son exchange recriminations, Shakespeare swallows tablet after tablet of poison. Alone and unconscious, Shakespeare is ignored by his daughter Judith, so intent is she on finding his will. Shakespeare dies while Judith repeats in disappointment: "Nothing." The "emptiness and silence" at the start of *Bingo* prefigure the death and "nothing" at the end – at the dawn of British capitalism.

Bond's Shakespeare is a far more socially sensitive writer than his Basho or Mrs. Rafi, and yet the most frequent scenic direction in *Bingo* is *"Shakespeare doesn't react."* His is a concentrated aria, penetrating to the ubiquitous suffering of victims. In scene 3 Puritans picnic near the gibbeted Young Woman, and they register no awareness of an abyss between such punishment and their prayers, but Shakespeare associates her fate with London bearbaiting at his theatre. In scene 4 Shakespeare hears the rebellious conspiracy counterpointed against Jonson's drunken confession of hatred.

By scene 5, however, Shakespeare himself stumbles drunkenly through the snow, oblivious to the rebellion against the land enclosure. At Shakespeare's bedside in scene 6 the poet hears the parallel intransigence of the oppressive Combe and the oppressed Son. What the director William Gaskill noted of Bond's *Lear* is just as true of *Bingo*: "I think the main moments are those when more than one thing is happening on stage at once."[11] In *Bingo* "one thing" is usually Shakespeare's failure to act against suffering, for all his residual sensitivity to it, couched in spare phrases.

While the antienclosure conspiracy is formulated in scene 4, Jonson confronts Shakespeare with the tattered remains of both their London careers, more usually seen as glories of British culture. Although Jonson disparages Shakespeare's late romances – "Your recent stuff's been pretty peculiar" – Bond implies the similarity of the two playwrights who have both failed to act toward social progress. Bond's Jonson accuses his Shakespeare of being "serene," although we have been witness to his deep disquiet. Jonson confesses to a hatred not only of Shakespeare but of their common art (as of Bond's own): "Fat white fingers excreting dirty black ink." Although Jonson spurns Shakespeare's compliment – "a very good writer" – he has no qualms about accepting money from the successful dramatist. Then as now, artists worry about survival and security.

Bond's Shakespeare is too guilt-ridden to write, but Bond situates his own fifth scene in a blizzard on the heath, which recalls the heath scene of *King Lear*. In Shakespeare's tragedy Lear rages against his daughters, and Bond's Shakespeare expands on the hate that Jonson confessed: "There's no limit to my hate." As Lear arrives at self-knowledge – "O, I have ta'en too little care of this" – Bond's Shakespeare realizes: "Every writer writes in other men's blood. . . . If I wasn't dead I could kill myself." Back in his room, before killing himself, Bond's Shakespeare revises Jonson's image of the writer: "White worms excreting black ink." At the threshold of death, Bond's Bard debases Jonson's "fat fingers" to "worms."

In the Introduction to *Bingo* Bond states: "I wrote *Bingo* because I think the contradictions in Shakespeare's life are similar to the contradictions in us." What Bond *preaches* is the contradiction of *artistic* endeavor in a *capitalist* society, which begins with the land enclosures of the early seventeenth century. What Bond *dramatizes*, however, is a hypersensitive artist whose verbal fluidity is

51

eroded by his witness to and participation in widespread social injustice.[12] New Place is not a home, although it was Bond's original title for his play.

Bingo (1973) and *The Fool* (1975) pivot on the same subject: the English writer's response to his time and society. *Bingo* is set in and around New Place, with a time span of a little over half a year. *The Fool*, in contrast, moves around Northborough, Ely, and London; the time span is some forty years of the nineteenth century, and the eight-scene plot rambles through several peripeteias – John Clare avoiding arrest, his refusal to expunge class criticism from his poems, his romanticizing of Mary while married to Patty, the latter's acquiescence to his incarceration in an insane asylum, Clare's brief escape from the asylum. Through all events Clare keeps writing: "Bin scribblin day-in-day-out for years." Bond's Bard and Clare both avoid social action, but their social sensitivity drives the one to suicide and the other to the madhouse.

The eight scenes of *The Fool* are more liberally populated than the six of *Bingo* – some forty speaking parts against twelve, many drawn from the life of John Clare. Martin Esslin has succinctly summarized the central difference between these two English poets who have attracted the English poet Edward Bond:

> The Shakespeare of *Bingo* is a highly successful artist who becomes enmeshed in society's guilt precisely *because* he is a financial success and has to invest his money, whereas *The Fool* shows the fate of an artist who cannot support himself by his writing. *The Fool* dramatizes the life story – and the bewilderment – of an individual of great talent who lacks the self-awareness which would enable him to master his personal destiny, just as he also lacks the historical and political consciousness that would allow him to make rational political decisions. . . . It is this lack of understanding which makes Bond's Clare a *fool*.   ("Nor Yet a 'Fool' to Fame . . . ," p. 44)[13]

Clare is also a fool in his entertainment of the wealthy, but he never acquires the witty wisdom of the Shakespearean fool.

Bond's play delays focus on Clare, for his early scenes offer a panoramic view of England in an age of transition: a squierarchy adjusting to capitalism while demanding feudal servitude from its workers, a clergy with eyes carefully averted from the here-and-now, Christmas alms dissolved into shrunken wages, petty thefts punishable by hanging, prizefighters maiming each other for professional gamblers, alcoholic Charles Lamb and his mad sister Mary, and homeless vagabonds roaming through the country.

For each social stratum of *The Fool* Bond creates a language. The play opens on a naïve Mummer's Play enacted by Lord Milton's tenants, but its coda is the lugubrious piety of the parson and the educated clichés of the gentlemen. When Clare becomes the pet of London intellectuals, we hear the pseudolyricism of Mrs. Emmerson – "It is my ambition to be at your side when the muse calls" – the gambling slang of the boxer backers, the sophisticated cynicism of Charles Lamb. Later there are vagabond Irishmen who sound like today's Cockneys. Bond's most musical language, however, is reserved for the poet Clare and his fellow villagers, whose idiom he echoes. Although the play is set mainly in Northamptonshire, the dialect is East Anglian, which has been praised by Bond: "I use it because of its curious concrete feel, its repetitiveness, it's like a sort of hammer knocking, knocking, knocking. But at the same time it can be very agile and witty. It's language which imitates experience." (Hay & Roberts, *Bond: A Study*, p. 200) Never mired in stiff syntax, Clare's compatriots express emotion through repetition of simple words, particularly "'on't" which can mean don't, won't, can't, shouldn't, wouldn't, am not. "On'y" and "'on't" pulse through John Clare's speech before he is reduced to slavering consonants.

John Clare, sometimes called the Peasant Poet, is Bond's fool of the title, who is robbed by society of the "bread and love" of the subtitle. Although Clare probably attracted Bond by his precise witness to the natural world, his pungent colloquial diction, and his unabashed class pride, there is no reference to the poetry until midway through the play, and there are no quotations at all from actual poems. For that poet in that cruel society Bond finds two main images – the prison (the setting of scene 4) and the madhouse (the setting of the final scene). Although these institutions confine Clare, they house the only cooperative communities in the play. The prisoners break out in a chorus of laughter at the news of their pardon – a chorus in which John Clare joins.[14] By the final scene in the asylum, the inmate John Clare speaks incomprehensible gibberish, but the inmate Mary Lamb deciphers his mumblings, translating them into our common English language.

At the last, Clare is deprived even of the words that he prized above "bread and love." During the course of the play, we have seen Mary give stolen bread to Clare, a warden give bread rations to prisoners, the Mary of Clare's fantasy give the condemned Darkie bread that he is unable to swallow, and Clare sell Mary to the Irish vagabond for a piece of bread and cheese. Emerging from his Mary fantasy, Clare appreciates the power of bread: "Bread goo from mouth t'mouth an' what it taste of: other mouths. . . . I am a poet an' I teach men how to eat." But the artist Clare does not teach them how to obtain the food to eat; or how to overthrow a system predicated upon slow starvation. Or indeed how to survive within the English society of his time. The critics Hay and Roberts argue for the hopeful ending of *The Fool,* which moves from dark early scenes to brilliant sunshine in the final scene, but no theatre wizardry can efface our last view of Clare in a wheelchair, *"a shrivelled puppet"* uttering gnomic gutterals. Like Shakespeare before him in Bond's work, the fool Clare has contributed to his own destruction, even though class-ridden England is finally to blame.

In *Bingo* and *The Fool* Bond's artist figures are inactive, especially if we compare them with Shepard's musicians, whose music we usually hear. Shakespeare's writing days are over, and Bond quotes none of Clare's lyrics. Yet Bond dramatizes their colleagues to convey the literary milieu – Ben Jonson in the one play and Charles Lamb in the other. The milieu is familiar in today's England, with its close-knit group centered in London, whence the literati look down upon the rest of the world. In both these plays, Bond locates his English artists on a larger social canvas, and it is in the textural specificity and authenticity of that rough English cloth that Bond has no match.

As opposed to such distinctive cultural icons as Clare and Shakespeare, Shepard's musical artists are barely distinguishable (except for Cavale, Hoss, Crow, and Dylan). In contrast, Shepard's few stage writers are incisively etched. If, like the musicians, they are to some degree autobiographical, they are also self-parodic.[15] In *Angel City* (1976) Rabbit Brown, ostensibly a writer although he is never so designated, is summoned to Hollywood. The only Shepard character to boast of being an artist, Rabbit looks like an innocent, traveling by buckboard and festooned with bundles. He acclimates quickly, however, and when he finally duels with the producer who summoned him to the infernal city, *"They were one being with opposing parts."* Writer and huckster, they both turn green, the color of American money and Los Angeles smog.

Earlier in the play, Rabbit proposes a threeway cooperation of Hollywood artists – the musician Tympani, the budding actress Miss Scoons, and himself. However, his purpose is obscure. Having announced that he is "ravenous for power," does he take this path to that power? By the end of *Angel City* Rabbit and Wheeler, shaman-writer and wheeler-dealer, are not only prey to the ooze of green liquid; they have themselves become actors in a disaster movie, transferred to the performance side of the stage screen. Despite the background horror, Shepard's dramatic critique of Hollywood is fanciful and funny, including mockery of the self-important artists.

Hollywood again looms over the writers in Sam Shepard's *True West* (1980), the last play in his "family trilogy." A well-groomed and well-educated Austin house-sits for his mother while he composes his "project" for a Hollywood producer. His ne'er-do-well brother Lee arrives from the desert, not only intruding upon the project – a word he pummels into ridicule – but casually pronouncing his own art "ahead of its time." Moreover, Lee can even wax critical when his brother lapses into cliché: "That is a dumb fuckin' line." In order to be alone with the producer, Austin reluctantly bribes Lee with his car keys, only to be excluded from a game of early morning golf – offstage. Abruptly, having lost a game or a gamble, the producer accepts Lee's idea for a Western movie, with its "ring of truth," and he demotes Austin to mere writer of the dialogue.

The two brothers thereupon abruptly exchange behaviors. Stealing like Lee, Austin has filled his mother's kitchen with *"a wide variety of models, mostly chrome"* toasters, and Lee comes to grips with Austin's typewriter, which he destroys with a nine-iron golf club. Nevertheless, after Austin toasts some bread for them, the brothers labor together over Lee's Western scenario, in which two men chase each other across the prairie: "What they don't know is that each one of 'em is afraid." Braving one another, the two brothers are hilariously timid before their mother, who returns unexpectedly to her demolished kitchen: *"the stage is ravaged."* Each of the brothers reaches toward the other's life-style: Austin yearns to live like Lee in the desert, and Lee appropriates his mother's best China because "I'm tired of eatin' outa' my bare hands, ya' know. It's not civilized." While Lee is preoccupied with the porcelain, Austin defensively wraps a telephone wire around his brother. Their mother having departed, Austin bargains with Lee: "Gimme a little headstart and I'll turn you loose." No sooner done than Lee springs up to block Austin's escape: "*the figures of the brothers now appear to be caught in a vast desert-like landscape.*"

What begins in familiar rival-brothers realism ends in a mythic image, which pleases Shepard *because "True West* doesn't end." Modulating an ironic line from *Waiting for Godot* – "Time stands still when you're havin' fun" – and a Ionescan profusion of objects, Shepard explodes the traditional American suburban kitchen, which cannot be the locus of artistic creation. Shepard himself thinks *True West* is "about double nature" (Dugdale, *File on Shepard,* p. 43), and he enfolds that idea into the play, when a drunken Austin tells his brother: "[The producer] thinks we're the same person." The play dances, however, around *two* brothers in a subtly symbiotic relationship.

Several critics interpret the play as a triumph of the old true West of Lee versus the new consumer West of Austin, but this view neglects the comic complexity of the brothers.[16] As early as *Cowboys* (1964) Shepard knew that the Wild West is a fiction, with its cowboys and Indians, its heroism and lawlessness, its veneer of male bonding. Shepard was not naïvely nostalgic for trigger-happy, sharpshooting heroes; his stage cowboys tend to be old men, ghosts, or composites. By 1980 Shepard was well aware that cowboy fiction was fostered by rampant Hollywood commercialism, to which he himself was "immune and contaminated at the same time." By 1980 it is impossible to know the true West, if there ever was one, but the two brothers – the wild man and the domesticated man – might join to create a new fiction, or they might destroy one another. In *True West* Austin excels at beginnings and Lee prefers endings; however Shepard may pose as Lee in interview and photograph, he resembles Austin in his explosive beginnings, and his endings are inconclusive.

It suits my Anglo–American comparison that Austin, setting artistry aside, accepts Lee's taunt: "You couldn't steal a toaster without losin' yer lunch." In Bond's *The Fool* bread is both the staff of life and the symbol of human community. In Shepard's *True West* toast is something of a joke, for Austin to butter and stack, for Lee to crush with feet and teeth. The image may serve to differentiate playwrights who resemble each other in their broad brushstrokes, their brilliant colloquialisms, and their *angst*-riddled humor. Bond's bread has to be theatricalized by actor and director; his scenic directions provide opportunities rather than instruction.[17] Bread for ill-gotten toasters is Shepard's culminating image of surplus food in pulverized families – the half-price artichokes of *Curse of the Starving Class*, the unearthed corn and carrots of *Buried Child*. Fortuitously linked by concrete stage images of bread or bundles, Bond's scenes are often arresting in their double focus, whereas those of Shepard erupt into the unexpected. It is somewhat surprising then that the two playwrights create comparable artists. Bond's attitude toward his artists is always adversarial, but he mitigates his critique between the villainous Basho and the finally inarticulate Clare. Shepard is invariably ambivalent; prey to the lure of fame and fortune, his artists yearn for purity or creativity. Both Bond and Shepard situate their several artists in moribund countries and cultures, but their artists nevertheless energize the stage.

Phrasal energies
Harold Pinter and David Mamet

Alan Ayckbourn and Neil Simon ground their several stage languages upon the firm foundation of shaky families. Edward Bond and Sam Shepard thread the figure of the artist through their far more varied plays. Harold Pinter and David Mamet share neither figure nor common ground, but they both pitch telling phrases with deadly accuracy. More than other contemporary Anglophone playwrights, they are verbal marksmen. Today the dramatic languages of Pinter and Mamet are enveloped in superlatives, but not too long ago their detractors denounced the English playwright for obfuscation and the American for obscenity. Recent plays of Pinter were also dismissed as political, and after *Oleanna* (1992) Mamet has been charged with misogyny, but I prefer to compare their taut, striking phrases.

Both Pinter and Mamet came to playwriting via acting, the Englishman in provincial repertory and the American under the aegis of Method practitioners. As playwrights, both men have battened on criminal films, and both have written screenplays that are not limited to crime. At the same time, both Pinter and Mamet derive obliquely from Beckett in their tacit acceptance of the proscenium, their sparsely peopled stages, the seriousness of their comedy, the resonance of their dialogue, and their common predilection for repetition. Pinter and Mamet stray from Beckett, however, in the localized time and place of their dramatic action, the one in England and the other in the United States.

"All we have left is the English language," chirps Spooner in Pinter's *No Man's Land*, and although Mamet characters do not credit the American language as their lifesaver, it is. If early reviewers praised Pinter at all, they did so for his tape-recorder accuracy of the lower-class idiom of East London. Comparably, Mamet's reviewers praised his accurate depiction of the low life of Chicago. The two cities are in fact some five thousand miles apart, but in the theatre we hear similar dialogue strategies from their denizens – strategies more subtle than electronic echoes. The sheer economy of phrasing is noteworthy; delivered explosively, words are short and sparse, recycled through obsessive repetition. A seeming lexical poverty nevertheless yields rare flavor as cliché is seasoned with incongruous jargon, and vituperation soars aromatically.[1] From menace to mannerism, Pinter, the conscientious objector, commands a verbal arsenal for his Lorenzian stage skirmishes. Mamet, a marksman who delights in firearms, appropriates several of Pinter's weapons, especially in his Business Trilogy (my designation of *American Buffalo* [1975], *Glengarry Glen Ross* [1983], and *Speed-the-Plow* [1988]). Mamet dedicated *Glengarry Glen Ross* to Pinter, whom he praises: "Pinter was probably the most influential when I was young and malleable ... *The Homecoming*, *The Basement*, especially the revue sketches. I felt a huge freedom because of Pinter's sketches to deal in depth and on their own with such minutiae" (Dean, "Musings," p. 13). I propose to examine "such minutiae" in the dialogue of plays of Pinter and Mamet.

I begin, however, with what often goes unheard in their dialogue – the titles of the plays, which are direction pointers to the interior. Pinter affirms: "My plays are what the titles are about" – itself a curious inversion of the expected: "My titles are what the plays are about" (Packard, "An Interview with Harold Pinter," p. 82). *The Room*, a theme as well as a place, is a shrunken version of Kafka's *Castle*.[2] *The Dumb Waiter*, a character as well as a prop, diminishes Beckett's waiters for Godot. *The Birthday Party* climaxes in a festivity that winds down funereally. The would-be caretaker in the play of that title, expelled from a sheltering room, is thrust into care for himself. *The Collection* is sexual rather than sartorial. With ruthless Ruth, a home may be coming after the curtain falls on *The Homecoming*, in a double entendre, one face whore and the other mother. Rival claimants of *Old Times* are dirtily buried when a newly bathed Kate declares her independence from old times. Expelled like the would-be caretaker, Spooner the would-be secretary finalizes his own exclusion from "a happy household" by consigning the host to an icy and silent no man's land. The lack of an article in the title *Betrayal* implies generalized behavior, for each of the play's three characters betrays the other two. In contrast, the single word *Moonlight* does not betray its threshold of otherworldliness.

Mamet's titles are less paronomastic, but they are never merely literal. *Lakeboat* is a reduced version of the American showboat tradition, and the circular absurdist tradition. *Duck Variations* mocks its own music, but elegiacally. *Sexual Perversity in Chicago* displays emotional perversity within easy urban sexuality. *American Buffalo* puns on a buffalo-headed nickel through which each one of three characters "buffaloes" the other two. *A Life in the Theatre* intercuts personal with professional moments in *two lives*, one actor at the rise of his career, and the other waning. Two Mamet plays with pastoral titles are mired in human cruelty – *The Woods* and *Glengarry Glen Ross*. *Speed-the-Plow* and *Oleanna* are ironic titles, for a Hollywood harvest is blasphemously blessed, and an ideal community harbors stage violence.

Below the titles, both playwrights are verbal engravers rather than muralists. Both dramatize against type of their respective countries. Modern American drama is anchored in the family play, whereas modern British drama has skimmed over various, usually genteel, professions. Despite an occasional butcher, driver, designer, or publisher, however, English Pinter's main plays are family based; conversely, those of the American Mamet take place in a shop, a radio station, a theatre, or especially in offices. Both in the Pinter family and the Mamet office, it's a man's world.

Most of Pinter's plays are structured in acts, whereas Mamet jabs with quick scenes. Indeed Mamet's shorter plays are largely duets, and the critic Richard Eder has quipped that the playwright was still waiting for Sophocles to invent the third actor. Mamet's longer plays resemble those of Pinter in a music-hall pattern where stage duologues are punctuated by a monologue. At tense moments in dramas of Pinter and Mamet, duets escalate to duels.

Pinter is reluctant to theorize about his drama. Mamet in interviews cites Aristotle and Stanislavski as tutelary deities, via Sanford Meisner's Neighborhood Playhouse in New York City. The intensity of their drama compels actors to "play the moment," and yet each play has an overarching action. In the words of Mamet's preferred director Greg Mosher: "You can't stage the text; you can only stage the action" (Kane, *David Mamet: A Casebook*, p. 238). Nevertheless, the playwright writes the text that the director stages as action. John Arden's felicitous comment on Pinter is thus equally valid for Mamet: "The slantindicular observation of unconsidered speech and casual action . . . illuminate[s] loneliness and lack of communication" (Marowitz, Milne, & Hale, *The Encore Reader*, p. 125). Speech may be "unconsidered" by the characters, but it is scrupulously considered by Pinter and Mamet, who mold dialogue with phoneme and phrase, syllable and sentence. Their shaping sounds, layers of lexicon, and contextual savor are not always appreciated. Acerbic John Simon has denigrated Pinter's language: ". . . only repetitions, insults, *non sequiturs,* and pauses. This too is a language, I grant you, but is it a language for human beings?" (Page, *File on Pinter,* p. 36)

The question deserves no answer, and I for one revel in the dramatic dynamics of that language. Both playwrights dabble in such soundplay as rhyme, chiming, and alliteration (Leech, *Linguistic Guide to English Poetry*, p. 95). Mamet has explicitly valued sound above sense: "Any language used on stage should be poetic, i.e. it should communicate the intentions of speakers and thus of the author, through tools of sound, rhythm, assonance, dissonance, meter, primarily, and only secondarily through the conscious understanding of tendentious expressions" (Dean, "Musings," p. 25). Pinter's soundplay is less obtrusive, like McCann's rhymes in his attack on Stanley in *The Birthday Party* – "porch/lurch/church"; or Goldberg's alliterative and repeated boast that he is "fit as a fiddle." Edward of *A Slight Ache* accuses the matchseller in dissonance: ". . . you sit like a hump, a mouldering heap." And Max of *The Homecoming* complains assonantly: "I suffered the pain, I've still got the pangs . . . ." Spooner of *No Man's Land* confesses to being a "betwixt twig peeper." Often this soundplay deflates the player, irrespective of his social class. One of Pinter's most enigmatic plays, *Moonlight,* is suffused in chiming; the dying protagonist can be sonically lyrical – "The past is a mist" – or vituperative – "voracious, lascivious, libidinous" or "blasphemy, gluttony, and buggery."

As early as Mamet's *Lakeboat* (1970) we hear the rhyme "larboard or starboard" and the alliteration "Sure as shit." In that play Mamet introduces a rhyme that he subsequently recycles in *Sexual Perversity:* "humping and bumping." Teach of *American Buffalo* inveighs dissonantly against "Fuckin' fakes," and he prods his colleague Don assonantly: "It's kickass or kissass." The hero-victim of

Glengarry is nicknamed Levene the Machine because of his (former) sales prowess, but he pleads: "I need the leads"; the rhymed one rhymes. In *Speed-the-Plow* rhyme connotes celebration; as producers of the Doug Brown buddy film, Bob assures Charlie about the women who will succumb to them: "It's Boy's Choice." Charlie flatters Bob: "You're Yertle the Turtle." Even out of context, Mamet's soundplay beats to a quicker tempo than that of Pinter, with characters constantly interrupting one another. Sometimes sheer speed of utterance reduces Mamet's Bernie, Teach, Moss, Roma, and Charlie to "blah blah blah." (In spite of Mamet's use of parentheses to signal an inner thrust to a sentence, I could not detect this in productions in either New York or London.)

Soundplay beats a tattoo through the dialogue of both playwrights, with the phoneme as its smallest unit. It is, however, the repetition of *words* and *phrases* that lingers in the memory. Comic when first heard, these repetitions can reveal the insecurity of the characters of both playwrights: Meg assures and reassures Stanley that "This house is on the list," and McCann insidiously offers him a "prospect." Rhythmed by hesitations, Davies's repetitions betray his anxiety in the very first moments of *The Caretaker:* "Sit down? Huh...I haven't had a good sit down...I haven't had a proper sit down...well, I couldn't tell you....."[3] Pinter's repetitions are sometimes immediate, sometimes separated by stretches of stage time, but manic Mamet is almost always immediate: George's "dying" ducks of *Duck Variations*, Bernie's "broads" of *Sexual Perversity*, "the deal" or "the book" in *American Buffalo*, "the leads" or "the board" in *Glengarry*.[4]

Not only does each individual character seek refuge in his own repetitions, but phrases are also bounced between two characters. At the close of each act of Beckett's *Waiting for Godot* the same words are spoken, but in different voices. So at the beginning and end of Pinter's *The Basement* the same words are spoken, but in the different voices of Law and Stott. In *The Homecoming* the link between Ruth and her pimp brother-in-law Lenny is forged onstage when she repeats his phrase about knowing Venice, if she or he had participated in the "Italian campaign" of World War II. Pinter's most striking example of verbal repetition in a different voice occurs in *No Man's Land*, where the title phrase is first uttered as a generalization by a hesitant Hirst: "No man's land...

does not move...or change...or grow old...remains...forever
...icy...silent." A similar passage virtually concludes the play
when Spooner situates Hirst in the bleak territory of the title, replacing the three-dot series by less hesitant commas, and intensify-
ing the negatives to "never"s: "You are in no man's land. Which
never moves, which never changes, which never grows older but
which remains forever, icy and silent." The words are almost identical, but Hirst's hesitations have been spliced into a death sentence by Spooner's four "which"s. Comparably, the opening and
closing of *Moonlight* reveals Bridget in faint light speaking about
the dark. In contrast, the initial and final phrases of Mamet's *Prairie du Chien* are less obtrusive: "I wish I could sleep like that."

If we momentarily ignore the lexicons of Pinter and Mamet,
rhythm distinguishes them. Pinter's silences are notorious, and
they are also graduated, lengthening from comma and dash, to period, to three dots, to *Pause,* and to the relatively rare *Silence* and
even rarer *Long silence.*[5] The only wholly silent character in Pinter is the Matchseller of *A Slight Ache,* a play conceived for radio,
but Pinter's quieter characters tend to dominate the prattlers – Bert
in *The Room,* Ben in *The Dumb Waiter,* Ruth in *The Homecoming,* Kate in *Old Times.* Pinter early recognized the power of quiet:
"The more intense the feeling, the less articulate its expression"
(Worth, *Revolutions in English Drama,* p. 90). For Mamet's characters, silence is retreat, but speech empowers. Thus Bernie Litko's
verbal perversity snuffs out his friend Danny's romance. Slow-
worded Bobby is the weakling of *American Buffalo,* but in *Glengarry Glen Ross* a harried, powerless Aaronow contrasts with a vicious, powerful Williamson, the two least loquacious characters. In
Mamet's duet plays each partner is usually accorded equal time;
thus, in the throes of *Oleanna,* the professor dominates the first
scene, but the student dominates the third.

Pinter and Mamet selectively repeat phoneme, word, and phrase,
but sentences form their most pervasive rhythms, adept as they
are at stichomythic duets that sometimes rise interrogatively. Like
a John Donne poem, Pinter's plays can begin with questions – *The
Birthday Party, The Dumb Waiter, A Slight Ache, The Hothouse,
A Night Out, The Homecoming, Old Times.* In Act II of *The Birthday Party* Goldberg and McCann shoot double-barreled questions at
Stanley; by Act III Goldberg warns McCann: "Questions, questions.

Stop asking me so many questions." But McCann pleads with Goldberg: "I was asking you, Nat. Honest to God. Just a question, that's all, just a question, do you see, do you follow me?" The two interrogators, Goldberg and McCann, may exchange questions, but their attack on an inarticulate Stanley accelerates to accusation. In a Pinter play of the same vintage Gus refuses to be the titular dumb waiter; he asks too many questions for his own good. The questions of Davies in *The Caretaker* reflect his uneasiness, and the anxious questions of Bill in *The Collection* also hang unanswered. Questions are enigmatic in *The Homecoming* until they point pragmatically to Ruth's future home. Mother and son exchange unanswered questions in *Family Voices*. In other words, certain Pinter characters at certain dramatic moments in many of his plays sting or flail interrogatively; the questions skewer a victim. In *Moonlight*, however, the questions of Andy, the dying protagonist, are largely rhetorical, and they tend increasingly to cluster.

Interrogation is also prevalent in Mamet, who conveys the insecurity of his characters in flurries of brief queries. A recurrent inquiry is "Am I wrong?" Gradually introduced in Mamet's early plays, questions become Danny's habitual rhythm toward Bernie in *Sexual Perversity* (1974), and questions punctuate the dialogue of the Business Trilogy. When questions go unanswered, the pace quickens. *American Buffalo* opens on Don Dubrow's "So?" which is at once expanded to "So what, Bob?" Levene's second speech in *Glengarry* protests, "Will you please?" Early in *Speed-the-Plow* a question is quoted from a stage book: "How are things made round?"

Mamet introduces his interrogative rhythms early, and they often recur. *American Buffalo* immerses us immediately in a catechismic conversation between Don Dubrow of the ReSale Shop and his gopher, the ex-junkie Bob. When the misnamed Teach intrudes upon this teacher–pupil pair, he cloaks his own questions in surmise about "the thing," "the job," "the mark," "the shot," "business." In *Glengarry Glen Ross* interrogation sometimes cedes to exclamation, but questions still govern the salesman Levene's pleas to the office manager Williamson; questions also stress the complaints about "leads" from the salesmen Moss and Aaronow, which mount toward an unstaged office trashing. It is also offstage that a detective questions the real-estate salesmen, but in the last moments of the play the honest salesman Aaronow phrases and rephrases questions as to the culprit, before he returns to business with another weary question: "Did the leads come in yet?"[6]

In *Speed-the-Plow* rising inflections signal exultation more often than solicitation of information on the part of the two self-styled Hollywood whores, Bob Gould and Charlie Fox. Once they grasp that the reigning male star is willing to make a buddy movie for them, Bob rhapsodizes: "The question, your crass question: how much money could we stand to make...?" But when Bob, skillfully manipulated by the temporary secretary Karen, betrays the "crass question" for a movie of edification, he awards Charlie the final favor of "one question" to Karen: "If [Bob] had said 'No' [to greenlighting the movie of edification], would you have gone to bed with him?" Karen's negative reply is Charlie's positive triumph, and he closes the play in a return to rhapsodic rhetoric, only perfunctorily interrogative: "What are we put on earth to do? ... Whose name goes above the title? ... Then how bad can life be?" *Oleanna* opens with John's question into the telephone, which he often rephrases or repeats, and his beating of Carol is punctuated by accusative questions: "After how I treated you...? You should be...*Rape you*...? Are you kidding me...?" The climactic rise is distinctively Mametic, whereas the enigmatic questions of Pinter characters have become bywords among an admiring "lickspittling herd of literati" (myself among them): "Is it nice? What are you drinking? Are you making me some kind of proposal? As it is? Same again?"

The *Village Voice* critic Ross Wetzsteon quotes Mamet: "I'm fascinated by the way, the way the language we use, its rhythms, actually determines the way we behave, rather than the other way around." To a large extent, however, stage behavior *is* "the language we use, its rhythms," as illustrated by Mamet's characters, beginning with *Sexual Perversity* and nowhere more pungently than in the Business Trilogy. Sharing this taste for interrogatives, the English dramatist and the American also sport rhythms that differentiate their dialogue. Pinter punctures stage speech with graduated gaps whereas Mamet characters rush pell-mell into a volubility that is only occasionally short-stopped by pauses. *Oleanna* is Mamet's pause-marked text, and when Pinter directed the play, he lengthened the pauses, so that the playing time was nearly an hour longer than in Mamet's own production.

When Pinter the playwright composes duets, they usually constitute an attack and defense – Mr. Kidd against Rose, Riley against Rose, Ben against Gus, Flora against Edward, and, most sharply in *The Collection,* James against Bill, Harry against Bill, and James against Harry. In these combats sheer speed of attack confers power. Mamet also structures scenes as duels, but at other times a duet can stumble toward tenderness – Danny and Deborah in *Sexual Perversity,* Don and Bob in *American Buffalo;* or even whole plays – *Duck Variations, Reunion, The Woods.*

Pinter's very first play, *The Room,* abounds in short-phrased duologues, and yet the play begins and almost ends in contrasting monologues. Opening the play, Rose's repetitions and self-contradictions cast doubt on her claim: "This is a good room." Bert's brutal description of his driving cues his final violence against the blind Negro. Again in *The Caretaker* (1959), Pinter counterpoints swift duologues against monologues, with Aston's recollection of shock therapy as the most electrifying example. Pinter himself has cast doubt on Aston's veracity (Bensky, "Harold Pinter: An Interview," in Ganz, ed., *Pinter,* p. 28), but in the theatre the monologue *sounds true,* breaking the rhythm of swift volleys. Other Pinter monologues are more aggressive – Mick's fantasy of interior decoration, Edward's tales of country squiredom, Lenny's rodomontades of cruelties to women, Deeley's version of *Odd Man Out,* Briggs's verbal labyrinth on Bolsover Street. These ploys are calculated to turn their opponent's ground to quicksand. *Old Times* opens on the duologue of Kate and her uneasy husband, Deeley, but Anna breaks that rhythm with her entering monologue. In Act I of *No Man's Land* Spooner's monological garland of Victorian phrases is punctured by Hirst's monosyllables. In Act II, however, Spooner rises to monologues consonant with Hirst's Oxbridge Colonel Blimperie, before he is rhythmically deflated by the colloquial thrusts of Briggs and Foster.

Monologue, duologue, stichomythic volley, varieties of interrogation, immediate and delayed repetition, all punctuated by measured pauses, compose the "Music in that Room" of Harold Pinter (Irving Wardle's phrase). Mamet resorts to similar sonic devices, but his monologues are shorter, his interrogations more rhetorical, his pauses less varied, and his interruptions more frequent.

Blatantly colloquial in lexicon, both playwrights deploy the sonic techniques of lyric poets.

The label of inarticulacy has dogged both Pinter and Mamet, but their main characters are not only inventively voluble; they even ruminate metadialogically. Gus and Ben argue about "light the gas/light the kettle," and Edward and Flora bicker about whether wasps sting or bite. Stanley teases Meg with the word "succulent," and Joey reflects on "going the whole hog." The faintly archaic monosyllables "lest" and "gaze" attract the attention of Deeley in *Old Times,* who pedantically explains his own use of the word "globe," rather than "world." His antagonist, Anna, describes Kate's reaction to having her underwear borrowed: "nonplussed, perhaps, is the word." *No Man's Land* is exceptional in that three of the four Pinter characters are writers, but it is Spooner alone who treats language trippingly on the tongue. Not only does he wax lyrical about the English language, but he is cheered by a metaphor, he boasts about his terza rima, and his locutions carry traces of Yeats and Eliot – for example, "Experience is a paltry thing" and "I have known this before," uttered three times.[7] So self-conscious is the dialogue of *Moonlight* that it his been mistaken as Pinter's parody of himself; the dying husband and his wife dessicate the meaning of "taking the piss," which epitomizes Pinter's method in earlier plays. In *Moonlight* the dying Andy refers to tautology, solecism, and contradiction, and his wife Bel praises him: "What a lovely use of language." So dense is the play that several reviewers quoted the character Jake: "What is being said?"

In the power skirmishes of Mamet's Business Trilogy, the main characters are loquacious. Moreover, they talk obsessively about "talk," so that that verb can mean speak, ask, boast, chat, describe, explain, comfort, confide, bargain, reveal, deceive, teach, intend, and even act. In *American Buffalo* Don oxymoronically explains to Bob: "Action talks and bullshit walks." At its least devious level, talk is praise: "Now you're talking!" But it can also be dispraise: "I don't want that talk." Or "He talks a good game." Or "That's 'talk.' Our job is to *sell.*" Talk can mean plan, when Teach avers that it is good "to talk this stuff out," but Don complains that Teach cannot "talk about how he will break in." In *Glengarry* Aaronow pleads with Moss: "We're just talking about [the heist]," but within a few seconds he protests: "We're not actually *talking* about it." For the gopher Bob, as well as the real-estate client Lingk, talk denotes urgency – "I got to talk to you" – and the grammar improves slightly in the Hollywood of *Speed-the-Plow* – "I have to talk to you." The effusive salesman Roma uses "talk" to mean "listen": "I can't talk now." In Levene's pleas of *Glengarry* "talk" is request, which the office manager turns to threat: "You'll talk to me." Similarly, the detective uses the verb as a form of coercion: "Mr. Levene, I think we have to talk."

Of the three Mamet business plays *Speed-the-Plow* harps least on "talk," substituting "say" and "tell," but "talk" is nevertheless meaningful when it does occur. Charlie's verdict about the *The Bridge* is "A talky piece of puke." The confession that Charlie elicits from Karen is punctuated by her repetitions of "We talked . . . ." When she shifts her verb from "We talked" to "We decided," Charlie has virtually won his case; there are no "we" decisions in Mamet's Hollywood. *Oleanna* is in part a play about language, and, metalinguistically, the word "talk" is quietly enfolded into the dialogue. The professor repeatedly protests to his telephone callers: "I can't talk now." The student is deaf to the professor's repetitive insistence on the gentleness of his pedagogy: "I'm talking to you as I'd talk to my son." After the student's threat: ". . . we're talking about it at the Tenure Committee Hearing," she refuses his pleas: "I'm talking *straight* to you. . . . I just want to *talk* to you." Other metadialogical remarks punctuate the play. The student's opening line requests a definition: "What is a 'term of art'?" This is a prelude to her other lexical questions – about paradigm, index, predilection, allegations, indictment. In the first scene the student accuses the professor of "lots of the *language*," and in the last scene again: "The language you use." Mamet's machine-gun barrage of "talk" and "language" reinforces their meaning, in contrast to Pinter's wider vocabulary for stage speech.

As reflectors of their respective countries, Pinter and Mamet use different lexicons. Pinter's colloquial vocabulary is virtually incomprehensible to an insular American: Units of money are bob and quid; unsavory monosyllables run rife among his lower-class characters – pong, kip, daft, prat, fag, sod, muck, bird, chuff, yob, git, slag, poof, ponce, on her tod, packed out, copped it, bang on the back seat, flake off, up my street. The milk is "off," and Stanley's birthday party is "laid on." Stanley affirms that Meg is "off her conk," and he is accused of leaving his girl "in the pudding club."

Meg, concerned about Stanley's health, asks whether he has "paid a visit," and Sam in *The Homecoming* confesses to feeling "peckish." In *Moonlight* the men are particularly partial to slang; in that respect, Jake and Fred show themselves as their father's sons.

Mamet's slang, as American as Pinter's is English, is familiar from gangster films and serials: fart around, skinpop, standup guy, sharp deal, up front, off the top, poop out, half a yard, hock, cruising, lame up, plunk down, front off, big deal, c-notes, stiff someone.

Artists of articulacy, both playwrights nevertheless allow their characters to succumb to cliché. As Christopher Innes discerns: "Goldberg and McCann are themselves clichés: 'the stage Irishman and Jew.' McCann whistles 'The Mountains of Morne,' utters stock laments like 'Tullamore, where are you?' and sings romantic ballads. Goldberg sentimentalizes his 'old mum,' a wife, . . . childhood innocence and 'gefilte fish,' while being given to [crackerbox] conundrums . . . and exaggerated ethnic expressions like 'Mazeltov!'" (*Modern British Drama*, p. 284). Goldberg summons clichés to counter early morning depression: "Whenever I hear that point of view I feel cheerful. Because I know what it is to wake up with the sun shining, to the sound of the lawnmower, all the little birds, the smell of the grass, church bells, tomato juice – " Just before their departure, Pinter's Goldberg and McCann pummel Stanley with a series of uplifting clichés toward living the good life. Indeed, Jeanette Malkin reads *The Birthday Party* as the coercion of Stanley into clichés of conformity, whereas she reads Mamet's work as a depiction of characters who can speak and think only in clichés. Exceptionally, the clichés of Pinter's *Moonlight* become a colloquial requiem. Early in that play Jake quotes a vicar at a business meeting in a brilliant parody of obituaries: "It was an act, went on the vicar, which, for sheer undaunted farsightedness, unflinching moral resolve, stern intellectual vision, classic philosophical detachment, passionate religious fervour, profound emotional intensity, bloodtingling spiritual ardour, spellbinding metaphysical chutzpah – stood alone." With comparably devastating lack of discrimination, Mamet's Teach draws upon gambling and business clichés: "All that I'm saying, there's the least *chance* something might fuck up, you'd get the law down, you would take the shot, and you couldn't find the coins whatever; if you see the least chance, you cannot afford to take that chance!" And, more briefly, Teach twists the cliché "It breaks my heart" to "It turns my heart the things that you do for the kid."

The characters of Pinter and Mamet occasionally quote their respective country's quasi-philosophical clichés – Pinter: "Well, there you are." Mamet, "Life goes on. That's the way it is. This is the way things are." In *Old Times* the statement and riposte through popular songs is itself a subtle use of cliché.[8] Several Pinter upper-class characters query, "Really?" and several Mamet lower-class characters assert, "You're goddamned right" or "You're fuckin' A."

In much contemporary speech obscenities are a cliché. As spelled out by David Lan's Willy in *Painting a Wall:* "They's just words that come out but they don't mean nothing so when they's out they's like bars around me – bars what keeps me doing the same things – thinking the same things – not letting me out to grow – to learn new words. . . . I can't go and talk to anyone 'cause all I can say is fuck and shit. That's not enough" (quoted in Birch, *Language of Drama,* pp. 51–2). Pinter's earliest characters did not use obscenities, and indeed in 1960 he opposed the tendency "to open up obscene language to general commerce. It should be the dark secret language of the underworld" (Bensky, "Harold Pinter: An Interview," in Ganz, ed., *Pinter,* p. 31). Yet Edward of *A Slight Ache* (1959, on radio) offers the Matchseller "Curaçao Fockink Orange" and "A Wachenheimer Fuchsmantel Reisling." Through the length of Pinter's career the very British "bloody" and the anational "bastard" are spoken by characters of all classes, but the vocabulary is most abrasive in *The Homecoming,* the last of his downmarket dramas. The play opens on a father–son exchange of insults, and soon the two older brothers volley vituperative adjectives.

Duff in the lyrical *Landscape* (1968) is the first Pinter character to punctuate his emotion with "shit," "piss," and "arse," but not until *Old Times* (1971) does "fuck" sound out loud and clear when an increasingly nervous Deeley ironizes about Anna's world: ". . . a lobster and lobster sauce ideology we know fuck all about." *No Man's Land* (1975) is rife with obscenities; Hirst utters "piss" and "shit" lightly, before he stutters his way into a waking nightmare: "Yes, yes, come on, come on, come on, pipe up, speak up, speak up, speak up, you're fucking me about, you bastards, ghosts, long ghosts. . . ." Foster and Briggs are free with such obscenities as "balls," "bugger," "cunt," and "fuck," climaxing in Briggs's anaphoric explosion against Spooner:

> To him? To a pisshole collector? To a shithouse operator? To a jamrag vendor? What the fuck are you talking about? Look at him. He's a mingejuice bottler, a fucking shitcake baker. What are you talking to him for?

In *Moonlight* Andy on his deathbed not only utters obscenities, but he also boasts: "I kept my obscene language for the home, where it belongs." Even when Andy enters the otherworldly upper area, he retains obscene language: "Bollocks to the lot of them." More automatically than Pinter's characters, those of Mamet exploit Anglo–Saxon monosyllables – the hard consonants and clipped vowels of "fuck," "suck," "cock," and "dick.[9] Like those of Pinter, Mamet's obscenities sometimes function literally, but they also shimmer in a wider spectrum of meanings.

Mamet juggles "balls." That monosyllable is of course slang for testicles, whence it connotes masculine courage, as when Don of *American Buffalo* instructs Bob in what is required to win a card game: "Skill and talent and the balls to arrive at your own conclusions." Partridge defines "to have someone by the balls" as "to have utterly in one's power," but Don extends this metaphor to a hilariously heroic dimension: "You take [Fletcher] and you put him down in some strange town with just a nickel in his pocket, and by nightfall he'll have that town by the balls." Unlisted in Partridge is "busting one's balls" or working against insuperable obstacles, and this is Roma's claim in *Glengarry*: "I'm busting my *balls*, sell your *dirt* to fucking *deadbeats* money in the mattress. . . ."

Less savory than "balls" are the connotations of "shit," which means excrement and is therefore a term of denigration – you're fulla shit, you're shitting me. By extension, shit becomes abusive, either in itself or in the compound "shithead." Teach can turn the epithet to sanctimonious morality: "Without [free enterprise] we're just savage shitheads in the wilderness." On the other hand, shit can imply value, as in Teach's ". . . a guy's lookin' for valuable shit" or Bob Gould's ". . . jolly *shitloads* of [money]." One of Partridge's definitions equates shit with blarney, and Mamet's characters express disbelief with the exclamation: "No shit." Related perhaps to this meaning is the amiable conversation connoted by "shoot the shit." In contrast, Partridge defines "shit-eating" as sycophantic, but the repetitions of "I eat shit" by the gopher Bob suggest a deeper self-abnegation, while in *Speed-the-Plow* shit-eating describes the sinister relation between Charlie Fox and the newly empowered Bob Gould.

Mamet is most versatile in modulation of the cliché "fuck." Far from Fred's description of his boatmates in *Lakeboat* – "They say 'fuck' in direct proportion to how bored they are." – the mono-syllable reveals the intensity of the feelings of Mamet's characters, either as a pleonasm – "How the fuck do I know? un-be-fucking-lievable." – or as an isolated invective, as when Teach intones five times: "Fuckin' Ruthie." With rare literalness Teach brags: "Guys like that, I like to fuck their wives." For Partridge "to fuck up" is "to fail dismally," and "I fucked up" becomes Bob the gopher's lita-ny in *American Buffalo*. Ruefully, Teach admits: "I fuck myself." The passive mode underlines failure, as in the remark of Fireman of *Lakeboat*: ". . . if she goes redline, you're fucking fucked." Un-listed by Partridge is the strong negative imperative: "Don't fuck with me" – Don to Bob, Teach to Don, Charlie to Bob. As "shit" can mean the opposite of excrement, so "fucker" can be a term of admiration, as can "son of a bitch."

At climactic moments Mamet gathers obscenities in bouquets. While Teach *"hits Bob viciously,"* he also beats him verbally: "Grace and Ruthie up your ass, you shithead; you don't fuck with us, *I'll* kick your fucking head in. (I don't give a shit . . .)" Blows do not rain down in *Glengarry*, but when Williamson the office man-ager punctures the lie of the star salesman Roma to his client, the businessman explodes: "You stupid fucking cunt . . . I'm talking to *you*, shithead . . . What are you going to do about it, asshole. You fucking *shit*. Where did you learn your *trade*. You stupid fucking *cunt*. You *idiot*. Who ever told you you could work with *men*?" Similarly macho, a frustrated Charlie *"hits Gould"* in *Speed-the-Plow*, punctuating the blows with obscenities: "I'll fucken' kill you right here in this office. All this bullshit; you *wimp,* you *cow-ard*. . .now you got the job, and now you're going to *run* all over everything, like something broke in the *shopping* bag, you *fool* – your fucken' sissy film – you squat to pee. You old *woman.* . . ." So automatic do obscenities become in many Mamet plays that he is hard put to wield one climactically – like the Professor's "cunt" of

Oleanna. The obscenities themselves are clichés, and yet Mamet milks them for many meanings.

More often than Mamet, Pinter relieves the monotony of cliché with inventive jargon, which the *Shorter OED* defines: "applied contemptuously to the language of scholars, the terminology of science or art, or the cant of a class, sect, trade or profession." Early in *The Birthday Party* Goldberg tries to assuage McCann's anxiety by adopting the evasive Latinisms of the law:

> The main issue is a singular issue and quite distinct from your previous work. Certain elements, however, might well approximate in points of procedure to some of your other activities. All is dependent on the attitude of our subject. At all events, McCann, I can assure you that the assignment will be carried out and the mission accomplished with no excessive aggravation to you or myself.

In attacking Stanley, however, Goldberg reduces philosophical jargon to nonsense:

> It's only necessarily necessary! We admit possibility only after we grant necessity. It is possible because necessary but by no means necessary through possibility. The possibility can only be assumed after the proof of necessity.

Such jargon would seem more consonant with the academic Teddy of *The Homecoming,* who brags about his "intellectual equilibrium" after the preemptive taunt of his pimp brother Lenny – "Do you detect a certain logical incoherence in the central affirmations of Christian theism?" During the scene cementing Ruth's prostitutional "home" coming, we hear incongruous jargons. The previously violent Max admonishes his pimp son: "I think you're concentrating too much on the economic considerations. There are other considerations. There are the human considerations. You understand what I mean? There are the human considerations." Given Max's play-long neglect of just those considerations, the repetition is wonderfully funny. At the same time it prepares us for the finale, when Max on his knees begs Ruth for a kiss.

In contrast to Max's sudden introduction of women's magazine sentimentality, Ruth, who never descends to slang or obscenity, adopts business terminology: "I would naturally want to draw up an inventory of everything I would need, which would require your signatures in the presence of witnesses. . . . All aspects of the agreement and conditions of employment would have to be clarified to our mutual satisfaction before we finalized the contract." In *Glengarry Glen Ross* the salesman Roma similarly refers to his client's marriage as a "contract" and a "bond."

Linguistically, each playwright reflects the decorum of his country. Pinter's characters reveal their class in clichés or jargon, whereas Mamet's misogynistic jargon spans the classless (but nonetheless hierarchized) worlds of boat work, office work, petty crime, real estate, Hollywood, and academe. Thus, Bert Hudd's jargon of aggressive driving in *The Room* is a world away from Flora's polysyllabic garden of *A Slight Ache*, written the following year: "You must see my japonica, my convulvulus. . .my honeysuckle, my clematis." Among Pinter's lower-class characters, it is usually the talkers who run to jargon, but the laconic Bert in *The Room* describes his hard drive before performing his harsh act, and the quiet Aston in *The Caretaker* verbally fondles the tools of carpentry (which Pinter eliminated in revision). Mick attacks Davies as much with the lexicon of interior decoration as with the Electrolux – a distinctively *English* lexicon. Teddy's family in *The Homecoming* offer Ruth emoluments of another class of interior decoration for her future flat in or near Soho's Greek Street. Although cricket is hardly an upper-class sport, Spooner elevates its terminology by incongruous attachment to Hirst's putative wife:

> How beautiful she was, how tender and how true. Tell me with what speed she swung in the air, with what velocity she came off the wicket, whether she was responsive to finger spin, whether you could bowl a shooter with her, or an off-break with a legbreak action. In other words, did she google?

The effect of such jargon is immediately hilarious but cumulatively threatening. As with cliché, jargon becomes an escape valve for the proximity of death in *Moonlight*.

Families figure so often in the dialogue of Pinter's plays that relationships can sound like jargon, from Mr. Kidd's Jewess mum in *The Room* to Spooner's malevolent mother in *No Man's Land*, via Goldberg's expanded family of *The Birthday Party* and the all-male household of *The Homecoming*. Of the last of these plays Ronald Knowles has observed: "We find primarily family, dad, father, mother, mum, son, brother, wife, uncle, and secondarily sister-in-law, brother-in-law, daughter-in-law, nephews, grandchildren, grandfather. These words occur approximately 130 times in the play" (in Bold, ed., *Harold Pinter*, p. 118).[10] Almost always, the jargon of family relationships – at least until Pinter's political plays of the 1980s – subverts that residual nuclear unit of modern society, which is rarely represented or even mentioned in Mamet's plays. (*Reunion* is an exception.)

Like nouns of kinship, the jargon of geography nourishes Pinter's drama.[11] His first two plays are unlocalized – "A room in a large house," "A basement room," and even *The Birthday Party* is set in an unnamed English seaside town – but Goldberg has London in his veins, referring to Charlotte Street near London University, the Ethical Hall in Bayswater, and Lyons Corner House at Marble Arch. Similarly, Mick of *The Caretaker* knows the London of Shoreditch, Aldgate, Finsbury Park, Putney. Fittingly, *The Homecoming* is set in "An old house in North London," but the references carry us around the city: Max and Mac once frequented the West End, Sam drives his clients to London Airport, the Savoy, the Caprice, the Dorchester, the Ritz Bar, and even Hampton Court. Lenny's haunts belong to another class – North Paddington, Greek Street, the Scrubs. Place names are duelling weapons of Anna and Deeley in *Old Times*: The former recalls bastions of culture – Albert Hall, Covent Garden, Kensington High Street, the Tate, Greenwich, Green Park; in contrast, Deeley goes to a pub off Brompton Road, and he mentions the Edgeware Road gang. Asserting her independence, Kate consigns Deeley, variously: "To China. Or Sicily." In *No Man's Land* Hirst, having met Spooner at the rather elegant pub Jack Straw's Castle, invites him home to a mansion in Hampstead, but Briggs relegates Spooner to a pub in Chalk Farm, called, like pubs all over Britain, The Bull's Head. It is against that background that Spooner boasts of his travels abroad to Lyon and Amsterdam, before admitting: "I wrote my Homage to Wessex in the summerhouse at West Upfield." In the unlocalized realm of *Moonlight* English surnames constitute a jargon of the two sons of the dying man.

Jeanette Malkin has contrasted the jargon of Pinter and Mamet: "In the plays of Pinter . . . jargon is usually a tool of intimidation; here [in Mamet's plays] it is the scum and essence of language . . . business terminology has invaded and colonized the minds of

Mamet's characters" (*Verbal Violence in Contemporary Drama,* p. 159) This is acutely observed, but both playwrights revel in the comedy of such jargons, which they intrude in incongruous contexts.

Set for the most part in the several workaday worlds of men, Mamet's plays display the particularly American business vocabulary of his characters:

American Buffalo draws from American gangster films – fin, lookout, kid's clean, set it up, mind the fort, a job cased, off the top, three-way split.

Glengarry Glen Ross is steeped in the unrealities of real estate – the key leads, board, kicked out, sit, on the plat, stats spread, call the shot, dollar volume, and the motto of the salesmen as epigraph: "Always be closing."

Speed-the-Plow views movie-making from a Hollywood perspective – bump, channels coverage, courtesy read, cross the street, greenlight, operative concept, promote, start to shoot.

Oleanna, in contrast, calls down a plague of jargon on both houses – academe and feminism:

Academe – criteria for judging progress, exploitation in the education process, posit orthodoxy, academic freedom, your political correctness.

Feminism – on behalf of my group, play the Patriarch, unlimited power, endured humiliations, you have an agenda, we have an agenda.

Mamet has affirmed in many interviews that he abhors the American business ethic, and he dramatizes that abhorrence, but, for me at least, the putative distance of comedy dissolves into affection for his characters who manipulate their limited vocabularies inventively and hilariously. Unlike Jeanette Malkin (*Verbal Violence,* pp. 160–1), I don't find it at all hard to like Mamet's characters who are trapped in capitalism, but my affection does not extend to either character of *Oleanna,* however the professor's final violence and vituperation were applauded by a few male members of the New York audience (but not in London).

Vituperation is so frequent in the mouths of both Pinter and Mamet characters that it borders on jargon. When Beckett's Didi and Gogo run out of activities, they seize enthusiastically on insult:

"That's the idea, let's abuse each other." But reciprocal tenderness seeps through their abuse. This is almost never true in Pinter's plays. Bert's insult is monosyllabic in Pinter's first play, *The Room*: "Lice." (The plural insults a black man and a woman.) Two years later in *The Caretaker* Mick attacks Davies vitriolically: "You're violent, you're erratic, you're just completely unpredictable. You're nothing else but a wild animal, when you come down to it. You're a barbarian. And to put the old tin lid on it, you stink from arse-hole to breakfast time."

Four years after that, in *The Homecoming* invective proliferates, beginning with a father–son exchange:

> LENNY: Plug it, will you, you stupid sod, I'm trying to read the paper.
> MAX: Listen! I'll chop your spine off, you talk to me like that!

Sam about Mac, but subtly enveloping Max:

> He was a lousy stinking rotten loudmouth. A bastard uncouth sodding runt. Mind you, he was a good friend of yours.

Max about Ruth:

> We've had a smelly scrubber in my house all night. We've had a stinking pox-ridden slut in my house all night. . . . They come back from America, they bring the slopbucket with them. They bring the bedpan with them.

In *No Man's Land* insults carry class resonance. Those of Hirst are aristocratically Victorian: "I'm beginning to believe you're a scoundrel . . . . I'll have you blackballed from the club!" But Briggs is vulgarly contemporary about Spooner in the passage already quoted as an example of obscenity. As can be seen even from these few quotations, vituperation is not necessarily obscene in Pinter's plays, but it is always beautifully rhythmed. Less inventive than the insults of Pinter, those of Mamet disparage others in racist, sexist, homophobic colloquialisms – fruit, mooch, deadbeat, nigger, jew, dyke, wog, fairy, Chink, Polack, chick, broad. Moreover, Mamet characters are freer than those of Pinter in scattering familiar blasphemies – God, goddamned, Lord, Jesus, Christ.

Pinter and Mamet occasionally erode words through slippage of meaning. The imagery of sight/blindness is pervasive in Pinter's work, and it is central to *The Birthday Party*. In the Act II attack upon Stanley, McCann witholds and then returns his victim's glasses, but Goldberg calls for glasses for the birthday party, and Meg announces: "Here's my very best glasses in here." Meg's "best glasses" provide no insight into Stanley's victimization. Faced with the Matchseller in *A Slight Ache*, Edward tries to salvage some security from the order in his house: "My desk was polished, and my cabinet. (*Pause.*) I was polished." Literally, this is absurd, but through slippage Pinter impugns Edward's mannered stance. So, Mick of *The Caretaker* undermines Davies in allowing "funny" to slip from "witty" to "strange." In *The Homecoming* glib Lenny enfolds slippage into his taunt of Teddy: ". . . Dad still plays a good game of poker, and does the cooking as *well, well* up to his old standard, . . . " (my emphasis). Max is unaware of his own slippage in describing his dead wife: "What a mind. *Pause*. Mind you. . . . " Deeley of *Old Times* slips easily from "trueblue pickup" to "trueblue generosity."

As with other lexical techniques, Mamet's slippage is more strident. Given the dubious ethics of business, one might expect slippage of such terms as "right" and "wrong."

DON: I'm just saying, something goes wrong. . .
TEACH: Wrong, wrong, you make your own right and wrong.

Don's "wrong" is merely awry, but Teach abnegates morality. Similarly, the meaning of "right" slips in Teach's admonition to Don: "You're right, and you do what you think is right, Don." In *Glengarry* the salesman Levene momentarily crows over the office manager Williamson, and the supersalesman Roma supports him: "He's right, Williamson." Whereupon Levene continues: "It's not right." As before, the slip is from correctness to morality. In *American Buffalo* the gopher Bob confesses: "I only went around to see he's coming out the back," and his employer Don remonstrates: "No, don't go fuck yourself around with these excuses." The first "around" is a directional adverb, but the second is an intensifier of an obscene verb which seems to mean "reveal your inadequacies." *Glengarry Glen Ross* sports a shift of meaning in a sight gag. Central to the salesmen's life is the black*board* on which their sales are graphed in chalk, but in Act II we read one of Mamet's rare scenic directions: "*A broken plate glass window [is] boarded up. . . .*" The star salesman Roma remarks: "You've got a *board-up* on the window." The two different boards are visible to us, both boding ill for the real-estate salesmen. More subtly, Pinter's Foster englobes the whole theater, including the audience, in his Act I curtain line of *No Man's Land:* "You know what it's like when you're in a room with the light on and then suddenly the light goes out? I'll show you. It's like this. *He turns the light out.* BLACKOUT."

The most insistent example of slippage in Mamet's Business Trilogy is the word "thing." At the most obvious level, things are visible material objects, like Teach's gun, the buffalo nickel, the junk of Don's shop, the leads of the real-estate office, or a contemptible book in Hollywood. Sometimes things are speech, but more often they are actions. The intended robbery of *American Buffalo,* like the buddy movie of *Speed-the-Plow,* is usually referred to as "the thing." Teach acknowledges that Don has done "things . . . for the kid." Things may also be events or qualities – "the one thing she's got, her *looks.*" Then again, things may be thoughts, as in "things on my mind," or abstract principles: "Things are not always what they seem to be." "Things get set." At their most threatening, things are akin to fate: "Things are going to fall around your *head.*" The three characters of *Speed-the-Plow* hammer at things, ranging over these meanings, and even the "Eastern Sissy" author of *The Bridge* is quoted by Karen: "That things were ending. *Yes.* That things *must* end." Charlie opens Act III with a shift from things as destiny to things as items on an agenda: " . . . the one thing . . . And the other thing . . . those two things, only, what I wanted to say to you." Since the characters of Mamet's Business Trilogy plays are much preoccupied with things, it is entirely fitting that that seemingly innocuous noun should embrace so much territory.[12] It is unlikely that any particular slippage is noticeable during an intense performance, but it *is* likely that such slippage contributes to the atmosphere of ambiguity in so many plays of Pinter and Mamet.

Such ambiguity is part of a context, where innocent words can become subversive in juxtaposition with their opposites. In Pinter's *The Room,* an uneasy haze pervades the simple but mysterious opposition of "in" and "out," "up" and "down," "cold" and "warm." The tone at first seems lighter in *The Birthday Party,* where the opening marital conversation pivots on "up" and "down," "light" and "dark," "boy" and "girl," but in retrospect these opposites are divested of innocence. Lenny of *The Homecoming* deliberately irritates his father with "passing the time of day here tonight," and the dying Andy of *Moonlight* praises their friend Ralph: "Never missed a day at night school." Max in *The Homecoming* utters one of Pinter's most celebrated oppositions: "You never heard such silence."

Like Pinter's *The Room*, Mamet's *American Buffalo* makes capital out of the play between "in" and "out." During the course of some twelve hours all three Mamet characters stumble into self-contradiction, with Teach offering the most blatant example: "I am calm. I'm just upset." Two characters present contradictory views of business:

DON: Things are not always what they seem to be.

TEACH: Things are what they are.

In *Speed-the-Plow* Bob Gould utters an oxymoron: "Money is not Gold."

Self-contradiction enhances the impression of illiteracy in Mamet's plays, but his characters intrude occasional sophisticated words into their banalities. As early as *Lakeboat* a drunken sailor pontificates: "Drink wine and it dehydrates you," yet he yearns for "cigarettes smouldering and chilled wine." Don of *American Buffalo* lectures Bob on "nutritive benefits"; Teach avers: "I am not here to smother you in theory." Teach excuses his gun in Latinate words: "All the preparation in the world does not mean *shit*, the path of some crazed lunatic sees you as an invasion of his personal domain." In *Glengarry* Williamson declares his obligation "to marshall the leads," and Levene speaks of "purloined leads," both dignifying the tricks of their trade.

Like their predecessors with lower incomes, Bob Gould and Charlie Fox stud their monosyllables with educated incongruities: Charlie utters the words "watershed," "pariah," and "a boon ... to assuage guilt"; Bob preaches about "addictive," "auspicious," "degradation," "depravity," "courage to embrace a fact." He teases Charlie about being Master of the Revels, and resurrects the archaic "Nary." But it is Karen who never soils her lips with obscenity and who almost always obeys grammatical rules; she is comfortable with polysyllables like "degradation," "despicable," "titillation," "companionship." Although Karen did not write the book sent for a courtesy read, she echoes its mawkishness. Mamet seems true to the phrasing of his characters, who rise above phonographic American realism to voice their sullied versions of the American dream.

The banal discourse of Pinter's characters blossoms more readily in incongruity, as in Goldberg's lucubrations on his family, or Hirst's memories of his past: "Constantine bowling, war looming." Spooner of *No Man's Land* thrives on incongruity, and he alone winds syntax in Jamesian arabesques, but even Pinter's lower-class characters tend toward correct grammar. A pimp is punctilious about verb tense; since Sam is "not even dead," Lenny corrects his father's "had" to "has." Max's interrogation of Teddy – "You been here all night?" – is ellipsis rather than illiteracy. Similarly, ellipsis abbreviates Max's threat to Lenny: "I'll chop your spine off, you talk to me like that."

Wetzsteon writes of Mamet's "utter clarity of total grammatical chaos," but there is method in that chaos. Innocent of class, Mamet's characters wallow in tautology and solecism, with ellipsis as their *lingua franca*, omitting prepositions, conjunctions, auxiliary verbs, or relative pronouns. As though the conjunction "if" were absent from the English language, Don instructs his gopher: "You're s'posed to watch the guy, you watch him." A dour and misogynistic Teach threatens: "She walks in back of me I'm going to hide my hand"; or "We don't care we wreck the joint up." But the joint that is wrecked is Don's Resale Shop, and it is wrecked by a Teach so frustrated that, exceptionally, he finds time and space for every syllable.

In *Glengarry* Levene pleads elliptically with Williamson: "I don't get on the board the thirtieth, they're going to can my ass." Moss threatens Aaronow: "They come to you. You going to turn me in?" In *Speed-the-Plow* the newly promoted Bob Gould crows to his underling: "Chuck, Chuck, Chuck, *Charles:* you get too old, too busy to have 'fun' this business; to have 'fun,' then what are you. . . ?" But Bob can still be instructed by Charlie: "You can't tell it to me in one sentence, they can't put it in T.V. Guide." Other words dropped in the verbal rush are with, in, to, of, what, who. Since nouns anchor the meaning for an audience, these missing monosyllables are expendable.

Even when they adhere to grammatical law, Mamet characters wrench syntax for emphasis: Teach declares: "A guy who isn't tense, I don't want him on my side." Levene mutters: "The Glengarry Highland's leads, you're sending Roma out." Bob warns Charlie: "To your face they'll go, 'Three bags full.'" Although such Yiddish gyrations do occur in colloquial American speech, Mamet's cunningly constructed run-on sentences are pure invention, never heard off the stage. Probably the most brilliant example of warped word order in all Mamet is Teach's explosion: "Only, and I'm not, I don't think, casting anything on anyone: from the mouth of a Southern bulldyke asshole ingrate of a vicious nowhere cunt can this trash come." It is quite a mouthful for an actor, and yet the syntax is relatively simple: The parenthetical apology separates the adverb "only" from the phrase it modifies ("from . . . cunt"); the run-on closes on a simple declarative sentence, with the subject intervening between the auxiliary and the main verb – "can this trash come."[13]

Mamet's grammar may sound anarchic (and funny), but it often makes a dramatic point. His characters can shift tenses – usually from past to the immediacy of the present. Subjects and verbs can disagree on number, and pronouns can run riot, as in the threnody of the unsuccessful salesmen, Moss and Aaronow, where "you" and "we" dissolve into "they"s without antecedent, climaxing in the desperate: "All of, they got you on this 'board. . .'" for their "board" is a form of coffin. Comparably, a grammatical subtlety predicts the end of *Speed-the-Plow*. When Bob and Charlie exult in their buddy film, they are careless of grammar, slumming in language, but after Karen seduces Bob with purity, Charlie is careful in phrasing his crucial question to her: "If he had said 'No,' would you have gone to bed with him?" In the face of her reluctance to reply, Bob repeats Charlie's question, but he amends it with the elision and mispronunciation that typified his earlier conversation with Charlie: "Would you of gone to bed with me, I didn't do your book." There is no question mark; Bob's rephrasing has answered his own question.

Mamet bases his grammatical chaos on the solecisms, digressions, and tautologies of everyday speech, but on stage they become symptomatic of the chaos in the seemingly different American worlds of petty crime, real-estate speculation, film production. Ineffectual as a thief, Teach is the champion verbalist of *American Buffalo*, but Roma of *Glengarry* excels both in verbiage and real-estate sales; he sells through his verbiage, which we hear as a stream-of-consciousness monologue enveloping his victim in per-

sonal concern. Thus, Mamet's skillful devices do not always serve his self-proclaimed critique of capitalism. In *Oleanna*, moreover, which is a critique of both academe and feminism, the professor alternates between a quasi-Jamesian syntax and Mametic fragmentation; the student alternates between a grammatically correct lexicon and similar fragmentation. There is, however, no ideological balance, since sympathy rests finally with a pedantic and patronizing professor, whose life is ruined by a cant-spouting, lying feminist.

In his Business Trilogy Mamet implies that the foulest obscenity is the word "business." Like four-letter words, this noun of twice four letters is occasionally comic, and it too undergoes slippage. Mentioned by Don to Bob early in *American Buffalo*, business is defined as "People taking care of themselves." In edging Bob out of the robbery, Teach admonishes Don: "All that I'm saying, don't confuse business with pleasure." Then within a moment: "And you cannot afford (and simply as a *business* proposition) you cannot afford to take the chance." Trying to edge Fletcher out of the robbery, Teach again invokes business to Don: "We're talking business, let's *talk* business: you think it's good business call Fletch in?" The curtain line of Act I epitomizes Don's misgivings about the whole enterprise: "Fuckin' *business*. . . ," but even in Act II an unteachable Teach continues to invoke business.

In *Glengarry Glen Ross* we see business in action, but we hear the word less often. Levene and Moss mention "doing business," but the meaning changes to a private domain, as Moss involves Aaronow in the planned robbery: "That's none of your fucking business. . . . My end is *my* business." In Roma's insult to Williamson, there is further slippage to "habit": "You know your business, I know mine. Your business is being an *asshole*. . . ." Roma can even disparage business when he presents the fictitious executive to his victim: "It's funny, you know, you get a picture of the Corporation Type Company Man, all business. . .this man, *no*." Finally, Roma repeats obsessively that his victim has "three *business* days" to annul the real-estate contract; fittingly, "business" has become an adjective for fraud.

In *Speed-the-Plow* Bob and Charlie burble happily about the movie business, which Bob praises as a "People Business." Charlie delivers a well-known one-liner, encapsulating his cynicism: "Life in the movie business is like the, is like the beginning of a new love affair: it's full of surprises, and you're constantly getting fucked." Karen, repetitively deprecating her own naïveté, announces her ambition "To think in a...business fashion." Obligingly, Bob instructs her: "This, in the business, is called 'a courtesy read.'" and "...that's what we're in business to do. *Make the thing everyone made last year.*" In his new quest for purity, Bob no longer flaunts "business," but a victorious Charlie circles back to Bob's earlier ebullient phrase: "Because we joke about it, Bob, we joke about it, but it *is* a 'people business' . . . ." The play's intention is for us to disapprove of those "people."

Sound and sense conspire in Pinter's enigmatic wit and Mamet's coarse comedy. Both playwrights have also composed in a minor chord. Pinter's *Landscape* (1968, originally written for radio, but often staged) and *Silence* (1969, which Pinter confesses "took the longest time to write"; Page, *File on Pinter*, p. 105) are more image-laden and more subtly rhythmed than his verse. The brief plays are abstemious of the invective and incongruities at the core of his comedy. They do, however, resort to repetition to hint at relationships between characters who never communicate directly. The title *Landscape* would seem to refer to Beth's beach, whereas Duff's speech moves from a pond in a park to a pub to Mr. Sykes's house, where he and Beth are both perhaps employed. Beth and Duff connect only in a few repeated nouns – touch, face, flowers, kiss – before the startling final opposition of Duff's verbal rape and Beth's gentle fantasy.

Landscape may be contrasted with Mamet's *The Woods*. Unlike Duff and Beth, Nick and Ruth almost always speak *at* one another, but they rarely communicate. Weekend lovers at a lakeside cabin in the woods, they reminisce, drink, quarrel, and finally cradle one another. Ruth repeats to a frightened Nick her grandmother's story about two children lost in the woods.[14] The contrast between Mamet's protagonists is less telling than those of Pinter in *Landscape*. Pinter's Duff abounds in active verbs, short phrases, abrasive locutions, whereas Beth is more leisurely and descriptive, drawing out the words. Although Mamet's Ruth talks more than Nick – "You talk too much, Ruth," Nick charges – they resemble one another in an idiom of short phrases, frequent questions, pointless repetitions. Often these lovers sound like children; like uninventive children, without the flare of a Bernie Litko or Teach.

Rather than this minor lyric mode, however, major dramas display similarities between the dialogue of Mamet and Pinter. Unlike certain plays of Simon and Ayckbourn, however, the works of Pinter and Mamet do not bend readily to larger comparisons of theme and structure. For example, duets drive toward different ends in two early plays, Pinter's *The Collection* (radio, 1961; stage, 1962) and Mamet's *Sexual Perversity* (1974), and extended comparison does not seem to me rewarding.

In more recent plays, however, theme and technique do repay closer study. Mamet has recorded his admiration for Pinter's *Betrayal*: "Take a play like *Betrayal*, a brilliant play that just puts everything backwards" (Savran, *In Their Own Words*, p. 135). Mamet's *Speed-the-Plow* drives forward rather than backward, but there are nevertheless analogies between the two dramas, separated by a decade. Mamet's *Speed-the-Plow* echoes Pinter's *Betrayal* in theme – male bonding is threatened by a woman. Mamet has revealed: "It's a play about my [*sic*] experiences in Hollywood – two producers and a secretary" (ibid., p. 143). But he neglects to mention the paramount point that the two producers are male, and the secretary female. *Betrayal* might be viewed as a play about Pinter's experiences in fashionable London – two book producers (literary agent and publisher) and a gallery manager. Again the crucial point is that the book producers are male, and the gallery manager female. In each drama the male members of the trio are virtual mirror images of one another, but whereas Pinter's Emma belongs to the smart world in which her husband and lover circulate, Mamet's Karen is "just a temporary" in every sense – without identifying background.

An often quoted Pinter remark, made long before *Betrayal* was written, nevertheless predicts the contours of both *Betrayal* and *Speed-the-Plow*: "I think I can say I pay meticulous attention to the shape of things, from the shape of a sentence to the overall structure of the play. This shaping, to put it mildly, is of the first importance." The "overall structure" of *Betrayal* is strikingly symmetrical, as Austin Quigley observed (*The Modern Stage and Other Worlds*, p. 230). The play begins after the end of an adulterous affair, and it ends with the beginning of that affair. Although the nine scenes of *Betrayal* move roughly backward through nine years, they are arranged symmetrically about the single scene set outside of London, where Robert the husband taunts his wife Emma into revealing her affair with his best friend Jerry.

1. 1977 – Emma and Jerry in a pub
2. 1977, later – Jerry and Robert in Jerry's house
3. 1975 – Emma and Jerry in a flat
4. 1974 – Three at Robert's house
5. 1973 – Emma and Robert in a Venice hotel
6. 1973 – Emma and Jerry in a flat
7. 1973, later – Jerry and Robert in a restaurant
8. 1971 – Emma and Jerry in a flat
9. 1968 – Three at Robert's house

It is in scene 5, just before Robert provokes his wife's confession of adultery, that he voices the play's theme and title: "Betrayal."

Speed-the-Plow is not quite as symmetrical in structure, but it too is carefully shaped, beginning and ending with the partnership of Charlie Fox and Bob Gould to produce a buddy movie:

Act I – Fox and Gould
    Fox, Gould, and Karen
    Gould and Karen; also Act II

Act III – Fox and Gould
    Fox, Gould, and Karen
    Fox and Karen
    Act III – (finale) Fox and Gould

Mamet's title is more devious. Unvoiced in the play, speed-the-plow literally requests a harvest blessing, in this case the final restoration of Hollywood decorum. "Plowing" is also a sexual pun, as the play's first director pointed out (Stafford, "*Speed-the-Plow* and *Speed the Plough*," p. 39).

My scenic breakdown reveals how both playwrights continue to build with duologues; what the breakdown does not show is the intrusion of monologue into that rhythm. In *Betrayal* monologue is a masculine province, from which Emma is barred. Jerry speaks inconsequentially until his final drunken declaration of love. Robert's three monologues all bear obliquely on Emma's adultery, but their surface subjects are "laughing Mediterranean" carelessness about mail, his own hatred of modern literature, and the male game of squash. Games go unmentioned in the gamelike repartee of *Speed-the-Plow*, and monologues rarely decelerate the pace. Toward the end of Act I, however, Bob Gould begins his seduction of Karen with short monologues about the movie business. In Act II, their rhythms reverse, when Karen lectures Gould in monologues inflated by random quotations from *The Bridge*. The confusions of Karen's curtain speech melt into the pointed clarity of "Here I am." Mamet opens his Act III with Charlie's stream-of-consciousness monologue, temporarily impenetrable to the news of Gould's betrayal. Once Charlie seizes the changed situation, however, monologue splinters into his successive assaults on friend and foe, which demand and receive response.

Like the monologue–duologue counterpoint, that of dialogue and silence is more distinct in *Betrayal* than in *Speed-the-Plow*, which nevertheless contains numerous pauses and one "long pause" – unusual for Mamet. *Betrayal* brims not only with pauses, but also with fourteen *Silences* that tauten tense moments. Between *Pause* and *Silence*, the three dots of Pinter's published text punctuate extreme anxiety of each of the three characters:

EMMA: [*to Jerry*] You know what I found out...last night? He's betrayed me for years. He's had...other women for years.

JERRY: [*to Robert*] The fact is I can't understand...why she thought it necessary...after all these years...to tell you ...so suddenly...last night...

ROBERT: [*to Emma*] A flat. It's quite well established then, your...uh...affair?

In contrast to the three-dot tenseness in the above passages, Mamet's three dots are puzzling, since they did not reflect the rapid-fire dialogue onstage in both the New York and London productions of *Speed-the-Plow*.

Within their "overall shaping" both playwrights "pay meticulous attention" to phonemes, and both playwrights limit soundplay to their male characters. Jerry and Robert never play squash in *Betrayal*, but Pinter plays with their sounds. Jerry's first extended speech about men drinking together burbles in p's and b's: "For example, when you're with a fellow in a pub . . . from time to time he pops out for a piss . . . if he's making a crafty telephone call . . . you can sense the pip pip pips." Robert, braving Jerry about betrayal, jabs with short *i* sounds: "You don't seem to understand that I don't give a shit about any of this. It's true I've hit Emma once or twice . . . The old itch...you understand." Perhaps the most lethal example of soundplay occurs in the Jerry–Robert confrontation of scene 2, the last in chronological time, where "No" and "know" are volleyed in the context of the old carnal meaning of "know."

Although Pinter is abstemious of rhyme and alliteration in *Betrayal*, his repetition is more frequent than ever before, erupting in such banalities as questions, exclamations, and routine courtesies. The opening scene, for example, pours out a torrent of "How"s and "Why"s, with few questions answered about the relationship of Emma and Jerry. The cliché toast over the many drinks consumed during the cheerless play is "Cheers." In this mannered society obscenities are rare: Once Jerry calls Robert a bastard, and is warned not to do so. Under stress, Robert inveighs against Venice: "They really don't give a fuck there." When Emma utters the word "fucking," she means it literally, but Jerry corrects her: "loving."

Occasionally, a verbal repetition underlines or undermines lexical meaning. Emma in scene 4 criticizes Casey's novel as "dishonest," and within a few moments Robert labels Casey as a "brutally honest squash player." Within another few moments Robert opens his monologue that will bar Emma from watching the men's game of squash: "Well, to be brutally honest. . . ." The subtext is honesty in marriage. In scene 5, obliquely confronting Emma with her adultery, Robert begins his monologue with the very English cliché: "To be honest. . ." but he still avoids direct reference to honesty in marriage.[15] Finally, Robert reduces Emma to *"Silence"* with: "To be honest, I've always liked [Jerry] rather more than I've liked you. Maybe I should have had an affair with him myself." Robert *has* had a kind of affair with Jerry – through the agency of Emma.

Like Pinter, Mamet reserves soundplay for the males of *Speed-the-Plow*, flaunting his full range of devices. Both Bob and Charlie alliterate: Bob refers sardonically to "fine folk," and Charlie denies wanting to "pee on your parade." Rhyme is a mark of jubilation, particularly on Charlie's part: "singing a song, rolling along." Charlie also repeats assonantly: "Douggie Brown . . . to my house." But Bob teases Charlie: "The Bitching Lamp is Lit." Repetition is swifter and more frequent than in any other Mamet play. At the play's opening Charlie utters four "Bob"s without succeeding in attracting his attention. Once attuned to the Doug Brown buddy film, however, Bob and Charlie in Act I finish each other's phrases and echo one another's thoughts in what Ann Wilson (in Kane, *David Mamet: A Casebook*, p. 156) names "the call-and-response ritual":

GOULD: I piss on money.
FOX: I know that you do. I'll help you.
GOULD: *Fuck* money.
FOX: Fuck it. Fuck "things" too...
GOULD: Uh huh. But don't fuck "people."
FOX: No.
GOULD: 'Cause, people, Charlie...
FOX: People...yes.
GOULD: Are what it's all about.
FOX: I know.
GOULD: And it's a people business.
FOX: That it is.
GOULD: It's *full* of fucken' people...
FOX: And we're gonna kick some ass, Bob.
GOULD: That we are.
FOX: We're gonna kick the ass of a lot of them fucken' people.

The repetition of short *u*, single words, and short sentences is familiar Mamet, but the jubilant obscenity is newly twisted to vengeful hostility in the Hollywood way. Unlike Sam Goldwyn, whose linguistic lapses were notorious, Bob Gould and Charlie Fox slum linguistically, but on the telephone to their superior, Ross, they speak correctly and respectfully. Inscrutable Karen is usually correct, although she does slip on "presumptious."

Betrayal and *Speed-the-Plow* sport soundplay, and they are similarly prolific in their range of repetition – word, pause, sentence, and scene. However, they are dissimilar in lexical variety. Not only does Pinter reduce his verbal palette, but he also refrains from highlighting single words. Mamet, in contrast, accords lexical range to his Hollywood sleazeballs: Latinism, Yiddish, Hebrew, bible, obscenity, cliché, movie jargon. Not to mention the vague religiosity of *The Bridge.*

Slippage is rare in both plays, but when it does occur, it is significant. Charlie and Bob are rhapsodic about their luck:

FOX: *These* are the films that whaddayacallit...(*long pause*) that make it all worthwhile.
GOULD: ...I think you're going to find a *lot* of things now, make it all worthwhile. I think *conservatively*, you and me, we build ourselves in to split, minimally, ten percent.

"Worthwhile" after a long pause is Charlie's token gesture toward the spiritual, but Bob brings him swiftly back to Hollywood economics. The slippage of "worthwhile" is the thematic summary of *Speed-the-Plow*.

Pinter's slippage blends more subtly with other verbal devices. In the final scene of *Betrayal* a drunken Jerry woos Emma with the richest lexicon of the spare play – "All these words I'm using, don't you see, they've never been said before." Paradoxically, Jerry woos with verbal rape: "I should have blackened you, in your white wedding dress," although Emma insists that she did not wear white at the wedding. Jerry gains verbal momentum in a rich rush, enhanced by slippage of the word "state." Banishment to "a state of catatonia" is the misery he will suffer if rejected by Emma. Surging on, Jerry shifts "state" from a psychological condition to a country ruled by a prince – "the prince of emptiness, the prince of absence, the prince of desolation. I love you." With Robert's implicit acquiescence, Emma rescues her prince from his lonely domain. She and Jerry "*look . . . at each other*" to end the play – and begin the affair that harbors betrayal.

The word "affair" does not dignify the few hours that Karen spends at the home of Bob Gould in *Speed-the-Plow;* he lies about his lust, first to Charlie and then to Karen, but when Bob responds to her rhetoric with repetitions of "I don't understand," he primes us for Charlie's repetitions of "I understand," before asking Karen the question that will incriminate her: "I understand. Karen. I *understand*. . .that things have been *occurring*. . .large decisions. . .do you follow me. . . ? [*Pause.*] Do you follow what I'm going to say?" It is quite a challenge to follow what someone *is going* to say, but the question alerts *us*, and *we* follow Charlie in his juxtaposition of "I"s against Karen's presumptuous "we"s, which undo her.

Soundplay, rhythmic counterpoint, lexical slippage, and areas of vocabulary are economically functional in *Betrayal* and *Speed-the-Plow*. So, too, is the rare imagery. Jerry and Robert prattle about the reluctance of boy babies to leave the womb, and Bob and Charlie prattle happily about their whoredom. More telling is a prosaic Pinter image, into which he enfolds residual jargon of family. In the first scene of *Betrayal* Emma recalls Jerry throwing her daughter Charlotte up and catching her, and Jerry adds that both families were watching. At the end of that scene, after Jerry knows he has been revealed to Robert as an adulterer, *he* recalls the scene with distinctive pronouns: "But he's my oldest friend. I mean, I picked his own daughter up in my own arms and threw her up and caught her, in my kitchen. He watched me do it." Four years earlier (but five scenes later) Jerry describes throwing Charlotte in the air while both families watched. Only when Jerry contrasts "his own" (daughter) with "my own" (arms) does he not have to be corrected by Emma as to the location of the event. By the end of the play Jerry has thrown over Emma (whom Charlotte resembles), and he has not caught her. Nor has her husband Robert. Perhaps she will be caught by Casey, the dishonest honest writer who brings profit to both men. Perhaps not.

As Pinter's jargon of family relationships crystallizes in this repeated image, his jargon of geography precipitates into what we see on stage. Inhabitually, Pinter provides no location for Jerry's house or Robert's; or for Emma's gallery, Robert's publishing firm, or Jerry's literary agency. We know only the address of the Kilburn flat for adultery, the setting for three scenes of *Betrayal*. Although other scenes are located in Jerry's house, or Robert's, or a pub, restaurant, or hotel room, all these rooms prove to be backgrounds for betrayal. Similarly, Mamet provides no Hollywood location either for Bob Gould's new office or his house, but both those settings prove to be backgrounds for betrayal. Verbally, however, Pinter plays the image of romantic Venice against the domestic flat that "could never...actually be a home." Comparably, Mamet plays the orotund prose of *The Bridge* against "a buddy film, a prison film, Douggie Brown, blah, blah, some girl...."

Although both plays function on realistic sets, the shaped language and its resonance lift them beyond realism into wider significance. Inconspicuously, too, the structure of both plays hints at the residual circularity associated with the theatre of the absurd. *Betrayal* opens on the meeting of Emma and a hungover Jerry, and it closes on a drunken Jerry gazing into Emma's eyes. *Speed-the-Plow* begins and ends on two Hollywood buddies together to produce a buddy movie – Mamet's most telling mise-en-abîme, since *Speed-the-Plow* is itself a buddy play. For all the specifics of their respective settings, the two plays share metaphysical absurdity.

More than the metaphysical subsoil, however, or even the theme of betrayal, the two plays echo one another's characters. Bobbie Gould figures in three Mamet plays, but *this* Bobbie is, despite his recent promotion, a spiritual brother of Charlie Fox. They have been underlings together for eleven years, during which they have absorbed the unethical ethic of Hollywood – "Get the Asses in the Seats." Overeducated and overambitious, they lust for power even more than for money or women. Clamped within the star system, they are indifferent to the filmic vehicle. Separately, they nod formulaically toward a larger purpose for film, but only Bob undergoes a temporary conversion to a movie with a mission.

Jerry and Robert are also spiritual brothers. Robert Downs is somewhat more of a rake, who has betrayed Emma with other women. Urbane and witty, he reads Yeats, vacations abroad, and keeps fit – the modern man about town who doesn't even have a nickname. Jerry, in contrast, is a nickname, and we never learn his surname; to rent the flat of his trysts he chooses the pastoral pseudonym of Green. More romantic than Robert, he also drinks more. His affair parallels Bob Gould's temporary conversion, but unlike Mamet's Bob, Pinter's Jerry never considers disrupting his career – or his domestic arrangements. Beneath their surface diversities, both Robert and Jerry thrive on betrayal.

Both plays dramatize female victims, but the two women are caught in different snares. Karen is suddenly sullied by Charlie, whereas Emma is continuously hounded. Wooed by a drunken Jerry in the last scene of the play, she announces her divorce in the first scene. During the course of her affair with Jerry, Emma tries to replicate a home in their flat – choosing the furnishings together and longing for more permanence. At the same time she plays the faithful wife to Robert, even to conceiving his child. When the men's ardor cools, Emma apparently begins an affair with Casey, who may in turn betray her.

Mamet's Karen, in contrast, has come to the right place at the right time – eager for "The making of decisions" in Hollywood. Critics are divided as to her sincerity, especially as played by Madonna with what Jack Kroll has called "seductive ambiguity." Mamet's longtime director Greg Mosher states flatly: "The attractiveness of [Karen] is her integrity" (Jones & Dykes, *File on Mamet*, p. 69) But integrity is not Mamet's forte, and Karen's didacticism mars her confession: "I knew what the deal was. I knew you wanted to sleep with me." Rather, Karen is understood by Charlie: "She falls between two stools." Condemning naïveté, Karen may be as idealistic as her pose, or she may not be wily enough to sleep her way to the top. "Between two stools," she remains inscrutable.

Finally, the game of squash, repeatedly mentioned in *Betrayal*, is an apt metaphor for both plays. A fast game in a walled court is what each woman is up against – the preservation of domestic decorum in the one play and the preservation of commercial viability in the other. For both *Betrayal* and *Speed-the-Plow* the noun "squash" puns on a verb that the *Shorter OED* defines: "to silence or discomfit (a person) in a crushing fashion." The parenthetical "person" is devastatedly female in both plays, in both Anglophone countries. And in both dramas the female is bludgeoned by precise and theatrical male speech.

Reading and teaching
Maria Irene Fornes and
Caryl Churchill

My next two Anglo–American pairings should be read in tandem, since they react to patriarchies on both sides of the Atlantic. Any fair-minded audience recognizes the sexist heritage of Eurocentric (but not only Eurocentric) drama, and early feminists expended a good deal of energy in proving that women characters of classical Western literature suffered from that bias. I suppose my pairing of David Rabe and David Hare treads that well-worn critical path, but I do not follow another such path, where superior women characters are found to populate plays written by women. Instead, I examine how actual writing, often a form of instruction, functions in the dramas of the women writers, Maria Irene Fornes and Caryl Churchill.

Contemporary critics of culture have assigned a privileged role to writing, in the wake of Jacques Derrida. French feminists have praised *l'écriture féminine* as fluid, open, emotional, polysemic, and, with imperturbable polarity, either subversive or nurturing. French feminist critics juxtapose *l'écriture féminine* against the phallogocentric discourse of the Western tradition. Only occasionally do French feminists penetrate specific texts, and then it is mainly poetry, fiction, or philosophy – genre designations that some feminists disallow. English and American feminists tend to be more aware than French of the contexts of texts. In the succinct summary of Elaine Showalter: "English feminist criticism, essentially Marxist, stresses oppression; French feminist criticism, essentially psychoanalytic, stresses repression; American feminist criticism, essentially textual, stresses expression" (quoted in Felski, *Beyond Feminist Aesthetics*, p. 20).[1] Although I am confused about what feminism entails, I do hew to the American stress on expression, and I have brooded about an *écriture féminine* in drama. With *l'écriture féminine* not so much in mind as in background, I compare the drama of American Maria Irene Fornes and British Caryl Churchill, both of whom have been claimed and disclaimed by different feminists.[2] The claimants couple them as women playwrights, and the disclaimants recognize that these dramatists have rejected the feminist label. I take it for granted that Fornes and Churchill are comparable on both these grounds, but what interests me is their dramatization of or by instruction, in which writing looms large.

Cuban-born Maria Irene Fornes (b. 1930), for whom English is a second language, contrasts with Oxford-educated Caryl Churchill (b. 1938), whose omnivorous reading puts scholars to shame. In their dissimilar ways, these two women playwrights have enlarged the contemporary stage. Neither writer strays from the genre of drama, and both playwrights have written more plays than they have published. Both have been associated with specific theatre groups: Fornes with the antiverbal fringe of New York's Off-Off Broadway of the 1960s and Churchill with the socially oriented Joint Stock Group of the 1970s. More praise has been heaped on Caryl Churchill than on Maria Irene Fornes, but the latter's subtleties are increasingly appreciated.

Although the plays of Fornes vary in subject, structure, and setting, they are alike in their preoccupation with the inner life of her characters – an inner life that eschews psychology. Rather, stage images such as writing help unveil that life, and nowhere more theatrically than in her first play, *Tango Palace* (1963, written obsessively in nineteen days). In spite of the title of royal resonance, we see only a property-strewn room, the habitat of Isidore, "an androgynous clown," who imprisons Leopold "an earnest youth." Their relationship involves, in Fornes's words, "a mentor of some sort and a student" (Betsko & Koenig, *Interviews*, p. 158). Inventive Isidore, the mentor, whirls capriciously through roles, as graceful as a tango dancer, whereas plodding Leopold seeks logic and sequence. "*Each time Isidore feels he has said something important, he takes a card from his pocket or from a drawer and flips it across the room in any direction.*" In the first of Fornes's three scenes the cards flutter so liberally that we soon suspect what Isidore affirms: "I never say a thing which is not an exact quotation from one of my cards." This is true not only of Fornes's character

Isidore, but it summarizes the method of any traditional actor, who quotes from a given script. More generally, we all quote the words of the language into which we are born, trapped as we are in what Nietzsche called "the prison-house of language."[3]

In Fornes's *Tango Palace* we in the audience cannot read the writing on the peripetatic cards, but we can read the tattoo on Leopold's chest: "This is man. Heaven or bust." Leopold's dogged celestial drive is implicitly opposed by Isidore's cards, whose aphorisms pop up out of context. Leopold resists Isidore's command: "Study hard, learn your cards, and one day, you too will be able to talk like a parrot." In Fornes's scene 2 Leopold tries to sort the scattered cards, but his attempt at order yields to conflict. In a mock bullfight, Isidore tangoes through six passes to the kill. In scene 3 Isidore and Leopold duel in beetle masks, then in words about death. This late in the play Isidore flips only one card – "Cleanliness is close to godliness" – an incongruous proverb in the shabby setting. When Isidore is stabbed by Leopold, the former reappears immediately as an angel, clutching stacks of cards. Leopold picks up a few cards, but *"Isidore shakes his head, and shows Leopold the cards he carries."* Even in heaven, speech is always already written.

Although Fornes was never again to stage the prison house of language so graphically, she did sporadically stage linguistic instruction, and indeed the very process of writing her next play relied on cards as a kind of self-instruction: "I put descriptions of characters on a number of cards and places on other cards, and shuffled them. I wrote *Promenade* like that" (Savran, *In Their Own Words*, p. 58). In that play Fornes substitutes numbers for names of characters; 105 and 106 anonymize prisoners in a world divided between the rich and the poor. Rather than the title's promenade, however, a swift chase absorbs the cipher-men, imposed by the several places Fornes had written on the cards. After digging their way out of prison, 105 and 106 attend a banquet, where they steal everything portable, including a woman who sings: "Yes, I have learned from life. / What surprises me / Is that life / Has not learned from me." But instruction is nowhere evident, as the characters tumble from a park to a battlefield to a mayoral party; the trio are pursued, on the one hand, by the jailer, and on the other, by the prisoners' mother. Finally, the large cast crowds into jail, but they soon disperse, leaving the original two numbered cellmates to close the play in song (with original music by Al Carmines, minister of the Judson Memoral Church in New York's Greenwich Village). Fornes's lyrics nod toward Marie Antoinette: "All is well in the city ... And for those who have no cake, / There's plenty of bread." Unlike the bread images of Bond or Shepard, the slang meaning of bread as money mocks the staff of life. Although Fornes's written cards triggered *Promenade,* the only writing actually staged is a letter by an anonymous soldier, improbably complaining about the quality of hamburger in a railroad dining car. Rather than writing or instruction, American film images fill the play, as they do in Fornes's *The Successful Life of 3* of the same year, 1965.

The number 3 of this title is an extended pun on that ancient subject of drama, the eternal triangle. A couple is named She and He, but the latter has a rival in the inevitable 3. Fornes's play skips through a sequence of events rather than a plot: He and She meet in a doctor's office; they marry; He deserts She; He and 3 share a household; 3 as thief is arrested by He as detective, but finally all three characters reunite to sing, sell candy, and fulfill the prophecy of the title – the *successful* life of 3 and of three characters. Learning is absent from the play, which I have summarized to suggest the charm of Fornes's early insouciance, climaxed by the finale's joyous "Song to Ignorance." In performance, Open Theater transformation exercises enabled the actors to shift instantaneously from one parodied film pose to another.

Obliquely, these lighthearted Fornes plays satirize social clichés: the institution of marriage (as well as the propensity to adultery) in *The Successful Life of 3* and the institution of prison in *Promenade.* Fornes's social critique remains oblique for her theatricalized protest against American involvement in the Vietnam war – *A Vietnamese Wedding* (1967). The whole play provides cultural instruction, and it stages writing among its artifacts. Four professional actresses draw ten participants from the audience to constitute a Vietnamese wedding party. Those audience members who enact the fathers of the Groom and of the Bride read ritually from their respective cards. The Groom burns red rice paper inscribed: "Rose Silk Thread God, / look after our marriage." Devotion is literally colorful, while the Vietnamese texts instruct American spectators in Asian ceremony. In contrast, another Fornes antiwar play, *The Red Burning Light* (1968), blends spy movie and TV advertisement in urging the audience to send for an "explosive book" before chanting a song of bombardment, but there are no actual books on stage.

With *Dr. Kheal* (1968) learning returns to the center of Fornes's stage. Like the academics in Ionesco's *The Lesson* and Adamov's *Professor Taranne*, Fornes's professor assumes omniscience, but, unlike his absurdist predecessors, he is alone on stage. Flourishing his pedagogy, Dr. Kheal chalks on a blackboard, a hubristic display of lecture subjects: Poetry, Balance, Ambition, Energy, Speech, Truth, Beauty and Love, Hope, Cooking, and, finally, Summing Up, whereupon he sums up: "Man is the rational animal." However, Fornes stages the man, Dr. Kheal, as a ridiculous animal, with inordinate ambition, and abstraction exemplified in his own blackboard lettering. Rather than lecturing on the announced topics, Dr. Kheal treats them as associational triggers. For example, to illustrate "Balance" he draws a kind of seesaw. "Energy" leads to charts, and "Speech" stresses the gap between words and ideas. Declaring that it is impossible to describe "Beauty," Dr. Kheal calls on an elusive Crissanda, a name that blends prophetic Cassandra into faithless Cressida. "Love" is quixotically coupled with mathematics, as Dr. Kheal chalks numbers on the blackboard. "Hope" inspires another drawing, after which Dr. Kheal concludes that man is superior to the spider. The instruction is, to say the least, quixotic, and we are the pupils. Although Dr. Kheal does not write his own name on the board, he does vocalize it, and we may recall it from the printed program: KHEAL hints both at healing and killing, a veritable prophecy of the effects of learning – in the drama of Maria Irene Fornes. We see Dr. Kheal write the subjects of his lectures on the blackboard, but we hear a series of verbal pirouettes that flout the very rationality he claims for man.

Jumping from the academic ivory tower to an old-fashioned saloon, Fornes opens *Molly's Dream* (1968, the first of her plays to be directed by herself) on a waitress reading from a Western magazine. It is, however, a magazine invented by Fornes, rather than an actual text, as in subsequent plays. The magazine inspires the waitress's dream about a West compounded of film echoes, fantasy, eroticism, and violence.

In these Fornes plays of the 1960s life is rendered lightly, sometimes with song and dance; we laugh at writing fluttering on cards, chalked on a blackboard, read aloud from a magazine. The critic

Scott Cummings has admirably summarized how Fornes's drama of this period epitomizes Off-Off Broadway: ". . . an overt and zestful theatricality, an almost self-consciously absurdist sensibility, a freewheeling sexuality, a rejection of dramatic logic and linear plotting in favor of transformational techniques, and a satirical thrust at such favorite political targets as the 'military-industrial complex'" ("Notes on Fornès," p. 92). What distinguishes Fornes's drama from others of its milieu is her light touch and her freedom from self-indulgence; the zaniness is somehow true to her characters, from Isidore with his epigrammatic cards to Molly with her romantic dream of the old West.

Preoccupied with administration of Theatre Strategy, an organization for producing new plays in New York City, Fornes wrote little during the 1970s. Her drama of the 1980s is at once more sombre and more sensitive to a global context for private lives. In that drama learning takes on a new importance, as Susan Sontag notes: "Character is revealed through catechism . . . people requiring or giving instruction" (Preface to *Plays*, n.p.) Fornes herself has acknowledged: "I feel that art ultimately is a teacher" (Savran, *In Their Own Words*, p. 56). Yet she avoids didacticism.

The Danube (1982), Fornes's response to a request for an antinuclear play, connects scenes through Hungarian–English language tapes, which symbolize at once the untranslatability of cultures and the drive toward doom in prewar central Europe, whose lifeline was the Danube River.[4] Although the beautiful blue Danube is a sentimental cliché, Fornes's *The Danube* shades into darkness as the play progresses. In fifteen brief scenes we witness the Hungarian sojourn of the American metalworker Paul, who marries Eve Kovacs in Budapest. After a mysterious illness (not explicitly linked to nuclear fallout), Paul recovers sufficiently to leave the country with Eve, who cannot persuade her father to accompany them.

The Danube starts in 1938, but, as Fornes's scenic direction specifies, the play "*soon departs from chronological realism.*" Geographical realism is also flouted: "*Painted backdrops, in a style resembling postcards, depict the different locations . . . At each change of scenery smoke will go up from three places on the stage floor.*" The visual artifice prepares for the aural artifice of the Hungarian–English language tapes. Although the characters, like those of Ionesco's *Bald Soprano*, sometimes sound like tapes, *The Danube* is neither satiric nor absurdist. Rather, it pivots on instruction, without ever lapsing into didacticism.

As the words of *Tango Palace* are often read from cards, those of *The Danube* often echo language tapes. In William Gruber's succinct sentence: "[O]ne could say that in this play egos are defined as echoes" ("Individuality and Communality," p. 183). Although I agree with Gruber that "Fornes tends to imagine character as a collection of things learned ... within a public sphere," I find the characters consistent, even though they are not traditionally coherent. Noteworthy are Paul's pro-American generalizations, which are obliquely countered by a restaurant waiter's generalizations about the differences between Americans and a "we," who may be European or Hungarian, or merely un-American.[5]

As Paul and Eve fall in love, Hungarian-language tapes are heard in the background. When Paul grows insensitive to the plight of a plague-infested Hungary, a scene's dialogue is repeated verbatim, with puppets replacing the live actors; as puppets, Paul and Eve prepare to flee the stricken city, but it is the live actors who actually leave, gun in Paul's pocket. Alone centerstage, Eve equates her death with departure from her Danube. Yet she does depart with Paul while her father calls her name. Is Paul the modern serpent, tempting her with American escape from a no longer Edenic Danube? Fornes provokes questions but does not offer answers.

From the echoic yet problematic instruction of *The Danube,* Fornes returns to instruction by print in *Mud* (1983), where the title element is the background for an aboriginal animality. In the play's opening line an illiterate Lloyd challenges the protagonist Mae: "You think you learn a lot at school?" Although she replies affirmatively, Mae is not able to read Lloyd's medical prescription, and she therefore welcomes Henry, who conveys the wonder of specialized dictionaries and is able to say grace before a meal. Haltingly, Mae reads from the one book visible on stage – about a starfish and then about a hermit crab. Although Lloyd slaps the book off the table, he understands that he is being displaced by the hermit crab Henry. Paralyzed from a fall, literate Henry mocks Lloyd's pathetic efforts to learn to read. Finally, Mae scorns them both, in her quest for "a decent life." When she announces her prospective departure, both men protest. However, Mae does leave, and Lloyd shoots her offstage. He carries her back to the visible mud for her

dying words: "I would die for [light]. Lloyd, I am dying." Just before her departure, however, Mae blossoms forth in a lyrical self-comparison to a starfish – a comparison firmly anchored in her previous laborious reading. As Fornes herself acknowledges: "What's wonderful about Mae is her love for knowledge" (Betsko & Koenig, *Interviews*, p. 166)

A Beckettian play of the lower depths, *Mud* reaches for a mythic dimension through instruction, but *Sarita* (1984) and *The Conduct of Life* (1985) approach naturalism more closely than any other Fornes plays. Only the geometric settings and the spare lyricism invite wider interpretation. Although neither play focuses centrally on writing, instruction nevertheless figures in the worlds on stage. The title character of *Sarita* is sexually obsessed with the ne'er-do-well Julio between 1939 and 1947, when she stabs him to death. Pregnant by Julio at age 14, Sarita reassures her mother: "I have to learn how to lead my life." The following scenes dramatize her failure to learn, although she pens three eloquent letters to Julio. The first is a long reproach, which dissolves under his caress. The second is an accusatory rejection, which is scornfully crumpled by Julio. In Sarita's third letter she threatens suicide, and the next scene finds her ready to jump from the top of the Empire State Building, but Mark, a stranger, restrains her with love. For three years Sarita tries to be faithful to Mark, but when Julio sends her a letter (which we do not hear), it is the beginning of the end for Sarita. Letters delineate the mounting intensity of Sarita's obsession, which she escapes only by murdering Julio. Learning has come too little and too late.

Sarita is set in a poor Puerto Rican household of New York City, whereas *The Conduct of Life* takes place in a privileged household of an unnamed Latin American country. As the one traces the evolution of sexual passion in a young woman, the other traces the evolution of a passion for power in a mature official, Orlando. In sharp contrast to *The Successful Life of 3*, which celebrates ignorance, *The Conduct of Life* laments both ignorance and the inefficacy of learning for the three members of an erotic triangle. Early in the play Leticia, the neglected wife of Orlando, wishes for sufficient education to enter a university as a step toward independence. Yet when her servant Olimpia struggles to learn to read, Leticia slaps the book from her hand. Orlando himself recites lyric poetry during sexual assaults on Nena, his illiterate sex slave. In this sombre play education is a sign of power – a power that is cruelly misused.

Fornes's *Abingdon Square* (1987) is a rare departure into the world of Henry James. Although her syntax is less convoluted, Fornes's dialogue is unusually formal in this play, with its occasional stylized quotation. The drama opens quietly on a middle-aged man, Juster, singing a Handel love song to Marion, a shy, teenaged orphan. By the next scene Marion is betrothed to Juster, but she asks for guidance from his son Michael, who is "the same age as Marion." Seven months after the marriage of Juster and Marion, he reads about plant fertilization, in actual quotation (as Fornes's note informs us) from *My Garden in Summer and Winter*. Marion reads a passage about plants that grow back at once after plucking. As is often true of Fornes, the symbolism is oblique: Juster is too old to be fertile, and Marion never quite recovers after he plucks her.

A year after their marriage, but immediately afterward onstage, Marion recites from a nineteenth-century verse translation of Dante's *Purgatorio*. In Canto II the voyagers "behold a vessel under conduct of an angel," and when Virgil counsels Dante to kneel to the angel, Marion faints. Having no guide of her own, Marion writes (unquoted) letters to her dead mother. Nearly two years after her marriage Marion tells her husband's son Michael of an imaginary love affair that she has recorded in her diary. Fittingly, Marion cowers among books when she sights the man she instantly recognizes as her lover, although she has not yet met him. With the admission of Marion's vulnerability, stage quotation dissolves into passions – Marion's adultery, Juster's jealousy, their reciprocal cruelties, and their final reciprocal tenderness. Embroiled in feeling, Marion and Juster are as uninstructed as the semiliterate characters of other Fornes plays.

Fornes's most sustained incursion of writing in her drama occurs in the opera libretto *Terra Incognita* (1993). Set in Palos, Spain, the port from which Columbus sailed to America, the contemporary play reflects upon the brutality of colonization of the New World. One of the five contemporary characters, Steve, speaks words that are read "for the most part from Bartolomé de las Casas's 16th century *History of the Indies*." That remarkable work, as the character Burt explains, was "a report [that de las Casas] delivered to the Spanish Crown as he pleaded for measures to protect the Indians." In Fornes's libretto, writing is first staged as the trivial diary entries of 20-year-old Amalia. Her friend Georgia also has a literary bent, for she analyzes Albee's *Zoo Story:* "If it's a question of life and death, does having a right to sit on a bench matter?" Amalia's brother Rob skims the stage property of a newspaper for accounts of contemporary American atrocities. Although the young people are not insensitive to global cruelties, they are immersed in personal concerns, and it is against those concerns that Steve reads from de las Casas. The three young people leave, while Steve remains alone on stage, facing front to read the most harrowing account of Christian decimation of the Indians: "If an Indian killed a Christian, by law, Christians could kill one hundred of them." Without music, the instruction of this libretto is didactic rather than dramatic; *Terra Incognita* is all too *cognita*. However, Fornes's words *were* written for music, which may mediate the message.

Although Fornes's more recent plays are far darker than her early ones, both groups contain a remarkable range of verbal instruction, visible in stage properties like cards, magazines, newspapers, and especially books; or audible in language records and recitations of poetry at problematic moments. Almost always, the style of instruction differs from the speech of her characters, which Bonnie Marranca has aptly described: "The dramatic language is finely honed to exclude excessive qualifiers, adjectives, clauses. . . . There is a purity to this language of understatement that does not assume anything, and whose dramatic potential rests in the search for meaning in human endeavor" (*Theatrewritings*, p. 72). In that search on the part of Fornes's characters, they are betrayed rather than fulfilled by staged instruction. Often incidental to the main plot line, sometimes ridiculous, sometimes even pernicious, staged writing is nevertheless imbued with the yearning of Fornes's cohesive but rarely coherent characters.

Between Fornes's early romps and her later explorations, *Fefu and Her Friends* (1977) is transitional, and it contains elements of both. It is Fornes's only all-woman play, which I will therefore juxtapose to Caryl Churchill's all-woman play, *Top Girls* (1982).[6]

Unlike Fornes, Churchill rarely gives central stage presence to writing or instruction. Although she, or rather her characters, do quote from the literature of our culture, they do so *sub rosa*, since

103

Churchill enfolds quotation into her own original dialogue. Caryl Churchill began to write plays in 1958, while she was a student at Oxford, and her sources were literary. One of them, *The Finnsburg Fragment*, dramatizes an Anglo–Saxon battle poem. Another play of that period infiltrates the Taoist *Lieh-tzu* into a drama about power struggles in ancient China. When Churchill's children were young, the abbreviated form of radio drama suited the time at her disposal, and she has praised that medium for its "movement between being inside someone's head and out among extraordinary events" (Introduction to *Shorts*, n.p.). For the most part, however, each Churchill radio play dramatizes *either* extraordinary events *or* the inside of someone's head. Like early Fornes, Churchill is obliquely satiric in these plays written during the adventurous days of the Third Programme of the British Broadcasting Corporation, under the sympathetic direction of John Tydeman. Churchill herself has described these radio plays "about bourgeois middle-class life and the destruction of it" (E. B. Weintraub, in *DLB* 13[1], p. 120).

In the Introduction to her collected stage plays, Caryl Churchill designates 1972 as her watershed year, because she then shifted from radio drama to the stage.[7] *Schreber's Nervous Illness* (1972), performed both on radio and the stage, is a particularly destructive play on "bourgeois middle-class life." A dramatization of the actual Daniel Paul Schreber's *Memoirs of My Nervous Illness*, Churchill's play allows the paranoid nineteenth-century German judge to *voice* what he actually committed to writing. Like Artaud in the intensity of mental suffering transmuted into corporeal pain, as well as in his monstrous megalomania, Schreber filled a thick book with the specifics of God's persecution of him, so that his body was "impregnated, twisted and mutilated, poisoned, infected, asphyxiated, emptied of or filled with fluids, invaded by 'souls' innumerable, hooked into by countless divine 'rays'" (Ganz, *Humor, Irony*, p. 265). Churchill's play is largely a monologue of quotations from Schreber's book (which also aroused the attention of Freud and Lacan, and which was the inspiration for Roberto Calasso's novel *The Impure Madman* [1974]). Churchill punctuates Schreber's self-dramatization by three other voices – a dry psychiatrist (whose clinical prose claims objectivity), soft, lisping Rays (who are God's main weapon against Schreber), and the mighty bass of God (limited to two sentences). Culling some forty pages from four hundred,

Churchill divides her play into seven sections. It is a skillful selection, whose headings trace an arc of Schreber's hallucinations, from the explosive opening – "God was always in a precarious position" – to Schreber's final animalistic bellowing, even after his release from the asylum. For all Churchill's fidelity to Schreber's *Memoirs*, however, her play is not a docudrama but a blend of persuasive fantasies and paranoia on a grand scale, in dynamic tension. *Schreber's Nervous Illness* predicts Churchill's ability to sift through masses of written material in order to build a *drama*.

Also written in the early 1970s, but for the stage, *The Hospital at the Time of the Revolution* is based on Frantz Fanon's "Colonial War and Mental Disorders." Churchill imaginatively expands on his Case #3 of Series B: "Neurotic attitude of a young Frenchwoman whose father, a highly placed civil servant, was killed in an ambush." Churchill blends a portrait of Dr. Fanon himself with excerpts from his cases to accomplish in a stage play what she had praised in radio – "movement between being inside someone's head and out among extraordinary events." Although Churchill draws upon various books for plays of this decade – Anglo–Saxon poetry, Taoist religious writing, a self-recorded case of paranoia, and modern anticolonial writing – a single source feeds each play. Thereafter her exploitation of sources grows more adventurously polyphonous.

Churchill herself has pointed to the books that influenced her first professionally produced stage play, *Owners* (1972), written in three days while she was recovering from a miscarriage. Eva Figes's *Patriarchal Attitudes* armed her with serious substance, and Joe Orton's *Entertaining Mr. Sloane* suggested the comic style. Figes's 1970 book was one of the first to document the exclusion of women from power in Western society, from the Greeks to contemporary marriage, and yet Churchill creates a powerful woman protagonist – her first top girl, an obsessive "owner."

Churchill prefaces her play with two contrasting epigraphs:

> Onward Christian Soldiers
> Marching as to war.

and

> Sitting quietly, doing nothing
> Spring comes and the grass grows by itself.

The dominant characters of *Owners* live by the first precept; the only man who attempts to live by the second dies in a fire.

Until the end, however, *Owners* is a wildly funny play. Like Orton, Churchill garbs the most outrageous behavior in formal English, and we laugh at this disparity. Churchill's intricate plot skips through burglary, bribery, adultery, kidnapping, pyromania, and several farcical suicide attempts. As in Orton's *Entertaining Mr. Sloane* all the characters are masters of cool depravity, and the protagonist Marion is upwardly mobile. Although *Owners*, produced at the Theatre Upstairs of the Royal Court, did not predict that Churchill herself would become a top girl of Western theatre, it did initiate her long association with the Court.

Traps of 1976, with its mischievous recollections of current English drama, was also relegated to the small Theatre Upstairs of the Court. In Churchill's view:

> Traps is about traps people get into with each other and also traps that the audience is led into by being given certain information. It sets up unresolved difficulties and tensions ... it's about the break-up of structures like the family, and people wanting perfection, and in a way the impossibility of that – yet in the end it's like saying, How do you get the goose out of the bottle? You ponder and puzzle – and all in a moment – it's out.   (Watts, "Interview with Churchill," p. 9)

Critics have doubted whether the goose is indeed out of the bottle, and Churchill's explanation fails to mention traps for the contemporary *playwright* as well as the audience. Her farce is a miscellany of echoes of plays in the public British eye: the ironing board of Osborne's *Anger*, the ineffectual card tricks of Storey's *Home*, the incest of Orton's *What the Butler Saw*, the mistreated baby – "it" – and the mending of a stage prop of Bond's *Saved*, the opening line of Griffiths's *Comedians*, the name of Brenton's Christie shared by two members of a couple, the city-to-country move of Wesker's *Four Seasons*, the comic paranoia of Stoppard's *Real Inspector Hound*, the ready rhetoric of suffering Royal Court protagonists (already mocked by David Hare's *Great Exhibition*). Churchill's main trap, however, is, surprisingly, Harold Pinter: the cluttered stage recalls *The Caretaker*, the sexual mix-and-match recalls *The Collection*, the plea to come home recalls *The Room*, the Christies' love play recalls *The Lover*. The phrase "I speak fluent jargonese" embraces many a Pinter play, and Churchill indulges in Pinter's verbal techniques of contradiction, tautology, disjunction, as well as repetition of word, beat, and gesture. Yet Churchill finally escapes from the trap of Pinter by her un-Pinteresque celebratory finale, where all the characters bathe on stage and then partake of a meal. *Traps* reveals a Churchill steeped in contemporary British drama, even as she grew more assured of her own distinctive difference, however her idiom varies with each play.

In 1976 Churchill began to work with two theatre collectives, where she was nourished by nondramatic books. *Vinegar Tom*, "Seventeenth century witchhunt; songs about women now," was conceived in cooperation with the Monstrous Regiment company, who suggested the subject of witchcraft. *Light Shining in Buckinghamshire*, "How the English Revolution didn't happen," was the first of Churchill's four collaborations with the Joint Stock Theatre Group. In *Vinegar Tom* Churchill evokes sympathy for several fictional women accused of witchcraft. She was inspired by her reading of *Witches, Midwives and Nurses* by Barbara Ehrenreich and Deirdre English and *Witchcraft in Tudor and Stuart England* by Ian Macfarlane. In the last scene of *Vinegar Tom* two women who have been hanged as witches reappear in the costumes of Edwardian vaudevillians; in light rhyme they identify themselves as "authorities" on witchcraft, Jacobus Springer and Heinrich Kramer, who then proceed to spout sentences from their monstrous book *The Hammer of Witches*, first published in 1486 but reprinted some thirty times by 1669.[8] Horror stories made for the bestsellers of the times.

Light Shining in Buckinghamshire responded to a request of the director Max Stafford-Clark for a play about the milennial spirit in the Crusades. However, in Churchill's own words: "When I read Cohn's *Pursuit of the Milenium* [sic] with its appendix of Ranter writings I was seized with enthusiasm for changing to the seventeenth century. . . . So there was a new direction for insatiable reading" (Ritchie, *Joint Stock Book*, pp. 118–19). By the mid-1970s "insatiable reading" was second nature to Churchill.

Churchill's title comes from a Leveller pamphlet of 1649, one of her extensive "documentary materials," which she lists as follows:

Fear, and the pit . . . Isaiah 24, xvii–xx
A Fiery Flying Roll Abiezer Coppe 1649
All Seems Beautiful . . . Song of Myself Walt Whitman
The Putney Debates 1647
The True Levellers Standard Advanced Gerrard Winstanley,
   1649
The English Soldier's Standard to Repair to 1649
The Moderate, a Leveller newspaper, 1649
The Sleep of the labouring man . . . Ecclesiastes 5

It is curious that the list separates Churchill's two biblical sources, especially since her ecstatically imbued characters also quote from the Bible's Pauline letters, the Book of Joel, and the Book of Revelations. During the workshop period with Joint Stock, "Each actor had to draw from a lucky dip of bible texts and get up at once and preach. . ." (Ritchie, *Joint Stock Book*, p. 119).

Churchill alerts us to the fact that "[t]he characters Claxton and Cobbe are loosely based on . . . two Ranters whose writings have survived," and which she read in the Appendices of Norman Cohn's *The Pursuit of the Millenium.* Although two and a half centuries separate the millennial Ranters from the paranoid Judge Schreber, they share the heady fervor of God's special attention. Both Claxton (or Clarkson) and Cobbe left their respective homes to become itinerant preachers of Levelling during the English Civil War. Their sensual and socialist beliefs were as abhorrent to the Puritans as they would have been to the Royalists, and both idealists were separately investigated by the same Parliamentary Committee in 1650, the very year in which the Ranters expected the Millennium. Unlike some of their martyred colleagues, both men recanted; after the Restoration Claxton joined a conservative sect, whereas Cobbe changed his name. However, both men published documents during the period of their fervor, and Churchill quotes intermittently from that passionate writing.

Churchill weaves the "ranting" of these historical characters into her own dialogue of fictional figures – a woman preacher, a socialist soldier, an egalitarian officer, and a woman vagabond. These characters stumble through history, which Churchill distills from the documented idealism of the Digger Gerrard Winstanley, and from the Putney debates in which Cromwell betrayed the radicals. Her skill in selection, condensation, and organization is tested to the utmost.

In her ambitious plunge into documented history, Churchill also flouts the age-old custom of drama whereby one actor plays one character: *"The characters are not played by the same actors each time they appear."* The idea started as an exercise while the script was not yet complete, but then Stafford-Clark and Churchill realized: "[P]erhaps there wasn't any need to write the missing scenes if it wasn't quite clear which character was which and different actors played the same character in different scenes" (Ritchie, *Joint Stock Book*, p. 120). With a mere six actors, Churchill conveys a large event involving many people, through rapid shifts of scene, quotation, and impersonation. *Light Shining* is a remarkable spectrum of republican, millennial shadings, where the "voices are surprisingly close to us" (Itzin, *Stages in the Revolution*, p. 284).

In 1978, Churchill wrote what she designates as her "only documentary play" for television – *The Legion Hall Bombing*. Sifting through nine and a half hours of trial transcript about a bombing in Northern Ireland, Churchill based a condensed and intense drama upon selective quotation, although she also interviewed "lawyers and other people involved with the case" (Cousin, *Churchill the Playwright*, p. 114). She added her own prologue and epilogue in order to cast doubt on the validity of a trial under the Northern Ireland Emergency Provisions Act of 1973: "There is no jury. The judge sits alone. And the rules of evidence have been altered so that a confession is allowed as evidence even if it was obtained by threats or force" (ibid., p. 115). Such courts, Churchill concluded, "were set up to make it easier to get convictions, and they have been successful" (Kritzer, *Plays of Caryl Churchill*, p. 57). The BBC modified Churchill's prologue and deleted her epilogue, whereupon she and the director Roland Joffe had their names removed from the credits.

Perhaps sensitized by this experience, Churchill in the same year wrote *Softcops*, which is, as Michael Ignatieff noted, "Foucault rendered as a music-hall turn and Victorian freak show," but set in Paris of the 1830s. Churchill draws not only upon Foucault's distinction between "hard" and "soft" policing, but also upon Jeremy Bentham's panopticon, and upon the memoirs of the reformed criminal Vidocq, who became the Chief of Paris Police. Despite

Churchill's debt to Foucault's *Discipline and Punish*, she rejects his optimism about the ultimate revolt of prisoners. Her fictional "softcop" Pierre, secure in his Benthamite panopticon, expands his surveillance to include not only criminals, but "the sick . . . the workers . . . the ignorant . . . the unemployed . . . the insane." "Softly" but stonily, Pierre smothers not only rebellion but any deviation from dominant law and order.

For her best-known play, *Cloud 9* (1979), Churchill again turned to the nineteenth century as the ancestor of the late twentieth. In collaboration with Joint Stock, and relying on such material as Kate Millett's *Sexual Politics* and Jean Genet's equation of colonial oppression with sexual oppression (in her reading of him), she first wrote what became Act II of *Cloud 9*. Dissatisfied with its "one of everything" sexuality, she hit upon the idea of staging the Victorian roots of sexual and racial stereotypes, in which she was aided by her reading of Frantz Fanon's *Black Faces, White Masks*.

The structure of two seemingly disparate acts was retained for *Top Girls* of 1982, where I halt for the moment. Churchill's subsequent drama draws on such various writings as Mary Chamberlain's oral history *Fenwomen*, Euripides' tragedy *The Bacchae*, the daily newspaper *The Financial Times*, Thomas Shadwell's play *The Volunteers*, and Bram Stoker's novel *Dracula*. About half of Churchill's major plays quarry written sources, and I know of no modern playwright whose yield is richer or more varied.[9] In *Light Shining*, with its polyvalent background and violation of the actor–character union, as in Fornes's *The Danube*, with its echoic texture, the very concept of dramatic character becomes prismatic. Unlike Fornes, however, Churchill rarely *stages* actual writing, or scenes of instruction.

I turn, finally, to a comparison of feminine writing in that rarity, the all-woman play – Fornes's *Fefu and Her Friends* of 1977 and Churchill's *Top Girls* of 1982. Written by seasoned women playwrights, these dramas are unusual in their all-woman casts, who are not wholly described by the plays' titles. The dramas are also unusual in the degree to which they depend upon or incorporate writing and/or instruction.

Fornes's title refers to Stephanie Beckmann and seven women who gather at her home. Fefu is an improbable nickname for Stephanie, which may be linked to the play's and Fefu's opening line: "My husband married me to have a constant reminder of

110

how loathesome women are." It is hard to take that remark quite seriously, and, similarly, it is hard to take the name Fefu seriously, compounded as it is of two syllables of distaste – Jewish Feh and American Foo. (Fornes is specific as to the pronunciation.) The other characters have more common names, five of them ending in the -*a* that denotes the feminine in several Western languages.

Generalizations about gender are delivered even before we know why Fefu's friends are dribbling into her New England country house on this spring day of 1935. Moreover, we soon see that stock prop, a shotgun, in the living room of this pleasant abode, and rather than arouse suspense, Fornes has Fefu shoot at her off-stage husband within the first five minutes of the action. Rooted in a Mexican joke, that shot seems to be a form of love (or hate?) play between Fefu and her husband, Philip, whose name means love. When all the women but Cecilia arrive at Fefu's house – Cindy and Christina, Julia in her wheelchair, Paula, Sue, and Emma – we learn that they have gathered to rehearse a program concocted to request funds for an educational endeavor. We also learn that a year ago Julia was paralyzed by a hunter's shot at a deer, although his bullet hit the animal and not the woman. With the arrival of Cecilia, Act I closes, but Act III will return the company of women to Fefu's living room.

Act II is staged inventively: The audience is divided into four groups, who are guided in turn to lawn, study, bedroom, and kitchen of Fefu's house, where four scenes occur simultaneously, each one played four times. With audiences cut to quarter-size confronted by actors at close range, these scenes are stripped for intimacy, and each one unveils a private nightmare: Fefu is hounded by a mangled black cat, Cindy is threatened by strange men, Paula has been abandoned by her lover Cecilia, but it is Julia who cowers obsessively as a victim of imperious anonymous males, and it is Julia's hysteria that is the most climactic of the four scenes, regardless of the sequence of viewing.

Fornes stages writing to rein these overwrought scenes. In the book-lined study Christina peruses a French grammar, while Cindy reads jokes from a magazine. Paula in the kitchen analyzes a love affair into its constituent parts; only with hindsight do we realize that her scribbled numbers add up to her past relationship with Cecilia. Outside on the lawn Emma recites Shakespeare's Sonnet XIV, which closes: "Thy end is truth's and beauty's doom

111

and date." How does the sonnet fit the action on stage, if it does? Perhaps it refers to the recently departed Fefu, or perhaps it predicts Julia's fatal wound, eclipsing her truth and beauty. Of the four brief scenes, Julia's alone is unrelieved by staged writing, whether in print, notes, or recitation, and yet her learning has been praised. After the final repetition of these intimate scenes, the audience returns to its seats to hear Paula at the living room piano singing Schubert's "Who Is Sylvia?" Although Fornes does not print the words, they come from Shakespeare's *Two Gentlemen of Verona*. Does the question extend to the identity of these women, where five names end in *-a*, like Sylvia?

In Fornes's Act III, instruction is centerstage, in the form of Emma's long quotation from the prologue of Emma Sheridan Fry's 1917 treatise *Educational Dramatics*. Although Fefu's stage friends and acquaintances were perhaps at school together, Emma seems younger than the others, and she dominates the program they are rehearsing. Sharing her name with an actual acting teacher, Emma also shares her pedagogic role. Emma Fry's prose is orotund, but Emma Blake vivifies it by her passionate delivery. The stage women applaud their Emma in her recital, belittling their own contributions as "blah-blah." Before didacticism can raise its ugly head, several women engage in a childish water fight.

The final mysterious confontation of Fefu and Julia is at once inevitable and shocking. Cindy has spoken of a hunter shooting an animal but paralyzing Julia; offstage Fefu shoots an animal but wounds and perhaps kills Julia. Fornes's play does not yield readily to a monolithic interpretation, and Fornes herself has called it plotless. What fascinated me in the one performance I saw was how Fornes staged feminine arias of vulnerability against a background of everyday women's games and activities into which writing is unobtrusively enfolded – Shakespeare, sardonic arithmetic, a French primer, a comic magazine, and, more blatantly, a long quotation about theatrical openness, programmed into a rehearsal. As in Fornes's later plays, stage instruction is a two-edged sword, capable of wounding those who seek it, but nonetheless tempting to women who have been deprived of it.

Like Fornes's women of the 1930s, Churchill's top girls also quote, but less recognizably. Her contemporary protagonist Marlene, to celebrate her promotion, invites legendary top girls to dinner – in order of appearance, the nineteenth-century British traveler Isabella Bird, the thirteenth-century Japanese courtesan and nun Lady Nijo, the apocryphal ninth-century Pope Joan, a woman warrior painted by Peter Breughel the Elder in 1562, and the patient wife Griselda, who suffers through Boccaccio, Chaucer, and Petrarch (and who is mentioned by Eva Figes as "the masculine ideal of womanhood"; *Patriarchal Attitudes,* p. 52). The gathering at the Prima Donna restaurant is never explained in realistic terms, but it is strained through the mind of Churchill's protagonist Marlene, a mind well-stocked in spite of her lack of formal education. Few audiences are familiar with all Marlene's guests, and this must be intentional on Churchill's part. She means us to be curious about these costumed women, as we would not be, for example, about such figures as Queen Elizabeth the First, or Joan of Arc, or Saint or Mother Teresa. Marlene's boast can be taken literally: "We've all come a long way" – all, including the audience.

Churchill's dialogue introduces us to each of the women, whose backgrounds she has studied in various sources. Churchill read about Isabella Bird in Pat Barr's *A Curious Life for a Lady:* curious because, after the age of 40, Isabella Bird traveled on her own to Hawaii, the Rocky Mountains, Japan, Malaysia, Kashmir, Tibet, Persia, Kurdistan, Korea, China, and Morocco. In the words of Isabella Bird's biographer: "She told her tales well, she seldom retraced her steps, she never outstayed her welcome" (p. 340). And she wrote best-sellers. Rather than tracing these voyages or these best-sellers, however, Churchill emphasizes Isabella's devotion to her sister Hettie, thus sensitizing us to the oppositional sisterhood of Marlene and Joyce.

Another writer, thirteenth-century Lady Nijo was one of several concubines of a Japanese emperor. Her autobiography was translated into English in 1973, as *The Confessions of Lady Nijo,* and Churchill is selective of details from Nijo's account of sexual bondage, ceremonial clothes, several lovers, unwanted pregnancies, and the imperial disfavor that drove her to become a nun. However, Churchill jumbles the events that Lady Nijo narrates sequentially, and the contemporary playwright highlights the book's single scene of revolt. Although it was customary for the emperor to beat his concubines about the loins in the belief that they would then produce male children, the women were resentful when he also allowed his attendants to beat them, and in the dark Nijo beat the emperor; but only in Churchill's play does she boast, "I hit him with a stick."

Nijo's boast triggers Pope Joan's Latin – a long and improbable quotation from Lucretius' *De Rerum Naturae.* Said to have reigned as Pope John VII from 854 to 856, Joan pops up in references from the thirteenth to the twentieth century, portrayed as so thirsty for learning that she disguised herself as a man, distinguished herself in brilliant disputation, became a cardinal and finally a pope. However, she was ignorant of biology, and, unaware that she was pregnant, gave birth during a formal procession, whereupon she was killed. The subject of tracts, plays, novels, and a film, Pope Joan is included in Platina's history, *Lives of the Popes* (1479). Churchill presents Joan as a virtual agnostic, reciting Lucretius in its original Latin, however few of us may recognize it.

Neither Churchill nor Marlene distinguishes between history and fiction in the guest list, and the newly promoted top girl has little rapport with Patient Griselda, who arrives two-thirds of the way through the opening scene, after which Churchill rarely quotes from her several sources. Griselda gives voice to a fragmented digest of Chaucer's Clerk's tale of exemplary patience. Griselda accepts her husband's destruction of her two children and her own displacement by a rich young wife, but her patience is finally rewarded by reinstatement to her exalted position. One of the Marriage group in *The Canterbury Tales,* Griselda's story is interpreted allegorically by the Clerk himself: "For, sith a womman was so pacient / Unto a mortal man, wel moore us oughte / Receyven al in gree that God us sent." Not a whisper of allegory do we hear in Churchill, who invents her Griselda's final line, with its bare hint of reproach for the exigent husband: "I do think – I do wonder – it would have been nicer if Walter hadn't had to."

Churchill's power of selection is evident in the patterns that govern the increasing chaos on stage. Three of the women have dead lovers or husbands, three have "passed" as men, and three have children. Churchill's two historical figures – Isabella Bird and Lady Nijo – are balanced by two fictional figures – Pope Joan and Patient Griselda. Odd women out are two characters without written source: the silent waitress who serves the dinner at the Prima Donna restaurant and the Amazonian figure who stomps out of a painting – Breughel's *Dulle Griet*, spelled Dull Gret and pronounced GREAT in Churchill's play. The mute waitress is treated by the top girls as a virtual slave, with scarcely a "Please" addressed to her, and not a single word of thanks.[10] Dull Gret, who utters only thirty-two words during the meal, is often held to represent covetousness, as in this comment of the Breughel scholar Fritz Grossman: "To gain her loot she would even storm hell" (*Peter Breugel*, p. 193). However, the painting does not portray Gret storming hell *for loot*, and whether or not Breughel subscribed to medieval misogyny, he painted a heroic woman, compounded of armaments, domestic utensils, and frenetic authority. Brecht celebrated Gret's subversive potential for his dumb Katrin of *Mother Courage*, and Churchill endows Gret with a biography of oppression and a spirit of rebellion. Like Beckett's mute Lucky, Churchill's nearly mute Gret is all the more forceful when she erupts in a vivid aria rhythmed mainly in the present tense and bristling with vengeance for victimized women who are not top girls. Moreover, as Linda Fitzsimmons has analyzed in precise detail, Churchill revised her text to highlight Gret's greatness.

Yet the dinner does not conclude on Gret's triumph but on a quotation (slightly altered) from Isabella Bird: "I knew my return of vigor was only temporary, but how marvelous while it lasted." The sentence reflects on any temporary triumph of top girls – especially since Churchill's characters have lapsed into laughing, crying, vomiting, stealing drinks. Earlier in the scene Churchill has assigned to Isabella, Nijo, and Joan the phrase "there was nothing in my life," which predicts Churchill's conclusion that there is nothing worthwhile in the lives of top girls like her protagonist Marlene.

In sketching Marlene's guests, Churchill quotes or paraphrases written sources for Isabella Bird, Lady Nijo, and Patient Griselda, but she invents dialogue for two legendary characters, Dull Gret and Pope Joan (even though Joan quotes Lucretius). Churchill blends deftly and dramatically, eschewing the sometimes lengthy diatribes of *Light Shining in Buckinghamshire*. She herself has called attention to the fragmented nature of the dialogue, which bespeaks the lack of community between these top girls of different cultures, and which in turn predicts the lack of community between the women in the contemporary scenes of the play, especially Marlene and her sister Joyce.

Top Girls contains Churchill's most skillful and ingenious dovetailing of documentary material with her own contemporary dialogue; the cross-cultural opening scene crackles with energy. Fornes's *Fefu and Her Friends* is more subdued, in spite of the gunshots at beginning and end of the play, and the free-spirited water fight. I am not suggesting that Fornes systematically controls her scenes through staged writing, but it remains a surprisingly recurrent mark of her dramaturgy, where "emotional complexity [is] conveyed through ruthless simplicity, moral concern ... through a wholly dramatic imagination" (Wetzsteon, "Irene Fornès," p. 42). In contrast, Churchill is more traditional in her dramatization – and manipulation – of material written in other genres, in the manner of Shakespeare. In *Top Girls,* however, that doubly feminine play (written by a woman and containing only women), Churchill not only exploits written sources; she also stages writing. At the Prima Donna restaurant we cannot read the menus, but we laugh at the contemporary orders of the anachronistic top girls. Later in the play, however, writing is serious: Marlene admits to her sister Joyce, "I can't write letters," and yet she has sent a postcard from the Grand Canyon to her castoff daughter Angie, who not only treasures it but reads it aloud to its insincere ending: "Wish you were here." Churchill's varied and sophisticated written sources of the opening scene of *Top Girls* precipitate down to her protagonist's postcard cliché, a guidepost on the way to the playwright's succinct conclusion about hard-driving top girls, past and present – "Frightening."

At a time of questions about the basis of gender, and of questions about the basis of conventional Western instruction, it seems to me significant that instruction is so central to the dramaturgy of these two women playwrights. Churchill's self-instruction, garnered in many kinds of books, is dramatized for covert education of her audience, but without blatant didacticism. In contrast, Fornes overtly stages the very process of instruction, and it rarely leads to enlightenment – except, occasionally, for us.[11]

Males articulating women
David Hare and David Rabe

Of my several comparisons, the Hare–Rabe juxtaposition is problematic, since the prolific Englishman is given to witty forays into
contemporary British institutions, whereas the American commands attention by his gritty brush with American misogynistic
males. Both men are, however, unusually sensitive to the position
of women in their stage patriarchies. While some feminists debate
whether men *can* be feminists, these two men dramatize moral
sewers in which women are degraded. Rabe's few marginal females
contrast markedly with the many vivacious women of Hare, who
stridently verbalize their discomfort in the upper echelons of
contemporary British society. Both dramatists write with a keen
awareness of masculine privilege in their respective countries, a
privilege that includes speech, but Hare's women characters are ex-
pressive on stage, whereas those of Rabe are barely articulate.

The American critic Philip Kolin has written: "If Miller, Williams, and Albee form a first generation triumvirate in the American theatre, then Rabe securely stands with Mamet and Shepard as
the triumvirate of the second generation of American playwrights
since 1945" (*David Rabe: A Stage History*, p. 98). It seems to me that
Rabe stands most "securely" with Mamet and Shepard in their
predilection for plays of male bonding and/or masculine maturation, so that they rarely endow their woman characters with dynamic dialogue. Turning from the all-American trio of playwrights
to an Anglo–American pair, I am fascinated by the different feminine speech patterns of Rabe in his few plays and Hare in his
many.

Born in 1940, David Rabe has summarized his biography succinctly: "I'd had a Catholic childhood in Dubuque [Iowa], played

football, gone to Loras College out there, and then to Villanova [University], in the East" (Kolin, *David Rabe,* p. 3). Although graduate study in theatre drew Rabe to Villanova, he left without a degree, and in 1965 at the age of 25 he was drafted into the United States Army. Instead of resorting to the several subterfuges whereby college men evaded military service, Rabe not only suffered basic training but completed nearly a year of duty in Vietnam, where he did not see combat. Afterward, Rabe used the words "catalyst" and "crucible" for the effect upon his drama of military service in a male army (ibid., p. 11).

After Rabe's return from Vietnam in 1967, that unhappy country became the background for his first play – *The Basic Training of Pavlo Hummel.* Theatre managers may have read Rabe's play in the context of the antiwar protests of "Angry Arts Week" of 1967; rather than a protest, however, *Pavlo Hummel* dramatized the war's impact upon an American combatant, with macho delusions of heroism. *Hummel* was rejected by several American regional theatres, as well as by Off-Broadway theatres in New York. In Rabe's view, it was accepted by Joe Papp for his Public Theatre "because he wanted new American political plays" (Savran, *In Their Own Words,* p. 197). Garnering rapturous reviews and miscellaneous awards, it ran for 363 performances in 1970–1 (Kolin, *David Rabe,* pp. 44–5). Before the opening Rabe was at work on his second drama with a Vietnam background, *Sticks and Bones,* which played briefly at Villanova University before Papp welcomed it to the Public Theatre, to considerably less applause. Rabe's third army play, *Streamers,* had a longer gestation period of some five years, and it was not produced until 1976. *Hummel, Sticks and Bones,* and *Streamers* are often called Rabe's Vietnam Trilogy, although there is no carryover of characters, and only the first play is set in Vietnam. However, the Vietnam War is the background of all three dramas, threatening as it was to every American male of draft age: "The question was never *whether* it would affect their lives disastrously, but only *when.*" (Berkowitz, *American Drama,* p. 144)

Women figure only briefly in Rabe's Vietnam Trilogy, but the feminine is held up to scorn in basic army training: "YOU LIVE IN THE ARMY OF THE UNITED STATES OF AMERICA ... WITH BALLS BETWEEN YOUR LEGS! YOU HAVE BALLS! NO SLITS." Completely absent from *Streamers,* women appear as Vietnamese prostitutes in the first two plays of Rabe's trilogy. Punningly named, Yen is treated as a commodity by Private First Class Pavlo Hummel. In a duel for her favors, Private Hummel kicks his sergeant rival in the groin. Instead of dying heroically on the battlefield, Pavlo dies stupidly in a brothel, for the sergeant fells him with a hand grenade. This first Rabe play sets a pattern for his women – objects of desire and therefore bones of contention between men who should be allies. We are offered no insight into the feelings of the women.

In *Sticks and Bones* the protagonist David returns from service in Vietnam to a family that Rabe borrows from a television series – his brother Rick and his parents Ozzie and Harriet Nelson.[1] Beneath the Nelsons' facade of patriotic pride in their blinded veteran son David, they gradually reveal their racism. Having persuaded David to abandon Zung, the prostitute with whom he had been living in Vietnam, the family are insensitive to his guilt: "I left her like you wanted." Haunting David surrealistically, the figure of Zung silently appears at critical junctures of his estrangement from his family. When Zung speaks a single line in Vietnamese (untranslated in the published text), Ozzie Nelson tightens his fingers around her throat and strangles her. Rick then suggests that his brother David commit suicide, and the family accommodatingly help him *"cut one wrist, then the other, as they talk."* Rabe's text leaves it open as to whether David actually or "only nearly" dies, but most productions imply fatality.

The male rivalry in *Sticks and Bones* is more subtle than in *Pavlo Hummel*, since father and son wrestle not for possession of Zung's body, but for a code of behavior. To Harriet's displeasure, Ozzie has trained David in competitive sports, and the father can even understand his sons' illicit sex. Odd woman out in her male household, Harriet finally accedes to the racist violence of her husband and younger son in this American Catholic family.[2] Concealed for much of the play, Ozzie's terror of miscegenation careens wildly from his son David to his wife: "Your internal organs – your internal female organs – they've got some kind of poison in them. . . . LITTLE BITTY CHINKY KIDS HE WANTED TO HAVE!" It is those unborn grandchildren that Ozzie strangles in the surreal Zung, but Rabe believes that contemporary American audiences share the guilt of the Nelson family: "I think the play succeeds in that it provokes even the most liberal of audience members to want to do something to [David], and so when it happens, they're

complicit in something they don't want to be complicit in" (Savran, *In Their Own Words*, p. 196). Foisting emotions upon an
audience is a precarious undertaking, and this particular "liberal"
audience member did not feel complicit with the murderous violence of respectable people in Rabe's stage world; nor were reviewers "provoked" by the blind veteran, David. As in the Greek tragic
tradition, David's physical blindness corresponds to a sympathetic
moral insight: "They will call it madness. We will call it seeing."

Madness and vision are more directly patterned on Greek tragedy in Rabe's *The Orphan*, which he revised in 1971 while also
working on *Sticks and Bones*. When Rabe saw a 1967 Off-Broadway
performance of *Iphigenia in Aulis*, he was inspired to write his
most ambitious – and most drastically revised – play.[3] *The Orphan*
conflates *The Oresteia* with the American sadism of the Manson-
directed massacre in California, and of the My Lai massacre in Vietnam. The orphan of the title is Orestes, whom Rabe viewed as a
parallel of patricidal American youth (Kellman, "David Rabe's *The
Orphan*," p. 88). Orestes is Rabe's protagonist, but he also gives
voice to several women characters. Greek tragedy is the source of
his Clytemnestra, Electra, and Iphigenia. In addition, three of his
four choral figures are women, as is a nameless cult member, the
Girl, and an equally nameless Speaker, who relativizes human
events by her far-flung images. Like Ariane Mnouchkine some
twenty years later, Rabe opens *The Orphan* on the sacrifice of Iphigenia, thus rendering Clytemnestra sympathetic. Rabe departs from
Greek tragedy in the simultaneous stage presence of *two* Clytemnestras, one "ten or fifteen years older" than the other. Of lesser
importance, Rabe's Electra blends the vengeful Sophocles heroine
and the demeaned princess of Euripides.

Rabe's *Orphan*, equating the Trojan and Vietnamese wars, extends his view of woman as a victim of violent males – Iphigenia
at the hands of her father, and Clytemnestra at the hands of her
son. Although Rabe follows Greek myth in this respect, he deletes
the goddess Athena, who exonerated Orestes's matricide. Athena's protection would be superfluous, for Rabe's Orestes comes to
realize: "I have killed my mother and there is no punishment."
Praised as an orphan by the Apollo Figure, Orestes is nevertheless
his father's son in injuring a woman – actually, two women, since
he slits the throats of both Clytemnestras. Rabe's title severs his

Orestes from his familial heritage, but Rabe's protagonist is seduced by and complicit with a contemporary Family, who kill mindlessly: "We went in there with knives as natural as the wind or rain or old age."

Rabe's Orestes tries to decipher his heritage – by means of questions, documents, and even hallucinatory mushrooms – but his women characters accede to patriarchal violence. Men murder Iphigenia, Electra, and both Clytemnestras on stage, in contrast to the offstage murders in Greek tragedy. Rabe compounds the cruelty since his contemporary Family members obey the ruthless behests of an Aegisthus and a Lieutenant to "kill some gooks." Aegisthus himself is slaughtered by the cult Girl and Orestes, acting in concert. No male is innocent of blood, but the nameless contemporary Girl is equally violent.

Of Rabe's characters in *The Orphan* only the female Speaker is aloof from bloody deeds. Unlike the male Figure who becomes Calchas in Act I and Apollo in Act II, the Speaker conserves her impenetrable identity, and she rarely addresses the characters directly. Objective and scientific, she drily describes the vast astral universe or the tiny electrical impulses within the brain. The director, Barnet Kellman, has attempted to explain the Speaker: "It is very important that the audience should not mistake her for an author's narrator. They must not think that she is giving the *correct* explanation for events, merely another explanation" ("David Rabe's *The Orphan*," p. 86). So unfeeling is she, and so oblivious of bloody events, that she does not so much explain as distance herself from human passion. It may be that the female Speaker is the other face of the cult Girl, the latter naturally sadistic and the former remote from humanity. For the first but not the last time in Rabe's plays, women can behave as ferociously or as coolly as men.

David Rabe is a compulsive reviser, and the final (1975) version of *The Orphan* opened in North Carolina two years after *In the Boom Boom Room* opened Joe Papp's short tenure at New York's Lincoln Center.[4] The latter play is unique in the Rabe canon in that the protagonist is a woman, one of six go-go dancers in the boom boom room of sexual titillation. In that context Rabe's indictment of lust – mainly male lust – resembles that of Shakespeare in Sonnet CXXIX: ". . . perjur'd, murd'rous, bloody, full of blame, / Savage, extreme, rude, cruel, not to trust."

Chrissy the go-go dancer has been viewed as a female version of the soldier Pavlo Hummel, but whereas women are a commodity for the fighting man, men are an emotional trap for the dancer: "We got no right to be bad to men. Nothin' ever works out for them." Despite childhood abuse, Chrissy is devoted to her father, Harold. Although she refuses "to hook on the side," she freely sleeps with her dates: "Maybe I'm a nymphomaniac. Sorta." Yet she is basically monogamous; attracted to Al, she breaks off with Eric, even though she is hypnotized by his astrological lore. When Al abandons her, she accepts solace from her gay friend Guy, but they fall out when he insults her dancing. Alone and resolute, Chrissy closes Act I in ambitious delusion: "I'm gonna be sittin' in fur, this mink curlin' down, and they polish me till I gleam, and I'm golden." The "they" are surely male, but the "I" will never gleam golden – in her poverty-stricken imagery.

Act II traces Chrissy's downward spiral: She rejects the lesbian advances of Susan and fails to find emotional sustenance in Eric or in her parents, who are immersed in their own sexual whirlpool. When the racist, sexist, criminal Al returns to her, Chrissy marries him in a go-go wedding, a victim of the romantic clichés of our culture: "It'll be what I dreamed of. I won't care about anything but him." In the very next scene, however, Chrissy and Al, each fatigued from the grind of demeaning work, charge one another with neglect. Al accuses Chrissy of "lesbian tendencies," and she taunts him about "lookin' at niggers" and then threatens to take black lovers. Stronger than Chrissy, Al rains blows down on her while she cries: "Don't hit my face, don't hit my stomach." The scene dissolves to Chrissy in New York, a topless dancer with a mask over her face. Half-heartedly, a nameless Man asks for our "undivided attention" to her.

Stephen Watt has argued that the finale of *In the Boom Boom Room* may represent an achievement on Chrissy's part: "Chrissy is developing a new dance, realizing one of the several performing selves dancing 'in her head all the time'; she has attained a new level of freedom, even if we are quite justifiably cynical about her new refuge" (in Zinman, ed., *David Rabe: A Casebook*, p. 61). I do not see how our cynicism can be justified if Chrissy has indeed achieved freedom. Chrissy's mask implies a scarred face; her virtual nudity is degrading since Chrissy has earlier declared to Susan that she "wouldn't . . . ever" dance topless. Whatever Chrissy may be dancing "in her head all the time," *we* watch the dance of a damaged commodity, who has been demeaned, successively, by her father, uncles, "friends," lovers, and, finally, by the nameless Man who introduces her to the audience: ". . . the little filly [in] her New York bare-boobie debut."

Rabe's scenic directions insist upon the "metaphoric realm" of the setting, and the play itself dramatizes the boom boom room as a sexual battlefield in which women are disadvantaged. As audience, we are oglers at the go-go dancers upon which the action begins and ends. Although the female dancers are mere background, two women are important in Chrissy's life. Her mother is not only fixated on her father, but she ends her pregnancies so that her body will still attract him. Yet Chrissy loves her father and hates her mother, who may have tried to abort her. For all the difference of their social class, Chrissy's mother and David's mother in *Sticks and Bones* are similarly subservient wives, but independent, bisexual Susan is a new departure for Rabe. Introducing the go-go girls to their public, instructing Chrissy in her dance steps, refusing the indignity of toplessness, Susan is scornful of men: "ther-a-pist. The Rapist." Yet even she is deferential to Tom, the unseen owner of the boom boom room, and even she sometimes enjoys sleeping with men. She shrewdly observes: "Nobody's very nice to you, are they Chrissy?" The Nobody is probably male. In teaching Chrissy the Jerk dance, Susan compares one gesture to being struck in the stomach: "They like that. . . . Up – hit, down." Again, the "they" is male. In "Up – hit, down," Susan paces Chrissy's dance – and summarizes her life.

However Rabe insists upon the "metaphoric realm" of the boom boom room, the play functions credibly at the realistic level, particularly in dramatizing Chrissy's limited lexicon. In contrast, *Goose and Tomtom*, also published in 1986, is a bewildering blend of an object-laden set à la Ionesco, a gangster idiom à la Mamet, a sexual battlefield à la Pinter, with Rabe's own characteristic stage violence, as well as a heretofore uncharacteristic fairy-tale quality. Rarely performed after a 1986 workshop production at Lincoln Center (with Madonna, Sean Penn, and Harvey Keitel), the play builds by recapitulation; again and again the characters repeat the inconsequential actions and dialogue in which they have been involved.

Moreover, verbal recapitulation is underlined by visual recapitulation in that, before our eyes, Tomtom makes drawings of the actions of the several characters.

At the surface level Goose and Tomtom are petty jewel thieves, as is Bingo of the equally childish name. The woman's name Lulu hovers between infantilism and sexuality, and the character Lulu is Rabe's most extreme example of the female victim; but when she is allowed to speak, she is astonishingly articulate. The sister of Bingo, Lulu has been kidnapped, gagged, blindfolded, and hung by her wrists in an offstage closet, to be "pumped" at male pleasure. In sharp contrast is the play's most powerful character, Lorraine. Nominally Tomtom's lover, she soon seduces Goose, and she stays "out all night" whenever she pleases. Goose and Tomtom accuse Bingo of stealing the jewels they stole for Lorraine, and, spurred by Lorraine, Goose kills him in punishment. Bingo's bloodstained sack disgorges diamonds, which gleam in the darkness. Mysterious invaders then abduct Lorraine. While Goose and Tomtom lose the ability to stand erect, Lulu sits *"unmoving though released,"* and the diamonds become the stars in the sky.

It is difficult to interpret the play. Like Mamet's *American Buffalo*, *Goose and Tomtom* is a parody of the macho underworld of film. Unlike Mamet's play, however, that of Rabe is also a fairy tale and a philosophic conundrum. What is less difficult to interpret is the role of the two women, Lorraine and Lulu, who are, like women in other Rabe plays, sexual commodities. In the words of Jennifer McMillion: "The women are at the root of the tribal rivalry in *Goose and Tomtom*, both as forces to be worshipped and obeyed and as possessions to be stolen" (in Zinman, ed., *David Rabe: A Casebook*, p. 183).[5] But not simultaneously.

Lorraine rules the roost. Taunting Goose and Tomtom about their toughness, she sticks pins into their arms, and with macho decorum they do not flinch. After "fuck[ing] that Goose's brains out," Lorraine removes his liver (offstage) and occasionally squeezes it in our presence, so that he screams with pain. Unlike the totalitarian "unseen hand" of Sam Shepard, the equally sadistic hand of Rabe's Lorraine exerts its power over Goose's liver that bleeds before our eyes. Lorraine's avidity for jewels provokes the friends' brutality toward Bingo, who defiantly declares: "Lorraine's a cunt." While Goose and Tomtom assault Bingo, Lorraine preens in garments of her wardrobe. Finally, however, Lorraine falls prey

to a nameless invader, who announces: "And so we lived, delighting in the grass, delighting in the sky, peeing standing up or squat-
ting. And then they came, the barbarians. . . . Though we could not
have before conceived of such deeds, we pillage and we are dismayed." During the play we have watched Goose and Tomtom pillage, and heard their intermittent dismay. Violence has spawned
violence. In Rabe's world sexual difference is at the root of male
violence: "There's somethin' very unfuckin' natural about broads."
With grim poetic justice, Rabe's victimizer Lorraine becomes the
victim of those who have responded to barbarians by becoming
barbarians.

An immobile Lulu remains onstage with the increasingly in-
fantile Goose and Tomtom. Earlier she has been assaulted by her
brother Bingo, pumped and gagged by Goose, chloroformed by
Tomtom – a graphic sequence of acts of sexual harrassment. In her
dignified words, which are at odds with the gangster colloquialisms of the other characters: "I am often kidnapped, you know,
and left like this to await some transaction both mysterious and
grand involving both myself and treasure." After the invaders
abduct Lorraine, Lulu announces that she is thirsty. Like Ruth's
thirst in Pinter's *The Homecoming,* that thirst is the prelude to independence and to a different kind of love: "a dismayed and hopeless love unlike anything of which they might have ever thought
their breathing little hearts to, before this moment, consist." "This
moment" does not arrive in *Goose and Tomtom,* which dramatizes one woman in the familiar but newly articulate role of victim, and the other in the newer but equally unidimensional role
of victimizer. The final reversal implies a resemblance between
the two women, which was earlier announced by Goose: "I love to
bang 'em, man. They got the plumbing, you know what I mean?"
Improbably as the play ends – upon diamonds becoming the stars
– the last human figure we see is Lulu, *"unmoving though released,"* the female victim somehow transcendant.

In a play of more realistic surface, *Hurlyburly* (1984, finally revised 1988), the resemblance among Rabe's three women characters
is patent. Perhaps the title, recalling the witches' chant of *Macbeth,*
reflects the male view of women as witches. Even the printed text
of what was originally entitled "Guy's Play" announces the gen-
dered society of the contemporary Hollywood setting, for Rabe lists
the male characters in one column and the females in another.[6]

Unlike the two-tiered dialogue of *Goose and Tomtom*, that of *Hurlyburly* is colloquial and obscenity laden – for men and women alike. Yet it is not naturalistic. Phil blends slang and abstraction in describing his brutality to his wife:

> She says some totally irrelevant but degrading shit about my idea and starts some nitpicking with which she obviously intends to undermine my whole Far Eastern theory on the balance of powers, and I'm sayin', "Wait a minute," but she won't. So WHACK! I whack her one in the face.

Into the Hollywood house rented by two divorced casting directors, Eddie and Mickey, three women are brought, one by one. Less complex than the Lorraine–Lulu contrast/resemblance, the three women of *Hurlyburly* are three levels of sexual commodity. At the apex is Darlene, a professional photographer and "dynamite lady," who is desired by both Mickey and Eddie. At the middle level is Bonnie, a nude dancer who is game for almost any kind of sexual sport. Finally 15-year-old Donna is delivered by Artie as "a CARE package" to fuck "Just to stay in practice. In case you run into a woman." Soon after Donna's arrival, Eddie and Phil follow her upstairs, presumably to fuck her seriatim. These women are not prostitutes, but they are nevertheless commodities – a sensual gratification to enhance the alcohol, marijuana, and cocaine of the males "bumping around in this vague, you know, hurlyburly, this spin-off of what was once prime time life."

In addition to these visible but rarely audible females, Rabe offers us portraits of offstage wives, viewed from the perspective of their estranged husbands. Phil, after beating his wife Susie, ruminates about his provocation: "Perverse is what she wrote the book on it." Eddie is married to Agnes, who taunts him by telephone when he is drunk: "You get off on it, don't you." Even less than in the case of actual women characters do we gain an inkling into the viewpoint of the invisible wives.

In Janelle Reinelt's succinct summary: "There can be little doubt that Rabe has written a critique of masculinist culture in this play" (in Zinman, ed., *David Rabe: A Casebook*, p. 197).[7] He does so variously: by showing us only the male view of women, by graphically depicting the pointless cruelties of four men of the masculinist culture, and above all by tracing the maturation of Eddie. Absorbed like the others in aimless indulgence of the senses, Eddie alone has no illusions about success in Hollywood, and he tries to disabuse the other men. More often than the others, Eddie voices concern for his far-off child, and Eddie alone desires some stability in a sexual relationship, even in Hollywood. When Phil kidnaps his own infant daughter, Eddie wonders: "Maybe if we kept her and raised her, she could grow up and be a decent human being." But decency is not yet his province, which he enters only after Phil commits suicide, leaving an enigmatic note: "The guy who dies in an accident understands the nature of destiny."

Eddie shifts mercurially from decoding the note to blaming Phil's wife for his death, to quarreling with his friend Mickey, to screaming at Johnny Carson on television. When Eddie himself meditates suicide with Phil's gun, he is interrupted by the unexpected return of teenage Donna. Touched by this "accident," Eddie apparently accepts her as the destiny that wills him to live. Declining Donna's monosyllabic offer to fuck, Eddie wishes her an innocent goodnight. At the play's beginning Eddie was asleep on the couch – "a mess." By the end of *Hurlyburly*, having offered Donna a tranquilizer, he stands tall while she falls asleep on that same couch. The death of his uncontrollable friend Phil has somehow led to Eddie's birth into a new and gentler manhood.

Although feminists have taken exception to Rabe's misogynistic males, the plays themselves seem to me to condemn these characters who are deaf to a woman's plea: "I am a form of human being just like any other, get it!" Rabe's women are invariably commodities in the male economy, who are rarely allowed to convey their feelings, much less to assert their own identity.

These replicated female products look nothing like David Hare's professional women, who are often the moral center of his plays. More than any other living male dramatist, Hare has given voice to women – on stage, film, and television. He has done so quite deliberately, having declared: "Looking at the world through the eyes of women is to see the world more clearly" (interview in *Time Out*). In quantity and quality, Hare's women are superior to those of Rabe; yet they too are counters in a male economy. In the lavish program notes of the Fall 1993 productions of Hare's trilogy at the National Theatre, women go virtually unmentioned.

A graduate of public schools and Cambridge University, Hare has drawn most of his characters – female and male – from his own middle class. Hare's men tend to accommodate to their privi-leged position in an immoral society – usually in England – but his women are less complacent. From the schoolteachers of *Slag* (1970) to the black barrister of *Murmuring Judges* (1991), Hare's wo-men fit badly into a bad society, and a few of his heroines "struggle . . . against a deceitful and emotionally stultified class" (Introduc-tion to *The History Plays*, p. 15).

Hare believes "that I didn't write until I wrote *Knuckle* [1974]. . . . Up till then I was writing purely satirical work" (Oliva, *David Hare: Theatricalizing Politics*, p. 165). It is therefore unkind to men-tion a "purely satirical work," but *Slag* (1970) is too heraldic to ig-nore. The very title prophesies other witty, enigmatic Hare titles – *The Great Exhibition, Knuckle, Teeth 'n' Smiles, Plenty, The Secret Rapture, Racing Demon, Murmuring Judges*. Never actually men-tioned in the play of that name, "slag" is defined in the *OED* as "a piece of refuse matter separated from a metal in the process of smelting"; presumably by extension, "slag" is British slang for the cheap "refuse matter" of female flesh, as in Hare's "I own up to the slag I want" (*How Brophy Made Good*), or "Couple of slags here say anyone fancy a blow job" (*Teeth 'n' Smiles*).

As the title *Slag* reverses the letters of "gals," Hare's play re-verses the sexes of *Love's Labors Lost* but borrows its basic situa-tion. Shakespeare's male scholars forswear intercourse with the opposite sex, and Hare's female teachers forswear intercourse with their opposites, thus losing all the pupils of their girls' boarding school. Disingenuously, Hare in 1975 defended his early play:

> The point is that [*Slag* is] really a play about institutions, not about women at all. . . . It's about every institution I had known . . . ever more baroque discussions about ever dwind-ling subjects. But it happens to be peopled with women, part-ly because it was the sort of play that I thought I would enjoy going to see – women on the stage, represented as I thought more roundly and comprehensively than was then usual.
> (*Theatre Quarterly* 5[19–20] [Winter 1975], pp. 110–11)

As recently as 1990 Hare claimed that in *Slag* he wanted "to cele-brate women" (Gaston, "Interview: David Hare," p. 216). Hare's ambivalent self-defense – a play "not about women at all" who are nevertheless well-rounded characters – was reflected in critical am-bivalence, even though *Slag* won him an award as the *Evening*

Standard's Most Promising Playwright. *Slag* also heralds Hare's preoccupation with crumbling British institutions, which resulted in his trilogy – one that lacks the violence of Rabe's trilogy.

Although *Slag* reads today like the witty, misogynistic romp of a clever young man, it does announce Hare's serious theme of living with lies, since that is what his English female trio do. Ann's lie is a facade of community, Elise's is her fantasy pregnancy, but the most blatant lie is Joanne's intransigent feminism. Implicitly, Hare espouses harmonious heterosexuality. Yet Hare gives his Elise a disarming line: "This is not the way women speak together, it's not the way they live. It doesn't ring true."

As Hare's dramaturgy grew in assurance, some of his women ring more true if no less didactic. Sometimes at the center and sometimes on the sidelines of their respective plays, Hare creates women who are burdened with a conscience often lacking in his men, and who flaunt that conscience expressively. A conscience who smokes, drinks, and runs a shady nightclub, Jenny Wilbur is a secondary but important character in Hare's favorite of his plays, *Knuckle* (1974).[8] Jenny bewilders the protagonist, Curly, who describes her in contradictory terms: "White-knickered do-good cock-shrivelling cow"; ". . . the hard, bright, glistening girl." Before Curly expresses these polar views of her, Jenny situates herself in the patriarchy:

Young women in Guildford must expect to be threatened. Men here lead ugly lives and girls are the only touchstones left. Cars cruise beside you as you walk down the pavement. I have twice been attacked at the country club, the man in the house opposite has a telephoto lens, my breasts are often touched on commuter trains, my body is covered with random thumbprints, the doctor says he needs to undress me completely to vaccinate my arm, men often spill drinks in my lap, or brush cigarettes against my bottom, very old men bump into me and clutch at my legs as they fall. I have been offered drinks, money, social advancement and once an editorial position on the *Financial Times*. I expect to be bumped, bruised, followed, assaulted, stared at and propositioned for the rest of my life, while at the same time offering sanctuary, purity, reassurance, prestige – the only point of loveliness in men's ever-darkening lives.

For all the difference in class and lexicon, Jenny's account of indignities parallels that of Rabe's Chrissy, Lulu, or Hollywood trio; but she speaks like a Cambridge graduate.

Three men are obsessed with Jenny: One threatens her with a knife, another commits suicide and leaves her a bar, and a third, Curly, announces: "I'm propositioning you." She of the "incandescent vagina" taunts Curly to uncover the truth about his sister's disappearance, and he finds that his father is the rankest culprit in Guildford. The self-styled "point of loveliness" for three men, Jenny Wilbur is a woman of principle, who does not fear male violence. In Hare's drama she remains subsidiary to the investigation of the "business practice" of father and son – that venerable theme of realistic drama.[9]

Hare conceived other supportive and conscience-carrying women, who are on the sidelines of masculine matters in their respective plays. The ambitious male journalist of his television play *Dreams of Leaving* (1980) is teased by an enigmatic beauty who challenges his accommodation with a crooked system, which he merely "dreams of leaving." *A Map of the World* (1982) and *Saigon* (1983), later paired as "Asian plays," trace Hare's emergence from English insularity to a broader canvas. The intricate plot of the former winds around a movie based on a novel, based on events into which I will not digress, but which tantalize an audience to decipher their location. All three genres – movie, novel, and "real" event – pivot on an erotic triangle; an Anglo–Indian novelist and an English journalist, political opponents, are also rivals for the sexual favors of the American Peggy. A minor character, Peggy has no connection with the world conference on hunger, the reason for the encounters of the other characters. The Anglo–Indian novelist, whom the "real" Peggy marries, summarizes his own fiction: "The actress questions her easy promiscuity and is made to realize adulthood will involve choice." In Hare's play, however, we have only his word for it, telling instead of showing Peggy's maturation, which is a minor matter in the world of men.[10]

The teleplay *Saigon* encroaches on Rabe's dramatic territory, Vietnam. At the end of the Vietnam War English Barbara, a blonde, "almost 50" bank official, engages in a love affair with a CIA agent who is half her age, while panic replaces orderly military withdrawal from Saigon. The play provides little confirmation

of CIA Bob's confession to Barbara: "Every time I saw you, you made me feel guilty.... That's why I stopped coming to see you." Still, that little marks Barbara as another Englishwoman of conscience. Like Jenny before her in Hare's work, like the several women in his later trilogy, Barbara is cleanly, and sometimes didactically, on the sidelines of the dirty world of men.

In *Pravda,* Hare's 1985 play cowritten with Howard Brenton, Rebecca Foley has a degree in investigative journalism, but she serves mainly to support her crusading journalist husband, and finally to condemn his acquiescence to the yellow journalism of a powerful publisher. For all her education, she remains on the dramatic sidelines of the duel between the powerful publisher and her journalist husband. In 1986 Hare created a pair of non-English, moral women for each of his one-acters about an imperiled marriage – *The Bay at Nice,* set in Soviet Russia, and *Wrecked Eggs,* set in the United States. In these slight plays, or those laced with peripheral women, Hare faithfully depicts the sexism of contemporary society, while investing the women with awareness of the immorality of that society, explicitly phrased in educated speech.

When women are leading characters in Hare's plays based in contemporary society – from *Teeth 'n' Smiles* (1975) to *Murmuring Judges* (1991) – Hare's attitude varies. Occasionally, the women are in the *Slag* lineage of living lies, but more often they are imbued with the moral fervor of the sideliners. Hare himself has insisted: "Women are characteristically the conscience of my plays" (Nightingale, "An Angry Young Man") Moreover, conscience is enhanced by consciousness of the cost of morality in modern Britain. Rabe's women suffer physically from male violence, but those of Hare are more subtly victimized.

Teeth 'n' Smiles is unique in Hare's oeuvre, uncandidly autobiographical, enfolding rock songs, and almost allegorizing the decline of England after the hopeful student revolutions of 1968. Set in 1969 at the Cambridge May Ball, the play was originally "to be all about Maggie, but actually she is only on the stage for about forty-five minutes" (Kerensky, *New British Drama,* p. 186). During that time, however, Maggie rises from an alcoholic stupor to martyrdom. Richard Cave evokes her admiringly:

> With the role of Maggie, David Hare has created one of the few characters on the English stage that bears comparison

131

with Genet's figures who similarly choose to be ritual scape-
goats for modern society . . . willing themselves to accept their
degradation as a way of revealing the moral bankrupcy of the
forces that have reduced them to such a state and thereby
discovering in themselves a new vigour and dignity.

(Cave, *New British Drama*, p. 195)

Hare endows Maggie with colloquial phrases that ring true for her
profession of popular singer: "I am the only girl singer in England
not to have been spun out of soya bean." "Can't go around with
blue balls all night." "Why are girls who fuck around said to be
tragic whereas guys who sleep about are the leaders of the pack?"

In an energetic exposition we learn that Arthur met Maggie
when he was a Cambridge student and she a 17-year-old folksing-
er. Writing her songs, shaping her persona, and claiming to love
her, "[Arthur] invents me." Apparently disillusioned that their
popular music inspired no revolution, and "frightened of being
happy because [she] felt it was wrong" (Page, *File on Hare*, p. 33),
Maggie spurned happiness with Arthur, substituting drink, self-
pity, easy sexuality, and easier deconstruction. She is scornful of
Arthur's (verbal) idealism: "It's all gotta mean something . . . that's
childish, Arthur. It don't mean anything." And although she is
also contemptuous of her manager's cynicism, her own heroism
borders on the cynical. When one of the band members conceals
his drugs in her bag, Maggie accepts arrest: "O.K. Try prison for a
while, why not?" Yet her acceptance of a scapegoat role does confer
a certain dignity upon her.

The first set and the first scene close on Maggie's song "Passing
Through," which confirms what we have heard about her: "If you
don't scream honey / How do they know you're there." In one way
or another, Maggie screams. In the second set Maggie insults the
Cambridge audience instead of singing, and she is punished beyond measure. In swift succession her manager fires her and announces Arthur's new love. Maggie accepts the band's betrayal and
disappears during their third set. But she returns in style, setting
fire to the concert tent, excoriating her manager, bestowing Arthur
on her rival, and finally turning her back on us: "Remember, I'm
nobody's excuse. If you love me, keep on the move." Maggie may
not spark a revolution, but "on the move" she threatens Cambridge with conflagration: "Police. Ambulance. Fire brigade. You

just got to score the air–sea rescue service and you got a full house." Arthur may have molded her art, but Maggie alone has the will to fail when the world around her is driving toward success.

Teeth 'n' Smiles (1975) is the only Hare play that can be meaningfully juxtaposed against a Rabe play – *In the Boom Boom Room* (1973). Played in several areas of a nearly bare stage, both dramas trace the deterioration of a female protagonist. Although Hare's Maggie and Rabe's Chrissy are both victimized as female fetishes, Maggie is cool about sex, whereas Chrissy romanticizes it. Chrissy is trapped by the poverty of her language, as much as by the poverty of her surroundings. Maggie is less voluble than Chrissy, but her language is witty and image laden. She can even compare the two countries of rock: "America is a crippled giant, England is a sick gnome." Hare would go on to create other witty women, but none of them can lacerate with Maggie's raw edge.

More educated and elegant than Helen Mirren's Maggie, Hare's Kate Nelligan characters shoulder the burden of conscience in his works of the late 1970s. A teenage heroine of World War II is common to the teleplay *Licking Hitler* and the stage play *Plenty* (both 1978). The very title *Licking Hitler* puns on the success and subservience of a British Political Warfare Unit, whose mission is to undermine German morale by broadcasting seemingly casual conversations between far-flung Germans during World War II. A member of that unit, lonely and young enough to sleep with her teddy bear, upper-class English Anna is raped by working-class Glaswegian Archie. Anna nurses her wounds in silence, and they begin an affair: "I don't know what he thinks about anything. We've never had a conversation. We just have a thing." Humiliating Anna during working hours, Archie finally terminates the "thing" by lying to his military superiors that Anna has "tried unsuccessfully to get him to sleep with [her]."

In a much criticized conclusion Hare resorts to anonymous voice-over to trace the postwar careers of the unit whose wartime mission was to lie. Archie filmed documentaries, and then Hollywood potboilers. Anna spent ten years in advertising before rejecting its lies; marriage, adultery, and promiscuity were punctuated by a hysterectomy. With no communication between them, Anna sees Archie's film and writes him "complaining of the falseness of his films, the way they sentimentalized what she knew to be his appalling childhood and lamenting, in sum, the films' lack of political direction." She too sentimentalizes when she closes her letter: "I have remembered the one lie you told to make me go away. And I now at last have come to understand why you told it." She then declares her love for Archie, but: "He never replied."

Hare has stated that ". . . both Anna Seaton and Archie Maclean are trapped in myths about their own past from which they seem unwilling to escape" (Introduction, p. 13). Anna's myth inflates a "thing" into love, and Archie mythologizes his working-class roots; but we see the play's events through Anna's eyes, and since she and Archie "never have a conversation," how does she recognize "the falseness of his films?" Feminists have criticized Hare for Anna's postrape affair with Archie, and the playwright has pleaded that "such things do regrettably happen" (ibid., p. 13), but the play itself does not grapple with *why* they happen. Does Anna submit to Archie through fear? Sexual attraction? Self-deception? If Anna is, as Hare claims, the conscience of the play, she should not be trapped in a myth about her past, including the myth of a meaningful love affair with Archie.

In *Plenty* Susan Traherne spends World War II in France as a subversive agent, and peacetime in Britain as an equally subversive agent.[11] Hare has described *Plenty* "as a play about the cost of spending your whole life in dissent" (Introduction to *The History Plays*, p. 14). He has also claimed that people can "go clinically mad if what they believe bears no relation to how they live" (Myerson, "David Hare: Fringe Graduate," p. 28). What enthralls in the theatre is the ambiguity of whether Susan Traherne's behavior is dissent or madness, or both. Clear, however, is the mounting desperation of Hare's most resonant heroine. Gordon Rogoff encapsulates Kate Nelligan's performance in that role: "Nelligan can come into a room with raging energy, only to expire slowly into a taut whisper, but always with a ping to everything she says that gives resonance to the thoughts below" (*Theatre Is Not Safe*, p. 237). It is Hare who rhythms those pings.

The play opens on a naked man in a nearly bare house – the obverse of plenty. Susan Traherne is on the point of leaving her husband and giving their Knightsbridge home to a longtime woman friend. The next scene flashes us back twenty years to wartime France, where a teenage Susan greets a British airman who has just parachuted down. Susan soon reveals her fear, and it is the man who saves their supplies from a rival claimant in the French Resistance: "Gestapo nothing, it's the bloody French." After the war Susan is restless and supercilious about "people who stayed behind," so that her future husband, Raymond Brock, asks: "You don't think you wear your suffering a little heavily? This smart club of people you belong to who had a very bad war. . . ."

Hare shades Susan's dialogue, however, not with overt suffering but with cutting deflation of an increasingly prosperous Britain. She leaves her export job and office "mating dance" to seek impregnation by a working-class stranger. After eighteen sterile months, Susan abandons that project, and when the young man appeals to her emotions, she shoots at him, but guns are not her forte. After the Suez "blunder or folly or fiasco," Susan is married to the diplomat Brock, and she is publicly scathing about the diplomatic corps. Susan imperils Brock's career by refusing to return to Iran with him, and yet she threatens a senior diplomatic officer with suicide if Brock is not promoted: "I think you have destroyed my husband, you see." But it is Susan who tries to destroy Brock, after destroying their common property: "A universe of things. . . . What are these godforsaken bloody awful things?" A few weeks after Susan abandons Brock, she shares a tawdry hotel room with the pilot whom she rescued during the war. When he leaves her, she slips into a drug-induced fantasy of the Resistance, where she responds radiantly to a Frenchman's welcome: "There will be days and days and days like this."[12]

Earlier, a perceptive Brock has charged: "When you talk longingly about the war . . . some deception follows." But longing talk about the war is itself deception for Susan, denying its danger and Anglo–French rivalry. Susan Traherne's dissent is ubiquitous; she is contemptuous of the English pride in plenty, of the hypocrisies of the British diplomatic corps, of the resolution with which individuals pursue their selfish goals. She confesses to the erstwhile pilot: "I have a weakness. I like to lose control." Like Anna Seaton in *Licking Hitler*, Susan Traherne is trapped in a myth about her glorious past, a myth she does not wish to control. For all their eloquence, both women accede to their victimization, like the very different characters of David Rabe.

Unlike Rabe, Hare usually provides female foils for his moral protagonists: Maggie's rival, the pragmatic but humane Laura in *Teeth 'n' Smiles*, is efficient and dependable. Susan's friend Alice in *Plenty* lounges in and out of love but finally resolves "to do good" to unmarried mothers, whereas socially useful action never crosses Susan's mind. Like Maggie before her in *Teeth 'n' Smiles*, Susan Traherne registers a self-indulgent dissent that serves no social purpose. Except for stimulating theatre.

Ten years later, in 1988, Hare brought his dissimilar females front and center in *Secret Rapture*. The Tory Marion is first seen removing a valuable ring from her dead father; tolerant Isobel, her sister, is last seen as a radiant ghost (in the original production, although not in either version of the published text). Drawing its title from Catholic theology, "the moment when the nun becomes the bride of Christ," or death, *The Secret Rapture* is Manichean, with its satanic and angelic sisters. Marion, a Conservative minister, lives a lie of pious public service, and Isobel harbors so rigorous a conscience that she refuses to expel their father's alcoholic (but witty) widow Katherine, another woman who lives a lie. In interviews Hare has insisted that the play is a modern tragedy, with "intractable goodness" as Isobel's fatal flaw. However, like Chrissy in Rabe's *In the Boom Boom Room*, Isobel is the victim of her lover in a patriarchal society. At the death of Isobel, her sister Marion undergoes a barely credible conversion to virtue.[13]

On the sidelines, or centerstage, Hare's women of education and principle tend to depend upon men. In *Knuckle, Licking Hitler,* and *Secret Rapture*, women are assaulted by men, and in Hare's three films (*Wetherby, Paris By Night,* and *Strapless*) women *need* particular men. As early as *Knuckle* Jenny rejects liaisons, but she thrives as a talismanic symbol in a bar frequented by men. Maggie's art in *Teeth 'n' Smiles* is as sexual as Madonna's, and Anna Seaton of *Licking Hitler* sentimentalizes her erotic "thing." Susan of *Plenty* sheds a husband for a nameless lover. Only in the film *Strapless* do two sisters weather affairs with men, maturing finally to become independent professional women "on their own."[14]

Some fifteen years later, Frances Parnell functions comparably in *Racing Demon* (1990), the first play of Hare's so-called trilogy. Like David Rabe's Vietnam Trilogy, Hare's three plays are linked only by theme – and by Richard Eyre's quasi-epic production on the wide stage of the Olivier Theatre. The first and third plays – respectively about the Anglican Church and the British Labour Party – display women on the sidelines, but the second play – about British justice – elevates women to protagonists. In *Racing Demon*

Frances is a sophisticated Londoner from an ecclesiastical family; she lacks Jenny's colorful language, but she too is aware of providing "the only point of loveliness in men's ever-darkening lives" – specifically, two men, both Anglican clergymen. Frances withdraws her sexual favors from young Tony when she is aware of his ruthless ambition, and she withdraws her comforting presence from middle-aged Lionel when she is aware of "Letting [him] imagine." A secondary character, Frances inherits Jenny's moral rectitude in a play about insidious business in the Anglican Church (which scants the controversial church problem of female clergy-*men*).

Two other women characters are neatly balanced in *Racing Demon*: Heather, the neglected wife of the humanistic clergyman, and Stella, an abused black woman evangelized by the unscrupulous clergyman. Ignorant of conflict within the church, these two women pay the highest price for it – sanity and freedom – but Frances retains both qualities as she flies away from an increasingly hypocritical England, to close this first play of Hare's trilogy on British institutions – and to escape the institution of the Anglican Church.

For those – male and female – committed to the institution of the British Labour Party in *The Absence of War* (1993), there is no such escape. The action centers on the election campaign of the Labour leader George Jones (played by the actor John Thaw, well-known on television).[15] The play's early scenes pivot on a career woman, advertising expert Lindsay Fontaine, who is introduced into the Labour team; but she soon fades from the main plot line, while Hare's depiction of election strategy centers on the male advisers of the candidate George Jones. Women serve him selflessly, but are denigrated by his self-seeking successor: ". . . all these women surrounding you telling you how marvellous you are." "These women" do much more than that, and yet Hare limns Labour politics as a man's world at the very time that women were being appointed to the actual Shadow Cabinet.

A woman does, however, provide a touching close to Hare's first act. As the veteran Barbara Castle was invited to the actual Labour Party rally in Sheffield, to show party continuity, Hare's fictional Vera Klein appears on the scene. Everyone pays her momentary homage, but they then turn their attention to the immediacies of the campaign, abandoning her. Ancient and frail, alone on the vast empty stage, the indomitable socialist asks: "When do we start?" In the second act female Lindsay triggers George's return to his own socialist roots, but it is too late; he has been spoon-fed too many speeches to improvise from his gut. He loses the election, for which Hare's women have worked indefatigably but incidentally.

In the second play of Hare's institutional trilogy, *Murmuring Judges* (1991), professional women sustain central roles – police constable Sandra Bingham and junior barrister Irina Platt. Deftly shifting between their respective worlds in contemporary London – the police station and the law court – and the prison that shades both worlds, Hare dramatizes British justice as an oxymoron: The overworked police cannot contain crime, the prison is governed by its own brutal laws, and the legal eagles fly by their own rarefied codes.

Although Sandra has had an affair with a seasoned detective, and Irina has known love in her native Antigua, Hare focuses on the professional lives of the two women – in a patriarchal context. Sandra, who has been brought up as a boy by her policeman father, is ambitious to rise in the force; Irina, who serves as the black female token of a prominent jurist, is ambitious to defend the innocent. Separately, both women are advised that they are members of "a team," but conscience as well as sex distinguishes them from their colleagues. Separately, the two professional women pierce to the lies that victimize an Irish laborer. Most reviewers complained of Hare's lectures in the mouths of Sandra and Irina – in Irving Wardle's phrase, "a pair of young puritans." Indeed both smart young women flaunt their consciences, particularly Irina on English prison and English privilege: "It seems so obvious to an outsider. Do you really not know? All this behaviour, the honours, the huge sums of money, the buildings, the absurd dressing-up. They do have a purpose. It's anaesthetic. It's to render you incapable of imagining life the other way round." Like other moral women in Hare's work, she too speaks like a Cambridge graduate, without a trace of her native Antigua.

To his credit, however, Hare has expanded his own ability to imagine life "the other way round." *Murmuring Judges* is not a Manichean reduction: The victimized prisoner is guilty, and the police show humor and humanity. The higher echelons of the judiciary are men of culture who welcome a black woman – provided she abides by their rules. Despite reviewers' contradictory complaints – on the one hand, that Hare was parading his research; on the other, that he was saying nothing new about judicial corruption – the playwright is theatrically informed and informative about the judiciary, at least to this theatregoer.

Hare's dramatic problem is his conscience-carrying women protagonists. Although one is black and the other white, they are both quite colorless on stage. In the theatre the villain usually steals the show, so that a playwright presents a virtuous protagonist at her or his peril. Dipsomaniacal Maggie of *Teeth 'n' Smiles* and hysterical Susan of *Plenty* may accomplish nothing constructive in the world, but they seethe with theatrical energy. In *Murmuring Judges* Sandra appreciates the rough masculine humor of the force, whereas Irina is impassive before the sophisticated wit of the leading members of the judiciary; but both are pale figures in their respective worlds.

Hare gives the two women a scene together, in which Irina appeals to Sandra to help her imprisoned client by incriminating the police: "You've chosen a woman. . . . You thought I'd be easier. I sort of resent that." Since *"both smile,"* the resentment dissolves into mutual sympathy – a sympathy that is dependent on their common sex. Hare mutes the articulacy of these women characters, to bolster their reciprocal understanding with scenic directions; but it was asking too much of actresses to follow these across the Olivier Theatre expanse: *"Irina picks up on [Sandra's] tone . . . Irina confident that she has Sandra's interest . . . Irina knows [Sandra] is still hooked . . . Irina makes a slight move toward [Sandra] with a card . . . a real warmth suddenly between the two women . . . they both smile together, joined by the thought"* (pp. 90–2). The thought in question is Sandra's remark that Irina's alternative law practice has no counterpart in the constabulary: ". . . there's nothing called the alternative police." Nevertheless *Murmuring Judges* closes on Sandra's decision to act as though there were, or eventually might be such an alternative. Instead of telephoning Irina with the crucial evidence, Sandra keeps it within the constabulary. In Hare's last scene a panoramic sweep against the prison background finally narrows down to Sandra, who steps to the center of the stage: "I want the Chief Superintendent. (*She waits.*) I wonder. Could I have a word?"

During the course of *Murmuring Judges*, however, Sandra has too many words, and Irina has even more. Unlike drunken Maggie, caustic Susan, or even tolerant Isobel, these female puritans are preachers whose sermons smother drama. We do not know how Sandra will fare in the police force; we do know that Irina will leave the British legal establishment. These Hare protagonists who rebel against injustice, and incidentally against sexism, are also his least theatrical women.

Dramatizing a panoply of middle-class women – from the singer Maggie to Dr. Lillian Hempel, from a diplomat's wife to a journalist's wife, and especially the professional women in British church, law, and the Labour Party – Hare indicts sexism, among other injustices; yet he himself finds it difficult to conceive of women who are independent of men. Rabe's women are blatant commodities in a masculine economy that he too indicts; in comparable worlds of the U.S. Army, Hollywood, and margins of crime, women are treated with matter-of-fact brutality. For all their praiseworthy indictment of the victimization of women in plays that differ as widely as their settings, neither Hare nor Rabe articulates the woman's point of view, much less her feelings.[16]

Englobing intimacies
Christopher Hampton and
Richard Nelson

The playwrights in my final Anglo–American pair are distinctive-ly readable as well as playable. Not only readable but well-read themselves, Christopher Hampton and Richard Nelson situate their dramas in a shrinking globe. Neither dramatist is linked with a particular style (like Bond, Pinter, and Shepard), a particular sub-ject (like Rabe), or a particular commitment (like Hare). Crafting dialogue carefully, Hampton and Nelson have similar dramatur-gical skills; on the one hand, they write witty, intimate plays in the comedy-of-manners tradition, and on the other hand, they com-pose larger dramas in a global context. Unspectacular, workman-like, neither playwright has been accorded the critical attention he merits.[1]

Christopher Hampton, born in the Azores in 1946, fell into play-writing almost by accident, whereas Richard Nelson, born in Chi-cago in 1950, grew up with theatre, since his mother was a dancer. Hampton has published only seven original plays, and I begin with a swift glance at his career. Born abroad to English parents, spend-ing his childhood in Egypt, he has been something of an outsider in England where he arrived at age 10, returning overseas to visit his parents on school holidays. While a student at Oxford, where he read French and German, he wrote his first play, *When Did You Last See My Mother?* (1964). After a university production, it languished in the Royal Court Theatre reject pile, where it caught the eye of the neophyte director, the late Robert Kidd, who snapped it up for his first professional production – a bare-bones perfor-mance on Sunday night. Under the aegis of the intrepid producer Michael Codron, the five-character, single-set play moved from the Court to the West End, where it ran for the contracted three weeks. Robert Kidd needed a translation of Isaac Babel's *Marya,* and he persuaded Hampton, who knew French and German but not Russian, to work from a literal translation – which became standard practice in London.[2] Awarded a traveling fellowship by Oxford, Hampton did research in Brussels and Paris on the relationship between the French poets Rimbaud and Verlaine; the resulting drama was *Total Eclipse* in 1968, while much of the university world was in turmoil, but not Oxford.

To encourage Hampton to enter the professional theatre rather than graduate school, the artistic director of the Royal Court, William Gaskill, invented the position of Resident Dramatist, launching Hampton on a career of playwriting, translation, adaptation, and screenwriting (and launching an impressive lineage of other Royal Court Resident Dramatists, including David Hare and Caryl Churchill).

Richard Nelson was drawn to theatre by the magnet of Broadway musicals, to which he was exposed as an adolescent. At the small liberal arts Hamilton College in New York State, Nelson had over a dozen plays produced, and when he received a travel grant, he went to Manchester, England, often journeying to London theatres. Upon his return to the States in 1973 Nelson worked as a journalist and wrote several plays rooted in current events, incorporating the viewpoint of the reporters of those events. The first to be professionally produced was *The Killing of Yablonski* (of the United Mine Workers) at the Los Angeles Mark Taper Forum Lab in 1975, and other productions followed in quick succession. Quite consciously, Nelson decided to translate and adapt classical plays (1) to educate himself, and (2) to earn a living in the American theatre, through percentages of the box office in 900-seat houses. "I wanted to follow the English example of Edward Bond, Howard Brenton and Christopher Hampton, who commission a literal, word-for-word translation and then work off that" (Savran, *In Their Own Words,* p. 165). At the same time Nelson wrote original plays, sometimes transferring mythological figures to the contemporary United States. Several of his early dramas graft fictional plots upon journalistic facts, while implicitly posing the question of the purpose of writing at all. What Nelson has said about his *Some Americans Abroad* holds for most of his plays: "Right there is my world – a world of displaced intellectuals, of Americans in confusion" (ibid., p. 169). Yet the confusion is mitigated, or at least mediated, by the unfailing articulacy of his characters.

Although Hampton is drawn to intellectuals outside as well as in England, he too dramatizes articulate confusion. Without any confusion, however, he has provided a guideline to his dramatic structures, which will serve me in my comparison of the two playwrights: "The pattern I've fallen into . . . is to write a 'small' play followed by a 'large' play, a fictional play followed by a play based on some documentary incident"[3] ("Christopher Hampton's 'Savages,'" p. 78). Hampton matches small with fictional, and large with documentary. Tracing Hampton's alternations chronologically, I was struck that Nelson makes comparable shifts, but less regularly, and that several plays of the two playwrights may be rewardingly paired and compared as to structure, subject, locale, or genre. What the "small" and "large" dramas share is the crystalline stage speech of an intelligentsia to which both playwrights belong.

Hampton's first "small" play, *When Did You Last See My Mother?* (1964), adds a contemporary twist to the hoary subject of a lovers' triangle. In the year before they matriculate at Oxford Ian and Jimmy share a flat. Adolescents discovering and troubled by their sexuality, the orphan Ian tongue-lashes the popular Jimmy about his easy conquests, male and female. When their physical fight climaxes in Ian's kiss on Jimmy's lips, the latter moves out of the flat.[4] A week later Jimmy's mother, emerging from "a fearful row" with her son, drives down to visit Ian, who plays upon her sympathy until he leads her "inexorably" into sexual intercourse. Another week passes, and after another row with her son, Jimmy's mother again visits Ian, but this time he taunts her: "Do you think I'd have made love to you if I didn't see [Jimmy] in you?" Horror-stricken, Jimmy's mother flees, and in the final scene Jimmy tells Ian of his mother's fatal automobile accident after "a row." When Jimmy blames himself for her death, Ian begins to confess his own guilt, but he stops short of full avowal. Only after Jimmy leaves does Ian accuse himself: "Always pleased to help people whose mothers I've seduced and killed." Self-disgustedly, Ian suspects that he will soon sleep with Jimmy, but onstage he seeks escape in television.

"When did you last see my mother?" is the question that Jimmy never asks Ian. Witty and even sinister, Ian is at once a self-indulgent egomaniac and a confused adolescent of eighteen – Hampton's own age at the time of writing. Unlike Robert Anderson in his *Tea and Sympathy* of the previous decade, Hampton dramatizes a love affair initiated by an adolescent and not by a mature woman. Yet Ian does not consciously conspire against either Jimmy or his mother. Ian is caught up in the momentum of his own rhetoric, and if he finally admits self-disgust, he and we know that he will not change his behavior.

Totally self-absorbed, Ian disdains a job, calls his neighbor a Wop, and turns off a television program about South African racism. Ian edits an anecdote so as to impose misery upon its protagonist, predicting his own impact upon those he meets. Insular but complex, Ian seethes with dramatic life. He is as witty as a Restoration rake, and as vituperative as an Osborne protagonist. Hampton's play is most scorching when there are only two characters on stage, Ian and his victim of the moment. Although Jimmy and his mother are his main victims, Hampton adds two incidental characters, male and female conquests of Jimmy, who become butts of Ian's invective. In spite of these superfluities, *When Did You Last See My Mother?* is remarkable in both control and compassion – in the first play of an 18-year-old playwright.

Violating chronology, I jump forward a decade to examine another Hampton "small" play – *Treats* (1976) – that prunes supernumeraries to etch a lovers' triangle. Written two years before Pinter's *Betrayal*, *Treats* also dramatizes a woman tossed like a ball between two professional men, but that had already been the basic structure of *When Did You Last*. The sharp-tongued journalist Dave might be an adult Ian, but the mother is replaced by the young professional Ann. As Kimball King notes: "Each of the play's nine short scenes explores the ambivalent *treat*ment of each character by the others" (Gross, ed., *Christopher Hampton: A Casebook*, p. 74; my emphasis). I would, however, substitute the word "cruel" for "ambivalent" – from Dave's physical abuse to Patrick's Ayckbournian insensitivity, backgrounded by Ann's dependence on a man, in spite of her occasional protests of independence.

Returned from an assignment in Nicosia, Dave finds himself ousted by Patrick from Ann's affections and her flat. The rest of the play perches Ann on a fulcrum as these two men seesaw for her favors, the one violent and the other placid, but both self-absorbed. Again Hampton's play crackles with the wit of a bright rake, targeting at once his rival and the object of his desire. In *Treats* Ann dismisses dull, stable Patrick with the obscene vituperation she has learned from Dave, who panics momentarily in fear of losing her. When Ann turns lovingly to Dave, however, he is *"stonefaced."* Dave needs Ann as a victim, not as a lover.

Taut of speech but roller-coasting in feeling, the trio of *Treats* ignore events in the world, and Hampton's epigraph (from the film *Casablanca*) implicitly condemns them for that: " – it doesn't take much to see that the problems of three little people don't amount to a hill o' beans in this crazy world." "This crazy world" barely pierces the consciousness of these "three little people," but Hampton gives *us* hints about events in that world. Ann is oblivious to an external world, Patrick listens abstractedly to the radio news, and Dave mentions parenthetically that the trio is within earshot of an IRA demonstration. Credible as Dave is in his erotic sadism, he is incredible as a journalist, since the profession demands obsessive attention to current events. Granted, the play dramatizes Dave's personal and not his professional life, but then Hampton should have given him a different profession. Dave's repartee is nonetheless striking in this bitter comedy of modern sexual manners or "treats."

What distinguishes Nelson's *Sensibility and Sense* (1986) is skillful weaving of "this crazy world" around his "three little people." A small play with five characters and a single setting, Nelson's drama was sparked by Lillian Hellman's libel suit against Mary McCarthy. For his fictional analogues of these left-wing writers, Nelson invents a shared husband; that is to say, Edward has in the past been married for three years to Elinor, but in the play's present he is married to Marianne. So the three characters may be loosely labeled a lovers' triangle. ("We've shared men all our life.") The rivalry of Marianne and Elinor turns, however, not on a man but on a sociopolitical gestalt. Two extratriangle characters set this rivalry in a broader context: The wealthy socialite Therese has actually fought in the Spanish Civil War, about which Marianne and Elinor bicker in their youth; her action thus devalues their words. The other minor character, Edward's nephew Peter, serves as a pale *raisonneur*; a generation younger than the principal characters, he helps them without understanding them.

Although *Sensibility and Sense* has a single setting, it shifts deftly between two time periods a half-century apart. The years 1986 and 1937 are projected at the starts of the first two scenes, but only the times of day are projected for the remaining ten scenes.[5] In 1937 the three main characters, editors of a left-wing literary review, come to a millionaire's vacation home to plead for money for their enterprise. In 1986 Edward and Marianne own that home. After a distinguished and profitable career as an educator, Marianne is so ill with cancer that Edward has to tend to her every need. Nevertheless, Marianne is intent on suing Elinor for libel in her book on left-wing intellectuals of their generation.

When the play opens in 1986, Marianne and Edward await the arrival of Elinor – to apologize for her book? To threaten lawsuit with countersuit? To gloat over a dying friend/enemy? Far from "try[ing] to *resolve* ... the personal, sexual and ideological tensions that have come to bedevil their relationships" (back cover of Faber edition; my italics), the two women express their similar, sometimes senseless sensibilities as they reenact their ancient rivalries, while Edward weakly tries to mediate between them or seeks escape in alcohol – in both time periods.

Nelson's three principals meet often in 1937, but he reserves a single scene for their confrontation in 1986, and that scene is noteworthy for its dramatic and economical summary of the dilemmas of the American left from the Spanish Civil War to the election of Richard Nixon. In the puzzled words of the younger Peter: "Seemed like they were splitting hairs. Both seem to have beliefs that are so much further to the left than the vast majority in this –" Perhaps the rage of splitting hairs precipitates Marianne's death (offstage). After her death Edward still attempts to mediate between his two wives: "That book kept her alive. . . . To get her angry. . . . That could keep her living." Elinor at first denies Edward's theory of her book's contribution to Marianne's sustained and sustaining fury, but then she appears to accept it before planning vengeance on her dead friend. Although Marianne wished no memorial service, Elinor proceeds to arrange for one – with Edward's blessing: "It'll be interesting to see who's left."

The pun neatly punctuates Nelson's play; that is to say, in the United States of the 1980s, who is left on the political left? In *Sensibility and Sense*, with its twist of Jane Austen's title, Nelson raises questions. Which is preferable: Edward's withdrawal into apolitical privacy, Elinor's fellow-traveling with communism, or Marianne's accommodation with power, from Kennedy to Eisenhower? The words "sense" and "sensibility" whisper through the play, so that we come to appreciate their sybilant overlap. Sense is never crudely common, as political causes are filtered through people. Subtly, Nelson elicits admiration for Marianne's rage while dying, as against her husband's alcoholic escape and her rival's quasi-penitential reminiscences. The world may be crazy, but in contrast to Hampton's erotic intellectuals of *Treats*, those of Nelson are absorbed in and by it.

I wanted to consider *Treats* with *When Did You Last See My Mother?* so as to examine the three triangle plays in sequence. In the rest of the chapter, however, I will move chronologically through Hampton's original works. Like the two early triangle plays, his second drama, the "large" and "documented" *Total Eclipse* (1968, revised 1981), dramatizes self-absorbed intellectuals who display only a niggardly awareness of the outside world. In a note to Nelson's large and documented *Two Shakespearean Actors* (1990) the American writes: "This play concerns imagined events surrounding the . . . true incident." The statement holds as well for Hampton's *Total Eclipse,* in which the French poet Paul Verlaine boasts of his role in the Paris Commune. He is, however, apolitical between 1871 and 1892, the timespan of Hampton's play. Although Verlaine's sentimentalized memories frame the play, Hampton's title refers to Arthur Rimbaud, whose extraordinary poetry suffered a "total eclipse" at the age of 20 – Hampton's age when he wrote the play. Rimbaud and Verlaine produced their best poems during the few years they lived together, even though they were often drunk, drugged, and violent toward one another.[6]

Total Eclipse is not only large, but also sprawling through time and place (even in the revised version, which was first directed by David Hare). We witness the Paris meeting of 16-year-old Rimbaud and 27-year-old, married Verlaine, with the former quickly dominating their aesthetic and their relationship. In spite of a large cast and multiple settings, the play never wavers from its focus on the two contrasted poets. For Verlaine poetry is an art admired in society; for Rimbaud poetry is a way of being – the poet is a virtual rival of God as Creator. Without quoting either poet, Hampton conveys their polarity.[7] Rimbaud's famous "long, immense et raisonné *dérèglement* de tous les sens" is not spoken but performed.

147

In a swift series of scenes Hampton traces the growth of Rimbaud's rebellious force and the corresponding enfeeblement of Verlaine, who not only abandons his wife and child but harms them physically. When a drunken Verlaine shoots Rimbaud in the hand, the latter blames him: "You missed." For Hampton's Rimbaud, death is preferable to the pragmatics of living. Although Rimbaud does not press charges against Verlaine, the latter is imprisoned for two years, during which he espouses religion. Upon his release Verlaine again seeks out Rimbaud, only to be told: "Anything that can be put into words is not worth putting into words." When Verlaine abjures his newfound faith and pleads with Rimbaud to rejoin him, the latter hits him *"carefully and methodically"* before leaving him forever.

Twenty years later Rimbaud is dead, and Verlaine is *"a derelict carnal hulk."* Rimbaud's sister visits Verlaine in a squalid Paris café. Speaking for her pious mother and claiming to speak for her deceased converted brother, she is in quest of Rimbaud's manuscripts "to destroy those of his works which we feel he would have destroyed himself." When she leaves, Verlaine tears up her address and wallows in absinthe memories of a Rimbaud who never was: "He's not dead, he's trapped and living inside me." Although Hampton's drunken daydreamer sentimentalizes the past, Verlaine does preserve Rimbaud's poems from the "total eclipse" desired by his pious family.

Actors rather than poets figure in Nelson's *Two Shakespearean Actors* (1990), and they do so in a comparably large and sprawling play – set somewhat earlier in the nineteenth century. Nelson's introductory note reads:

> The play concerns imagined events surrounding the following true incident: on Thursday 10 May 1849, while the English actor William Charles Macready was performing *Macbeth* at the Astor Place Opera House in New York City, a riot erupted which resulted in the death of thirty-four people and the injury of over a hundred more.

Like *Total Eclipse, Two Shakespearean Actors* shifts through several settings, but, unlike Hampton's play, it concentrates the action within a single week. Like *Total Eclipse, Two Shakespearean Actors* houses a large cast, but its focus only slowly narrows down to its eloquent protagonists, the English actor William Macready and the American actor Edwin Forrest.

Hampton forgoes the temptation to quote from his poets, but Nelson indulges in histrionic displays by his actors. Not only does he stage an abridged *Macbeth* (*pace* Tom Stoppard), by zigzagging between two different theatres and two radically different productions, but he also shows us Forrest in his most popular role as the Native American Metamora.[8] Nelson's play is full of delicious tidbits to delight a theatrically knowledgeable audience – greenroom gossip, stage accidents, the actor who dries, the actor who drinks, and especially the actors' grandstanding, whether on or off the stage.

Although Nelson's many actors are immersed in theatre, his two principals nourish their monstrous egos within the theatre conventions of their respective countries. Thus, Macready is patronizing to the Americans: "Here I have found in New York, an American group of – Which is almost like a group of English actors. I can't say more." Given the "almost," he need not say more. Forrest in turn boasts of owning "the only First Folio in the New World" but mistreats his English wife. Nelson delays the confrontation of Forrest and Macready until midway through the play, when they are invited to supper by a fatuous Dion Boucicault. Icily polite at first, the two stars in their cups agree on the sanctity of art:

MACREADY: The world should be left behind. In the dressing-
    room.
FORREST: It certainly should not be brought on to the stage.

But when Macready is onstage shortly afterward, the audience in the "real" world pelt him with missiles, and there is a "deafening cheer" at the announcement: "Macready has left the theatre!" Nelson does not allow *us* to leave the world behind.

New York's anti-Macready feeling arises from populist distaste for the culture and breeding of the moneyed classes, which looked to England for its models. A doddering Washington Irving – "I have been criticized for being – European" – promises Macready police protection and reminds him of his duty to spread culture. More shrewdly, Macready offers his actors an increase in their box-office percentage if they brave the American audience, and the English group agree to play *Macbeth* again.

In the ensuing violence of May 10, 1849, Nelson's bewildered Macready faces the armed mob with his stage sword, but a more practical actor leads him to safety – in Forrest's dressing room. At first critical of Macready's conduct, Forrest is puzzled that the mob shouted his name, and he agrees to provide refuge for his fellow-actor. Occasionally interrupted by cries and gunshots, the two Shakespearean actors companionably examine costumes, analyze audiences, and delve into such performance details as Macready's little dance in *Hamlet*, Forrest's asylum visits before enacting Hamlet's antic disposition, line readings for *Othello*, and credible humps for Richard III. As the two veteran Shakespeareans emote in the empty theatre, Forrest shouts to the invisible mob: "Leave us in peace." But violence accelerates outside the theatre, and Macready's actor friend hurries him off to Boston. As he leaves, Macready invites Forrest to England to "get away from all these troubles." Forrest counters with the last line of the play: "I'm away from all these troubles here." Macready nods before departing.

Like Hampton's poets, like several contemporary intellectuals of both playwrights, the actors shut their eyes to "all these troubles." Yet Nelson makes *us* aware of their intrusion, and he even hints that "troubles," public or private, can enhance a performance. When Forrest's wife has left him, the American actor is a moving Othello in his empty theatre. In that same theatre, Macready recites Lear's great speech that terminates: "Here I stand your slave, / A poor, infirm, weak, and despised old man." It is also a portrait of a cultivated English actor in populist America.

Theatre lacks a proverb about artists, which would correspond with: "Satire is what closes on Saturday night." Yet artists are notoriously difficult to stage. Despite Hamlet's unprincely predilection for actors (shared by Polonius, of all people), Shakespeare himself stages them rarely. In later periods of theatre expressionism is the heir of Romantic drama in staging poets but stifling drama. By the second half of the twentieth century it is therefore something of an achievement to *dramatize* artists at all, and I have already commented on Bond and Shepard, working through their own artistic sensibilities by way of the artist figure. In *Total Eclipse* and *Two Shakespearean Actors* Hampton and Nelson are constrained by the history of their actual artists, but they nevertheless manage to dramatize different aesthetic views without taking sides, and without sacrificing the histrionic appeal of their poets and actors.

Neither Nelson nor Hampton resorts as frequently to artists as do Shepard and Bond, but they do so again in adaptations of classical dramas. Thus, Hampton's historical poets of *Total Eclipse* are followed by fictional counterparts in his "small" *Philanthropist* (1970), which was consciously patterned on Molière's *Misanthrope.* Transplanting Molière's play to England "in the near future," Hampton peoples it with a playwright and a novelist, as well as academics who are as self-absorbed as other intellectuals on Hampton's stage. The novelist recognizes the basis of his own success, but his dictum also fits Hampton's two professors: "Self-obsession combined with the ability to hold opposite points of view with equal conviction" – especially since these intellectuals are virtually without convictions. *The Philanthropist: A Bourgeois Comedy* takes place in a Britain where the government ministers have been assassinated by a madman disguised as a woman: "Nine of them he got, and several others wounded.... It's not going to make much difference, whatever happens." Unlike Molière's noblemen, whose lives revolve around the king's court, Hampton's bourgeois intellectuals are callously indifferent to the assassination of government figures.

Hampton not only transfers Molière's *Misanthrope* to a modern university town like Oxford, but he deliberately subverts the theme of the seventeenth-century drama. In his words: "I got the idea one day of writing a riposte to *Le Misanthrope* in which the central character would be completely opposite, yet the same things would happen to him" ("Christopher Hampton's 'Savages,'" p. 66). More recently, Hampton explained: "It seemed to me that in an age of rudeness a man who is incapable of being rude to anyone would very likely succeed only in raising hackles wherever he went" (Bayley, "Profile," p. 21). What might be a mere exercise, however, is in fact a scintillating comedy of manners, interspersed with eighteenth-century opera arias. *The Philanthropist* is the most frequently performed of Hampton's plays.

Molière's social misfit Alceste is remodeled into Philip, who likes everyone and everything because he is passionate about nothing. Alceste and Philip are polar opposites:

[Alceste's] is a flamboyant role, one of energy and attack, of passion hand in hand with melancholy, of desperate and irrational love coexisting with venomous anger. It is part of

151

Hampton's larger theatrical audacity that these values are cast in negative, as it were, in the creation of Philip, an embodiment of a philanthropy potentially too passive to hold the stage. . . . Indeed, Philip repeatedly rejects the asocial stance of misanthropy, and his every action is motivated by a desire for company. . . . The energy of Alceste is alien to him, and the passions of love and fury unknown. Philip exemplifies a spirit of emotional detachment.[9]

(Gross, ed., *Christopher Hampton: A Casebook*, pp. 43–4)

Although Hampton's Ian, Dave, Verlaine, and especially Rimbaud are not emotionally detached protagonists, they do, in their self-absorption, screen out the world. So does the academic philologist, Philip.

Hampton's comment on his "riposte" cites only his protagonist, but the other Molière characters also have their analogues. Célimène is matched by Philip's fiancée Celia, after whom his "colleagues lech." However, the *prude* Arsinoé, who is enamored of Alceste, is "riposted" by the *promiscuous* Araminta, who spends the night with Philip. Hampton splits Molière's versifier Oronte into two writers – the dramatist John, who commits suicide in the first scene, and the novelist Braham, who sleeps with Celia after dominating the conversation at Philip's party. In this sparkling comedy of manners Hampton even manages to parallel Molière's "reasonable" couple, Philinte and Eliante. A totally mute Elizabeth is a contemporary approximation of reasonable Eliante, but Philip's fellow-don Donald is a blend of Molière's conciliatory Philinte and the malicious *petit marquis*.

Those familiar with Molière's comedy can take pleasure not only in the character parallels and ripostes, but also in familiar scenes: the reluctant critiques of art, the lawsuits merged into literary criticism, the decorum of coupling and uncoupling, the pernicious prattle about those absent from the stage, the flirtatious tendency of the heroines. Even though Molière's Célimène–Arsinoé confrontation is one of the greatest scenes of the French theatre, Hampton bravely essays a Celia–Araminta confrontation, and if it does not match its model, it is nevertheless amusing.

In the comedy of manners tradition, Hampton's dialogue glistens. Braham the cynical writer is in the lineage of the Restoration rake: "Masturbation is the thinking man's television." Although

Donald disapproves of Braham, he too coins epigrams: "I think we're only capable of loving people who are fundamentally incompatible with us." Philip is not consciously witty, but his word-juggling game nevertheless results in an aphorism: "Imagine the theatre as real." Which is what we bourgeois have been doing through the performance of Hampton's "bourgeois comedy," where the several intellectuals fence verbally.

Nelson not only matches Hampton in (irregular) alternations between small and large plays, but he also wrote a middle-sized riposte to a classic play – a modern classic. Nelson's *Bal* (1979) is based on Brecht's first play, *Baal* (which is itself a riposte to Johst's *Lonely One*). Nelson's omission of the letter "a" in the name of his protagonist excises Brecht's association of his hero with the Phoenician fertility deity.[10] Brecht countered Johst's expressionist portrait of the solitary suffering artist with that of an earthbound poet who indulges his senses, regardless of how others may suffer.

Nelson's Bal is not a poet but a "totally grotesque" mechanic (played, however, with energy rather than grotesquerie by Jim Belushi). Bal's faithful companion is Johnny, a blend of Brecht's Johannes and his Ekart, who are both betrayed by his Baal. Although Nelson shrinks Brecht's twenty-two scenes to ten, he includes most of the original events by telescoping several scenes. Brecht's translators, Manheim and Willett, list "nine basic scenes which recur in the same order in every [Brecht] version [of *Baal*], together with four others which are cut only in the 1926 text" (*Complete Plays,* vol. I, p. 350). It would be tedious to list the scenes, but they dramatize Baal's "seductions" of the wealthy wife Emilie, the innocent teenager Johanna, the wayward Sophie, and his companion Ekart. (I place "seductions" in quotation marks because Baal's approach is direct and often brutal; yet he does not rape but somehow attracts his victims.) Nelson expunges Brecht's homosexual element, but he too depicts a protagonist who devours women – not unlike the historical Brecht. As in Brecht's *Baal,* Nelson's bourgeois Emily also grows hysterical; his deflowered Johanna also drowns herself; his Sophie and her infant are also abandoned by Bal. Even more than Brecht's insatiable Baal, Nelson's Bal inflicts pain on the victims of his appetites.

Brecht's Baal is a cabaret poet, as was Brecht himself, and the German playwright's drama is enlivened by the songs of Brecht/ Baal, for which Nelson substitutes brief quotations from Shakespeare. Although Brecht traces Baal's life from triumph to death, the leitmotif is the image of an unattainable sky. Brecht's Baal, aware of his own transience, responds to the sky's permanence as well as its lofty beauty, however he may be mired on the earth.

In contrast, Nelson's Bal is a mechanic who is fascinated by the working of his own mind, and he reasons compulsively (as does Brecht in his theoretical writings). Nelson's Bal utters any thought that enters his head, and he often ratiocinates about those thoughts. He writes down his dream, aware that he is thereby structuring it. He repairs a generator, but then systematically destroys it. Not only does Nelson's Bal steal Johanna from Johnny, but he precipitates her suicide by taunting her: "I'm probably not going to be able to resist telling [Johnny]. Just out of curiosity, I suppose. To see his reaction." To see *her* reaction, Bal persuades Sophie to kiss a corpse. Bored with Sophie, Bal foists her upon Johnny, but then spoils their pleasure by scrutinizing their coupling. Before Johnny hangs himself, he imitates Bal in his detached attitude toward his own death: "So here – at the point of suicide – I find that my greatest concern is in finding something interesting to say." And he coins an oxymoron, labeling himself "a hopeless optimist. That's me alright."

Nelson's Bal is surprised at Johnny's death, and he is surprised that he is disturbed by it – a feeling he soon smothers. Noticing that he is seated at a table and drinking, he meditates on his physical stance:

> I remember seeing a movie once where a man sat in just such a position as this, holding just such a glass out in front of him. He talked to himself too. (*Pause.*) Ever since then, this position has become for me – the drowning one's sorrows position. (*Breaks the position, nods.*) We never stop learning how to behave.

It is the play's last speech, uttered by an analytic protagonist who has no sorrows to drown, and who does *not* learn how to behave with compassion.

Both Hampton and Nelson subvert classical plays to their own purpose. Hampton remains in the comedy of manners tradition, but dramatizes the narrowness of that tradition in a time of social crisis. Nelson preserves a mythic protagonist in an expressionist form, and into that myth he enfolds Brechtian ratiocination. Lean-

ing on Brecht's play and perhaps on his biography, Nelson creates
a protagonist who neither murders nor dies (as does Brecht's Baal),
but who constantly examines his own thoughts. Brecht's vigorous
Baal exploded the lachrymose German stage with sharp vulgar
dialogue that continues to attract actors, despite Brecht's subsequent disapproval of his early creation. Nelson's ratiocinative Bal
subdues the antisocial sensuality of the original, and, like Hampton with his Philip, he risks an undramatic protagonist: "You take
what we're seeing to the extreme and this is what you get" (Savran, *In Their Own Words*, p. 176).

Basing the sequence of my investigation on Hampton's alterna-
tion between small fictional and large documented plays, I have
found that certain Nelson plays resemble them in subject (a lovers' triangle), genre (the comedy of manners), or form (riposte to a
classic). The next pair are similar in locale and in political background. They are both set in modern, unstable Latin America –
Hampton's in Brazil and Nelson's in "an unidentified Latin American country." However, Hampton's play is intricate in plot and
political texture – his largest play – and Nelson's is quite small.
I restrict my comparison to comparables.

Hampton's *Savages* (1973) intertwines three strands:

1. the ironically designated "savages," Brazilian Indians who
   are brutally destroyed by modern "civilisation";
2. the rich lore of the Indians, whose study is the hobby of a
   minor British diplomat, Alan West;
3. the kidnapping of West by Marxists whose spokesman,
   Carlos, is himself a middle-class intellectual.

Only the last of these strands has its parallel in Nelson's *Principia
Scriptoriae* (1986).

Hampton's large-scale *Savages* was provoked by an article in the
Sunday Times of February 23, 1969; the journalist Norman Lewis
documented the genocide of the Cintas Largas Indian tribe. Hampton journeyed to Brazil and did extensive research on this all but
extinct "savage" civilization. The play also offers us the imaginative legends of several Indian tribes, for which Hampton consulted a number of sources, indefatigable scholar that he is. There are
then two document strands in *Savages*, Indian legends and the
genocide of a particular Indian tribe. In performance, however, the
legends are heard as the prose poems of the protagonist, Alan West,

155

a fictional poet-diplomat whose imprisonment constitutes the third plot strand. Although documents outweigh fiction in *Savages,* Hampton's play is structurally balanced between the Indians and West. The deteriorating condition of the Indians, dramatized largely in flashback, parallels the deteriorating situation of the hostage Alan West in the ongoing action. Since it is far harder to stage the extermination of a people than an individual, tension is centered on the confrontation between Western West and his Brazilian captor Carlos, between the ironic minor poet and the idealistic minor revolutionary, who finally assassinates his captive.

Nelson's *Principia Scriptoriae* is a less ambitious play, but it too pairs a Western writer with a Latin American youth, and it too resorts to flashback. In the main, however, the action divides chronologically between 1970 in the first part of the play and 1985 in the second; only the final scene returns to 1970. Although the play is structured in scenes rather than acts, the first part dramatizes the captivity of the American Bill and the Latin American Ernesto, recent graduates of American universities and would-be writers. Frightened though they are in their incarceration, the two young men try to converse about literature, only incidentally contrasting American democracy with the right-wing dictatorship of the unnamed Latin American country of their prison. After they are tortured individually offstage, Bill and Ernesto persist in talking about literature and especially about their own future writing. With some irony, Nelson projects over each scene a well-worn "principle of writing" – the title of the whole play.

In 1985 Bill returns to Latin America as a journalist covering a meeting of Writers for Human Rights, and Ernesto is the secretary of the country's left-wing Minister of Justice. An international committee of writers is trying to obtain the release from prison of a (fictional) right-wing poet whose work Ernesto had praised to Bill when they themselves were in prison. The left-wing minister schemes to obtain the release of a political prisoner in Honduras, who is not a writer. While the minister and the international writers jockey for the life of the aging poet, Bill and Ernesto show the committee the scars of their own imprisonment. Alone together in Ernesto's home, the two ex-prisoners come to understand how their cultures have changed them, but they renew their friendship in agreement about the naïveté of their youth.

The final scene of the play returns to 1970, with Bill and Ernesto blindfolded and tied back to back, expecting their imminent execution. Bill composes an autobiographical story, but their fear keeps intruding, and although their bonds preclude physical movement, they hug one another verbally. The Ernesto of 1985 has been a mere pawn for his Minister of Justice who considers culture a political weapon, but the Ernesto of 1970 reassures Bill: "Other writers are always sending telegrams to get other writers out." Perhaps. Or perhaps it is dumb luck that their guard fires a gun into the air, and the two blindfolded young men receive a new lease on life: "I'm still here."

Nelson indicts the political dictatorships of the left *and* the right in their contempt for cultural figures, and Hampton indicts revolutionaries *and* the military–industrial complex in their genocide of the Indians. In Hampton's *Savages* the cultural cleavage between the Briton and his Latin American captor results in the death of West – a death publicized throughout the stage world, whereas the many Indian bodies go unremarked. In Nelson's *Principia Scriptoriae* there is no cultural cleavage between Bill and Ernesto when they face death together, but their friendship barely survives in the political opposition of their maturity. Locale and flashback technique are minor similarities in these two plays of Hampton and Nelson. Their profound resemblance rests upon a dramatization of the helplessness of writers – no matter how eloquent – in a world of power politics; there are no *Principia Scriptoriae*.

Hampton's analysis of his playwriting rhythm – a small fictional piece followed by a large documentary drama – dates from the production of *Savages* in 1973, which was duly succeeded by the three-hander *Treats* in 1976. Although Hampton writes slowly, he was not idle in the years between his original plays, for he produced translations, adaptations, and screenplays.[11] *Tales from Hollywood* (1982) also conforms to the pattern he noted, being quite large and largely documentary. I again pair it with a small Nelson play, *Some Americans Abroad* (1989), since both dramas set characters outside of their native lands and both are steeped in literature.

Unusually for these playwrights, both plays were commissioned; moreover, each play was commissioned by a theatre in the country of the other, Hampton's *Tales from Hollywood* by the Los Angeles

Mark Taper and Nelson's *Some Americans Abroad* by the Royal Shakespeare Company. Since funding for Hampton's play required a Los Angeles setting, the Associate Director of the Taper obligingly suggested possible subjects to the Briton, and Hampton's imagination responded to "the European émigrés and refugees from Fascism" (Introduction, p. 7). Nelson was evidently allowed carte blanche as to subject: "I thought that the idea of Americans confronting the culture of London, and specifically the culture of theatres like the RSC, was very suitable" (Jackson, "Principles of the Faculty," p. 15). The two plays are separated not only by thousands of miles but by several decades of Western history; yet both playwrights dramatize a group reaction to a foreign culture.

Hampton selected *writers* among the Hollywood refugees, and he researched his subject thoroughly. Not only did he plunge into books (a few of which he lists in the Faber edition of the play), but he interviewed several of "the surviving émigrés and those involved with them." For this viewer, who has read some of the background material, Hampton achieves credible thumbnail portraits of Thomas and Heinrich Mann, and of Bertolt Brecht. Through the Central European colony in Hollywood, Hampton threads a wholly fictitious plot centered on the writer Ödön von Horváth. As Hampton restricted *Total Eclipse* to Verlaine's viewpoint, so *Tales from Hollywood* is seen through the eyes of Horváth.

The historical Horváth was, in the words of Hampton's protagonist, "a German-speaking Hungarian born in an Italian town now part of Yugoslavia."[12] Too modest to expand on his contribution to Austrian theatre, Horváth had staged freaks, drunks, and abused women, rendering their dialogue with rare authenticity. Although his talent was recognized in Austria, he was not well enough known to provoke the Nazis, as did the Mann brothers and Brecht. Nevertheless Horváth was happy to leave Central Europe for Paris to discuss a possible film of his novel, and there he was killed in 1938, in an accident during a storm "when a branch of the chestnut tree under which he was sheltering fell on his head" (Hampton note, n.p.).

Hampton resurrects Horváth to be both the narrator and protagonist of his play.[13] The falling branch is seen, but, as Hampton's Horváth explains: "[it] landed on the back of my companion's head. ... He died instantaneously. And this was the incident which prompted me to make the following remark: Why is it people are so afraid of the Nazis? Why aren't they afraid just walking down the street?" Hampton leaves it to us to judge Horváth's ingenuousness about these nameless "people" and their fears. Although Hampton's protagonist is explicit about his belief in chance, he nevertheless intervenes in his own destiny by fleeing from Europe, and then from his Nazi uncle in Virginia, in the hope of becoming a screenwriter in Hollywood.

Hampton was too young in 1956 to experience the strong impact of Brecht's Berliner Ensemble on the London theatre, but he lived in its aftermath, resistant to Brecht's didacticism. While some of Hampton's colleagues were adapting and directing Brecht in the 1960s and 1970s, he translated the plays of Horváth, and for his own *Tales from Hollywood* he adapted the very title of that playwright's *Tales from the Vienna Woods*. As Horváth's grim and brutal drama gives the lie to the saccharine Vienna of Strauss music, so Hampton's refugee Europeans cast a shadow on the glitter of Hollywood. Hampton looks hard at his refugee writers, who are contemptuous of American film vulgarity but who also yearn for its spoils.

Among the German refugees Hampton's Horváth is an outsider, not only in his Austrian nationality. A lover of wine, women, and freaks, he responds warmly to Hollywood. Hampton's Act I curtain line is Horváth's: "After two years in Los Angeles, I knew I was home." To enhance that knowledge (and improve his English), Horváth has an affair with the fictional Helen Schwartz, an American Jewish screenwriter. Bored with the earnest proclamations of the German exiles, Horváth resists Brecht's efforts to indoctrinate him: "I've never understood why a love of mankind in general should so often be accompanied by a profound dislike of the individual." Horváth wryly describes Brecht's farewell to the real America when a fictional America had loomed so large in his early plays: "[Brecht] left America for good, flew back to Europe and entered into his kingdom."

Actual German writers are background figures in Hampton's play, but Heinrich Mann's wife Nelly is in the dramatic foreground, spouting vigorous colloquialisms. Hampton's Horváth is sensitive to her mounting isolation that culminates in suicide. In a last meeting of Horváth and Heinrich the senile old man recalls Nelly's love. He is deluded in imagining that he will return to East

Germany as President; Horváth describes Heinrich Mann's death in his sleep, in Hollywood. It is the play's last reference to its historical background.

The fictional Horváth, who has always resisted commitments, praises the courage of his Jewish Communist mistress in refusing to name names to the infamous House Un-American Activities Committee. Unprompted, Horváth confesses to her that he was once a passive Nazi: "So, my boot also was on your people's faces." Yet Horváth follows this confession with a quip about his Nazi party membership: "Only thing I can say in my defence. I never paid the dues." Nor is Hampton's Horváth quite ready to pay the demeaning dues for success in Hollywood, so he prepares to return to Europe. After a last interview at the palace of a film executive, the fictional Horváth dives into the swimming pool, hits his head, and reclaims the death that eluded him in 1938.

Against the German refugee background *Tales from Hollywood* builds tension through contrasts: the dissimilar Mann brothers, frustrated Nelly against active Helen (both Jewish), mellow Horváth against didactic Brecht. In productions of Hampton's play (including the TV adaptation) the minor role of Brecht is more dynamic than that of Hampton's favorite, Horváth. When I mentioned this to Hampton, he replied: "Perhaps he *is* more dynamic." What Hampton has undertaken bears some analogy with his *Philanthropist*. As that play presented a passive, basically undramatic protagonist, so does *Tales from Hollywood*. However, Hampton enhances the witty repartee of the earlier play with spectacular sight gags involving Tarzan, the Marx Bros., Garbo, and even the figure of Death from Cocteau's *Orpheus*. Verbal quips of the comedy of manners give way to satire of the long-windedness of Thomas Mann, the self-importance of Heinrich Mann, and the formulaic theatre devices of Brecht (entrance through the auditorium, projections of time and place, half-curtain, white light, and a scene summary: "TWO FELLOW DRAMATISTS REACH THE PARTING OF THE WAYS").

Tales from Hollywood is both rich and selective in its presentation of the predicaments of Central European refugees, but it is also a Hampton play in raising the question of the behavior of intellectuals in times of crisis. Hampton's Horváth, refusing commitment, believes in chance: "And those of us who by chance had not been murdered had to consider whether or not we should go home and

try to make our peace with those who, by chance, had not murdered us." Not by chance but by Hampton's design, however, his
Horváth faces two ethical choices. Habitually accepting any woman who offers herself to him, Horváth nevertheless rejects the
advances of Nelly Mann: "It was just the image of that old man
sitting alone in that tiny house on South Swall Drive, waiting."
Dissimilarly, he rejects a durable affiliation with his courageous
Jewish mistress, by confessing his brief Nazi past.

For all Hampton's convincing rendition of Horváth's acclima-
tion to Hollywood, the play's strength lies in the juxtaposition of
two cultures, presented through the eyes of a Central European
writer. The play's emotional center, however, is not a writer, but a
former barmaid, Nelly Mann, better known as the model for Dietrich's performer in *The Blue Angel*. A tower of strength in times
of crisis, Nelly is utterly unable to function in the relative harmony of Hollywood. A sensual woman married to an ineffectual old
intellectual, she seeks escape via the familiar paths of alcohol, fast
cars, and young lovers, while she voices intolerance toward her
race, which precludes her return to Berlin: "She was frightened
they'd find out she was Jewish." Despite the contrast between two
Jewish women, Nelly and Helen, the plight of the Jews is as marginal to these transplanted German celebrities as the plight of the
"savages" was to the white men of Hampton's earlier play. But *we*
are made aware of brutality on the margins.

A smaller play, Nelson's *Some Americans Abroad* presents
American intellectuals who navigate through London and Stratford culture but are totally insensitive to actual English people. On
the face of it, this Nelson play is more instructively compared with
one of Hampton's "small" plays, most obviously the academic *Philanthropist*. More telling than its size, however, is Nelson's presentation of characters who fit badly into another culture. Moreover, the respective backgrounds lend themselves to illuminating
contrast: In the one play German émigrés cannot accommodate to
American vulgarity; in the other American tourists vulgarly over-
praise British culture, particularly its canonized writers.

Early in *Tales from Hollywood* Heinrich Mann asks Horváth,
"How is it we've managed to be so lucky?" And in their last meeting, the old widower again asks: "How was it we were so lucky?"
Although Hampton intends the repetition to have an ironic edge,
these refugee writers *were* lucky, and some of them were aware of

it, in a period when few indigenous American intellectuals were aware of *their* luck during World War II. Such intellectuals, a few decades later, people Nelson's *Some Americans Abroad* (1989), where the word "lucky" is also repeated. Nelson's intellectuals are American academics who batten on English culture, but the word "lucky" is first heard on the lips of the wife of an American professor who has retired to Jamesian Sussex: "We consider ourselves very lucky. . . . Very lucky." The assistant professor, who is not being reappointed, is encouraged by the department chair: "You're attractive to a lot of colleges already, Henry. You just need to get a little lucky." The play shows both "lucky"s to be hollow.

Three American academics, the English department chair and his male and female colleagues, are herding their students through theatre in London and Stratford. Accompanying them at his own expense is the luckless faculty member and his wife; unknown to this untenured instructor, someone else has already been offered his post. Other Americans are resident in England – the racist former chair (with wife) and a former student who has married an Englishman. Of some dozen Nelson characters none is English, but English landmarks are wittily if schematically seen – Luigi's Restaurant in Covent Garden, Foyle's Bookshop, the Buffet of the Lyttelton Theatre, Waterloo Bridge, the RSC Memorial Theatre, Trinity Church Garden, the Arden Hotel in Stratford, Westminster Bridge, and full circle back to Luigi's.[14]

At a time when the literary canon was under attack in actual university departments of English literature on both sides of the Atlantic, these academics are unaware of it. Not only do they dutifully make the Stratford pilgrimage, but they discuss Shaw, respect Henry James's Lamb House, read aloud Ben Jonson's tribute to Shakespeare, recite Wordsworth's sonnet at dawn, and they even sing "God Save the Queen." At a time when the British economy is bolstered by such academic tourists, they quibble about their expenses without checking customary prices in their host country. So fatigued with their whirlwind theatre program that they are scarcely able to distinguish one play from another, the faculty members nevertheless utter opinions about its quality.[15] Theirs is the cultured green and pleasant land that they themselves had been spoon-fed as undergraduates, and they spoon-feed it to their students.

The protagonist is the new department chair, Joe Taylor, and like Hampton's protagonist Horváth, he twice has to decide matters of ethics, but, unlike Horváth, Joe twice fails the test. One problem faces Joe for the duration of the play: the duty to inform the untenured professor that someone else has already been offered his post. Not only does Joe *not* tell Henry; he implies to Henry's wife that he has informed the luckless instructor in a particularly humane way. Joe then proceeds to ask professional services from Henry, and in his final gesture of the play Joe accepts Henry's contribution toward paying the bill, and then leaves a measly tip at Luigi's Restaurant.

Money is secondary in Joe's second ethical problem. A female student charges Joe's colleague Philip with "what you tried to do to me in the car." Instead of immediately facing Philip with the accusation of sexual harrassment, Joe seeks advice from his female colleague (who has been sleeping with Philip), from his predecessor as chair, and even from his dean in the States. It is, however, on Joe's own initiative that he "solves" the problem by buying the student's silence with dinner and a passing grade. Assuring Philip that he believes his outraged denial, Joe refuses to acknowledge that his two colleagues have been sleeping together: "I don't know anything!" Earlier he had told Philip: "It's the Dean's policy to not get involved if he can help it." By the end of the play we realize that Joe has the makings of a dean.

Although my summary sounds like the portrait of an academic villain, Joe is merely someone who prefers "to not get involved," and Nelson foreshadows this in his use of the word "complicated," which Joe applies indiscriminately to the world and the check at Luigi's. Joe also repeats the cliché "Trust me," but by the end of the play he is revealed as thoroughly untrustworthy. Joe opens the play protesting that he is against nuclear war, but the action shows him incapable of coping ethically with the small skirmishes of his profession. Old friends, Joe and Philip in their youth demonstrated against the Vietnam War, and Joe protests that he is still "a goddam liberal." Yet both faculty members keep silent when the former chair utters snide remarks about Jews and blacks. So does their female colleague: Not only does she sleep with Philip, but she bludgeons the harrassed student into submission to authority. We never know whether Philip actually molested the student, but we do know that all the faculty members behave despicably toward someone in their care.

Although the discrepancy between academic preaching and practice is a truism, Nelson dramatizes it skillfully. The dichotomy is perhaps too evident, between instructors of the humanities and humane behavior, but Nelson displays keen insight into the small clichés of inhumanity – the chair who lies about being American and who relies on his daughter's spying, the retired chair who poses as an English squire, the transplanted American who is impervious to British comedy, the ubiquitous American suspicion that the English are taking advantage of them, the academic snobbery toward unacademic Americans, the appreciation of theatre seat location rather than of the theatre production, the dwelling on the symbolism of literature rather than on its experiential thrust.

Some Americans Abroad (the "some" is significant) is of course a slighter play than *Tales from Hollywood*, but they both dramatize a situation of displacement, and they both ponder the ethics of intellectuals, the one in the comic mode and the other with pathos. Both plays isolate intellectuals in unfamiliar surroundings. Hampton's Brecht objects to being called an émigré: "I was driven out. I'm an exile." Nelson in an interview acknowledged: "Many of [my plays] are about writers . . . but they are all about exiles" (Jackson, "Principles of the Faculty," p. 15). Theatrically, the situation of the exiles is enriched by the presentation of the host country. Hampton displays Hollywood legends – Tarzan, the Marx Bros., Garbo – and he cunningly contrasts two fictional studio executives: the vulgar and ignorant Charles Money, who first interviews Horváth, and the suave collector Art Nicely – "The Renoirs are kind of fun."

Hampton's satire is mordant about Hollywood's reaction to World War II:

The following weekend the Japanese attacked Pearl Harbor. We show folk knew where our duty lay and we were not slow to retaliate: all performances of *Madame Butterfly* at the Met. were cancelled and Greenwich Village Savoyards withdrew *The Mikado* from their repertoire. All the Japanese gardeners in Hollywood were fired. In the case of an air raid,

Variety advised its readers to seek shelter in the Nora Bayes Theater, on the grounds that it had never had a hit.

Nelson's English background is also satiric, if less spectacular, with its projections of Waterloo and Westminster Bridges, as well as Big Ben and the Memorial Theatre at Stratford. Nelson has his academics read only the opening lines of Ben Jonson's tribute to Shakespeare, with their disdain for "some infamous Baud, or Whore, / Should praise a Matron" – repeated in the reading. And he has them sing the unfamiliar second verse of "God Save the Queen" with its prayer against her enemies, which is not irrelevant to the stage action: "Confound their politics / Frustrate their knavish tricks." The very absence of English characters from the play highlights the American isolation in England, underlined in the published text by the laconic statement, "All the characters are American." Although the American Anglophiles are familiar with the monuments of English literature, they utter conventional clichés, if they bother to comment at all on the plays they see. Joe regrets missing *Antony and Cleopatra* because he is writing an article about it. These academics are drawn to Simon Gray, an ex-academic who writes plays about academics. *Les Liaisons Dange-reuses* is currently successful, and it enables Nelson to cue us into his own plot ramifications of entangling alliances. The new play at the Royal Court is something "very political," whose name no one can remember. No one comments on the politics of contemporary Britain.

A realistic play that moves forward during a week of chronological time, *Some Americans Abroad* indicts the selfish isolation of *all* the Americans we see. An inventively framed play that depicts Central Europeans in Hollywood during a critical decade of Western history, *Tales from Hollywood* is chary of indictment. In their own ways and plays both Hampton and Nelson are aware of the global context in which their characters, like us all, live. And that context lives on their stages.

Fortuitously, too, their work glances at aspects of stage language that I have examined in this study. Like Simon and Ayckbourn, their bent is comedic, but *their* witticisms fit their characters. Although neither of them can match Ayckbourn's inventive stagings, Nelson is attracted to projections, and Hampton's large plays exploit visual aspects of theatre. Like Bond and Shepard, Hampton and Nelson sometimes stage artists, but unlike the elder pair, they are ambivalent about artistic ethics in times of crisis. Unlike Pinter and Mamet, the younger intellectuals lack colloquial versatility, but, within their educated limits, their dialogue flows rhythmically and dramatically. The protagonists of both Hampton and Nelson tend to be men, and yet they occasionally offer sharp insight into their woman characters – Jimmy's mother, Nelly Mann, a dying Marianne. Less inventive than some of their colleagues in languages of the stage, less experimental than some of their colleagues in the language of stage dialogue, Christopher Hampton and Richard Nelson nevertheless ground their drama in articulate thinking beings who spur *us* to think through our feelings.

Notes

Introduction

1. In 1992, for example, Michael Billington demurred in *The Guardian* that an American import – John Guare's *Six Degrees of Separation* – usurped the stage of the Royal Court, with its tradition of presenting new *British* drama. In parallel fashion in 1993 Jonathan Kalb objected in the *Village Voice* to the Off-Broadway production of Caryl Churchill's early plays, when those of (unnamed) Americans languish in libraries.
2. Ms. Fornes's name is spelled here as it is most often cited in the critical literature, without diacritical marks. This, I understand, is also the playwright's preference in Anglophone publications.

1. Funny money in New York and Pendon: Neil Simon and Alan Ayckbourn

1. Simon and Ayckbourn also share the following details: (a) Homage to *The Importance of Being Earnest*, since English Cecily and Gwendolyn figure in Simon's *The Odd Couple*, and a scribbled country address leads to mistaken relationships in Ayckbourn's *Relatively Speaking*. See Kalson, in *DNB* 13(1), p. 18, for an extended comparison of *Relatively Speaking* with *The Importance of Being Earnest*. (b) Un-Wildean is the treatment of suicide as farce by both Simon and Ayckbourn: In the former's *The Odd Couple* the friends of unhappy Felix walk him strenuously around to counteract the effect of deadly pills, and so do the acquaintances of Roland Crabbe in Ayckbourn's *Taking Steps*.
2. The blurb about Ayckbourn in the program of *Time of My Life* cites "stage manager, sound technician, lighting technician, scene painter, prop-maker, actor, writer and director" – in short, an all-around theatre man.
3. *The Odd Couple* became the basis for a television series starring Tony Randall and Jack Klugman, but Simon was not its author. In 1985 Simon reworked the play for a female odd couple.

4. The lithe, charismatic Tom Conti played the protagonist in the first London productions of early Ayckbourn plays, but ungainly Michael Gambon of the puzzled demeanor enacted the protagonist of *Chorus of Disapproval, Man of the Moment,* and *A Small Family Business.*
5. Rare in Ayckbourn's dialogue, puns often figure in his titles.
6. Simon's *Jake's Women* experiments with the play of past against present, facts against fantasy. That play suffers from analogies with Arthur Miller's *After the Fall* (1964), as does Simon's *Chapter Two.* Similarly, *Brighton Beach Memoirs* (1982) echoes the Depression-era salesman father and two sons of Miller's *Death of A Salesman* (1949). Gerald M. Berkowitz hears the voice of Odets in Simon's *Brighton Beach Memoirs:* "Like [Odets's plays] it uses the native American dramatic form of domestic realism, here tempered with warm and unobtrusive humour, to depict a society in crisis and transition, through its reflection in the everyday lives of ordinary people" (*American Drama of the Twentieth Century*, p. 174).
7. English friends have objected to my designation of Ayckbourn's world as "middle-class." They insist that his characters are "lower middle-class." I am sufficiently dubious about this point to confine it to a note.
8. Richard Meryman describes (in tedious adoration) the out-of-town adventures of Simon and *The Gingerbread Lady.* I am grateful to Kent Nicholson for supplying me with this article.
9. The program of the first London production of *Just Between Ourselves* pictures a man and woman pried apart by a large automobile, but the unmoved car is a symptom, not a cause of the bad marriage of Dennis and Vera.
10. Ayckbourn's *Man of the Moment* intrudes television into "live" scenes – another variation on the play within the play.
11. The 1993 movie of *Lost in Yonkers* (shot in Kentucky!) dwells in loving detail on the candy store. It also materializes Bella's beloved Johnny, and it introduces gratuitous wisecracks.
12. It is piquant that Ayckbourn likens playwriting to furniture making: "I always compare [playwriting] with furniture making rather than with any other kind of writing" (Page, *File on Ayckbourn*, p. 92).

2. Artists' arias: Edward Bond and Sam Shepard

1. Richard Gilman's Introduction to Shepard's *Seven Plays* suggests that the American playwright "must . . . have been influenced . . . by certain aspects of Pinter and, more recently, by Edward Bond," but he does not elaborate. Shepard's *True West* deploys pauses in Pinter's rhythmic fashion, but I am dubious about a Bond influence.
2. Each playwright has set minor works in the country of the other: Shepard in *Geography of a Horse Dreamer* (1974) and Bond in *A-A-America!* (1976).

3. In a letter to the critic Doris Auerbach (Dugdale, *File on Shepard*, p. 61) Shepard does *not* mention Brecht's estrangement as a quality that attracted him. However, Shepard refers to Brecht's "duality," by which he may mean estrangement.

4. In an interview with Carol Rosen ("Silent Tongues," *Village Voice*, August 4, 1992, p. 36), Shepard affirmed his loss of interest in "the exploited artist as hero," but none of his protagonists quite conforms to this stereotype. Drake is exploited by his brother and his manager, but he is neither the hero of the play, nor heroic in character.

5. For information on rock music in Shepard's plays, see: Robert Coe, "Image Shots Are Blown: The Rock Plays" in Marranca, ed., *American Dreams*; Bruce W. Powe, "*The Tooth of Crime*: Sam Shepard's Way with Music" in Parker, ed., *Essays on Modern American Drama*. DeRose comments on the live band accompaniment to Shepard's *The Unseen Hand*, *Operation Sidewinder*, *Mad Dog Blues*, and *Back Bog Beast Bait* (*Sam Shepard*, p. 50). This was also true of *A Lie of the Mind*. Shepard himself is not a singer, and although most of his musician characters are, it is as composers that they suffer. By the 1990s almost all rock composers are also singers.

6. Ann Wilson, "True Stories," in Wilcox, ed., *Rereading Shepard*, p. 103. For surprising appreciation of Dylan as lyricist, see Christopher Ricks, *The Force of Poetry*, Oxford: Clarendon Press, 1984, passim.

7. Although Shepard cannot read music – or so he told me in 1976 – his scores are published in the Grove Press edition of *The Tooth of Crime*, but not in the Bantam or Faber editions of *Seven Plays*. By the 1980s other composers produced scores for Shepard's lyrics in *Tooth*. Shepard told Carol Rosen that he considers the play dated: "There's this pretense of being a commentary on pop culture" ("Interview with Shepard," *Modern Drama* 36 [1993], 11).

8. Cf. Johan Callens: ". . . the trancelike simultaneity of enactment and observation, sensory experience and understanding [of] Tympani" ("Between the Margin and the Center," p. 8).

9. Like Ann Wilson, but on more formal grounds, I consider *True Dylan* "untrue." That is to say, however factual the Dylan–Shepard meeting may be, their conversation is shaped like a play.

10. In the same year as *The Bundle* (1977), Bond wrote a ballet *Orpheus*, a story in six scenes, in which, according to Philip Roberts: "The conventional myth of Orpheus losing Eurydice because he looked back is modified by Bond, so that Orpheus is now caught between two deadening worlds, that of hell and that represented by Apollo. . . . Orpheus smashes his lyre and, with it, Apollo's control." However, Bond's Orpheus fashions even more beautiful music from the broken lyre, inspiring Eurydice and the hell dwellers to emerge into life on earth. Thus, Orpheus blends the artistic talent of Basho with the social purpose of Wang in Bond's musical fantasy. Although Bond has not published his *Orpheus*, he graciously allowed me to read it. I cite the excellent account

of Philip Roberts, "The Search for Epic Drama," pp. 459–60. For a detailed description of the ballet, see Clement Crisp, "Orpheus," *Financial Times* (March 20, 1979). Bond has also written fifteen "Part Songs for Chorus" entitled "Orpheus and the Wire," published in his *Poems 1978–1985*, London: Methuen, 1987. Elizabeth Hale Winkler comments perceptively on both ballet and poems (*Function of Song*, pp. 135–6).

11. Cf. G. Dark, "Production Casebook, No. 5: Edward Bond's *Lear* at the Royal Court," *Theatre Quarterly* 2(5) (1972), 25. Alistair Stead has directed my attention to the double focus of Shepard's *Suicide in B-Flat*.

12. For a less sympathetic view of Shakespeare, see Hay and Roberts, *Bond: A Study*, pp. 179–99.

13. Shepard has also titled a play for a fool protagonist – *Fool for Love* (1983) – but the fool is a cowboy, not an artist.

14. According to Hay and Roberts, Bond intended Clare's laughter as "a wholly natural and spontaneous reaction to an absurd and unjust situation" (*Bond: A Study*, p. 208), but I defy any theatre spectator to understand that. Similarly, Richard Cave writes: "Clare's laughter is not as it might seem manic, but the mark of a profound engagement, an awareness of the full demands upon him as man and poet. His patrons will seek to trivialize that awareness and, when he resists, will interpret it as a sign of madness. Bond defies us to judge that laughter insane"(*New British Drama*, p. 286). Again, this seems to me to load the laughter with a burden it cannot carry. For a nuanced reading of class conflict in *The Fool* see Jenny S. Spencer, "Edward Bond's Dramatic Strategies" in Bigsby, ed., *Contemporary English Drama*, pp. 134–7.

15. It is this comic level that is ignored in Sheila Rabillard's stimulating analysis of Shepard's author plays as subversions of author-ity; see "Shepard's Challenge to the Modernist Myths of Origin and Originality: *Angel City* and *True West*," in Wilcox, ed., *Rereading Shepard*, pp. 73–92.

16. See especially Tucker Orbison, "Mythic Levels in Shepard's *True West*," in Parker, ed., *Essays on Modern American Drama*. William Kleb, however, writes that "past and present [West] both dissolve" ("Worse Than Being Homeless," in Marranca, ed., *American Dreams*, p. 123).

17. Bread can, of course, be theatricalized in production, and it has been theatricalized in stage presentations as different as the Bread and Puppet Theater and the Maly Theater's *Brothers and Sisters*.

3. Phrasal energies: Harold Pinter and David Mamet

1. In her detailed examination of verbal violence, Jeanette Malkin tends to equate cliché with jargon, but the two verbal techniques seem to me quite distinct.

2. Pinter in 1992 wrote the screenplay for Kafka's *The Trial*.

3. In my quotations from Pinter and Mamet, I do not separate the drama-

tists' three-dot punctuation from the surrounding text, whereas I do space my own ellipses.

4. Leech, *Linguistic Guide to English Poetry*, pp. 72–83, is exceptionally lucid on poetic repetition.
5. In a cartoon, a spectator at the (silent) Short–Kasparov chess match (which took place in the Savoy Theatre) inquires of his neighbor: "Is this the new Pinter?" *(Independent,* September 9, 1993).
6. Although Mamet has dubbed Aaranow "a raisonneur" who is troubled by corruption, that salesman resignedly resumes his occupation in a corrupt enterprise (cf. Jones & Dykes, *File on Mamet*, p. 61)
7. "An old man is but a paltry thing / Unless soul clap its hands and sing" *(Sailing to Byzantium).* "I have known them all already" *(The Love Song of J. Alfred Prufrock).* In *Moonlight* the coarse son Jake improbably quotes from *Four Quartets:* "All will be well. And all manner of things shall be well."
8. These are subtly analyzed by Dukore, *Harold Pinter,* p. 95.
9. Mamet has been quoted: "If you say 'cunt' or 'cockteaser,' what you say influences the way you think, the way you act, not the other way round" (Jones & Dykes, *File on Mamet,* p. 18). I think, however, he is placing the cart before the horse. Mamet's blend of foul language and stage violence, so different from Pinter's cooler expletives, would be fodder for Britain's censorious Mrs. Whitehouse, one of whose diatribes is headlined: "Foul language's link with violence" *(The Times,* July 23, 1991).
10. Ronald Knowles, "Names and Naming in the Plays of Harold Pinter." Also suggestive in the Bold volume is Steven H. Gale, "Harold Pinter's *Family Voices* and the Concept of Family."
11. Among other failings, Pinter's political plays lack geographic specificity.
12. With less slippage, the word "things" also echoes through *The Woods,* but it lacks thematic relevance.
13. Cf. Dean, *David Mamet: Language as Dramatic Action,* pp. 111–12, for analysis of what she calls an "aria of hatred."
14. Mamet exploits the mise-en-abîme or embedded device in other plays:
    The Woods dramatizes two (adult) children (emotionally) lost in the woods, where one tells a story of two children lost in the woods. (Other details common to frame and embedded story are a lost bracelet, violence against a woman, and return to the past.)
    Dark Pony dramatizes a frightened child reassured by the story of a dark pony who reassures a frightened boy.
    Sanctity of Marriage dramatizes an ex-husband's failure to spend the night with his wife, who recalls his earlier failure to visit a church that was emotionally important to her.
    Prairie du Chien explodes in violence after we listen to a Gothic melodrama of violence.
15. Cf. Ben-zvi, "Harold Pinter's *Betrayal,*" p. 231.

4. Reading and teaching: Maria Irene Fornes
and Caryl Churchill

1. I would shift the proper nouns: "Lacanian" rather than "psychoana-lytic" for the French, and "socialist" rather than "Marxist" for the English. The locus classicus for *l'écriture féminine* is Hélène Cixous's "Le Rire de la méduse," most readily available in English in Elaine Marks and Isabelle de Courtivron, *New French Feminisms*, New York: Schocken, 1981.

2. See, for example, Gayle Austin, "The Madwoman in the Spotlight"; Helene Keyssar, "Drama and the Dialogic Imagination"; and Lurana Donnels O'Malley, "Pressing Clothes / Snapping Beans / Reading Books."

3. Fredric Jameson borrowed that phrase as a title for his influential book.

4. Comparable is Caryl Churchill's use of Romanian language tapes in *Mad Forest*, although influence is unlikely. My reading of *The Danube* does not quite harmonize with Fornes's own description of "a play about a nice family that is being destroyed" (Betsko & Koenig, *Interviews*, p. 164).

5. Fornes suggests *"that Mr. Kovacs, the Waiter, the Doctor and the Barber be played by the same actor."* Although Ayckbourn uses the same technique in *A Small Family Business* and *Time of My Life*, the effect here is more interrogative than comic. In other words, the same stage device in a different context elicits a different audience reaction.

6. *Top Girls* was preceded by Churchill's all-women plays *Perfect Happiness* (1973) for radio and *Turkish Delight* (1974) for television, neither of which has been published. The version of *Fefu* in *Word Plays* differs slightly from that published in *Performing Arts Journal*, mainly in scenic directions, but also in tightening the final confrontation between Fefu and Julia.

7. That was also the year that, by mutual decision, Churchill's barrister husband left private practice to work in alternative law.

8. Ironically, the final sentence of the introduction to the English translation of *The Hammer* – by Pennethorne Hughes – sustains devaluation of women: "Thousands of men's bodies, and of women's, [the book] sent to a horrifying death." Since women constituted the vast majority of the martyred witches, they merit more than the afterthought "and of women's."

9. I doubt that Churchill realizes how much she has relied on written sources: "Most of the plays I've written have been without any research, from what I already knew or what I imagined" (Betsko & Koenig, *Interviews*, p. 81).

10. Cf. the character added by the director Anne Bogart to her 1992 production of Clare Boothe Luce's 1936 all-woman play *The Women*: "Anne added the character of a washerwoman ... who scrubbed,

172

wiped, mopped or plunged in virtually every scene. This character revealed the pervasive class-consciousness of the play, and represented
the army of women who keep things in shape as other women [top
girls] lunge and plot" (Todd Salovey, "Violently Awake!" *Theatre Forum* [Fall 1992], p. 71).

11. Scrappy notes are Fornes's own way into a play, which never begins
with a blank page.

5. Males articulating women: David Hare and David Rabe

1. Rabe's protagonist bears his own Christian name – a fact he disguised
by listing the author as D. William Rabe.

2. Cf. Rabe's own view of the play: "In *Sticks and Bones* the fundamental
conflict is about how to talk about experience. The family wants to use
clichés. David wants to use poetry" (Savran, *In Their Own Words*,
p. 205). David's "poetry" is less resonant than that of his successors
in Rabe's work, especially Goose and Tomtom. My point, however, is
that the woman Zung is virtually silent, and the woman Harriet wields
fewer clichés than her husband Ozzie.

3. Barnet Kellman supplies a detailed account of Rabe's revisions of *The
Orphan*. As I write – 1993 – Manson has become a cult figure, although
he is serving a life sentence for his brutal murders. Irony is too soft a
word to describe this phenomenon.

4. Although the three-act version of *In the Boom Boom Room* played at
Lincoln Center, Rabe's revision returned to the original two acts.

5. I agree with McMillion's view of the two women in *Goose and Tomtom*
(Zinman, ed., *David Rabe: A Casebook*), but I believe that she oversimpli-
fies this complex Rabe play.

6. I summarize the 1989 Samuel French edition of *Hurlyburly*, which Rabe
prefers to either of the Grove Press editions. The Hollywood plays of
the other two members of the "second generation triumvirate" also
dramatize male bonding – Shepard's *Angel City* and Mamet's *Speed-
the-Plow*.

7. Reinelt has written a measured feminist critique of the women of *Hurlyburly*, to which I am indebted, but she tends to equate the four men,
whereas I believe that Rabe achieved his intention: "The emotional core
of *Hurlyburly* is that Eddie and Phil have to be friends" (Zinman, ed.,
David Rabe: A Casebook, p. 224) .

8. *Knuckle*'s inclusion in the Faber volume of Hare's *The History Plays* is
puzzling, since *Teeth 'n' Smiles*, set in the "revolutionary" year of 1968,
would seem more suitable. Jenny's position is so secondary that John
Bull, in *New British Political Dramatists*, barely mentions her in his
astute analysis of *Knuckle*.

9. Benedict Nightingale, in "An Angry Young Man," comments on Hare's
surprise at receiving letters of thanks for the father–son subject "he
thought not central to it at all."

10. The bare-bones situation resembles Tom Stoppard's *Night and Day,* where a woman in Africa (rather than Asia) is erotically involved with two English journalists. See Cave, *New British Drama,* for a much more sympathetic view of Peggy.
11. Hare's film of *Plenty* displaced Kate Nelligan with the film star Meryl Streep, and he revised the flashback to straight chronology. The product is a conventional film, about which Hare confessed to Georg Gaston: "I found the work of turning the play into a screenplay extremely difficult." And – I would add – unsatisfactory.
12. Hare directed *Plenty* to preserve the ambiguity as to whether we see Susan's drug-induced fantasy or her memory of actual events. See, for example, Mel Gussow's review in *The New York Times* (July 30, 1978).
13. The London production of *Secret Rapture* titillated by its Edwina Currie details, whereas the New York production leaned on Margaret Thatcher. The latter version was the occasion of Hare's heated diatribe against the *New York Times* reviewer, Frank Rich.
14. Strapless gowns are, however, a faulty metaphor for female independence.
15. Habituated to the intimacy of television, Thaw played intimate scenes close up, "leaving vast open spaces on the huge stage of the Olivier. . . . The director, Richard Eyre, had to tell him: 'You've got to stand 15 yards away and yell. Yell quietly'" (*The Observer*, 3 October 1993, p. 23).
16. The harshest judgment of Hare's women characters charges: "Essentially, Hare does not write about women at all but as blanks on which he can imprint an external, male pressure; and to such pressure they respond only with pain or madness or, if they are secondary characters, with baffled dismay" (Chambers & Prior, *Playwrights' Progress,* p. 186). It is true that Hare's women suffer male pressure, but that pressure erupts into their articulate scorn for the established verities. It is also true that Hare's secondary women characters are often dismayed, but they are rarely baffled. Gradually, Hare's respect has grown for his women protagonists – Maggie Frisby, Susan Traherne, Jean Travers, and Dr. Lillian Hempel, but only PC Sandra Bingham and barrister Irina Platt virtually dispense with masculine succor.
    A cogent article on the whole question of Western conscience-carrying women was written by Katha Pollitt, "Are Women Morally Superior to Men?" *The Nation* (December 28, 1992).

6. Englobing intimacies: Christopher Hampton and Richard Nelson

1. Hampton garnered early plaudits because his first play was produced when he was still in his teens. Nelson caught the influential attention of

Michael Billington, who protested in 1992 against the early closing of the RSC production of his *Columbus,* a large play that does not fit my scheme.

2. *Marya* is not mentioned in the *Sunset Boulevard* program, which lists Hampton's translations: "Four plays by Ibsen; two plays by Molière; three plays by Odön von Horváth; and Chekhov's *Uncle Vanya.*"

3. At the time this statement was made Hampton could not have predicted his involvement in a mammoth musical, *Sunset Boulevard* (1993).

4. Ann Wilson seems to me dead wrong in her use of *When Did You Last* as a weapon to bludgeon Freud. Hampton does not replace "the [homophobic] censure of the state . . . by that of the playwright" ("Love Under Censure," in Gross, ed., *Christopher Hampton: A Casebook,* p. 37). What the play censures – if anything – is self-serving cruelty, regardless of sexual orientation.

5. Nelson first uses projections in *Between East and West* (1984), and he thereafter remains partial to them.

6. I disagree with Ann Wilson's reading of the play as "an implicit castigation of homosexuality" ("Love Under Censure," in Gross, ed., *Christopher Hampton: A Casebook,* p. 37). What concerns Hampton is the effect of sexuality on poetry – a difficult concern to dramatize, and yet *Total Eclipse* has been widely staged. It is Hampton's favorite among his plays.

7. The published play does, however, list his scholarly sources, including the complete poems of both poets.

8. I believe Nelson's intention was to contrast the two approaches to staging Shakespeare, but the RSC production seemed to me a rather facile caricature of both *Macbeths,* as well as of *Metamora.* No reviewer suggests this, so perhaps the particular performance I saw suffered a lapse into the "grotesque exaggeration" mentioned by Nelson. The American dramatist also makes Forrest a political innocent, rather than the jingoist depicted by Jeffrey D. Mason in "The Politics of *Metamora,*" in *The Performance of Power,* Sue-Ellen Case and Janelle Reinelt, eds., Iowa City: U. of Iowa Press, 1991.

9. Ben Cameron reads *The Philantropist: A Bourgeois Comedy* with discernment in Gross (ed., *Christopher Hampton: A Casebook*), and I am indebted to his insights.

10. Besides inventing the originating circumstances of *Baal* (which he claimed was written in four days on a bet), Brecht revised the play several times and published four somewhat different versions. Details are given in the Editorial Note of vol. I of Brecht's *Complete Plays* (which are not yet complete).

In a personal communication Richard Nelson has informed me that he thinks of his *Bal* as a descendant, rather than an adaptation, of Brecht. He wished to oppose Brecht's immoral character with an amoral one, but I find moral standards confused in both plays.

11. Hampton adapted Laclos's novel *Les Liaisons Dangereuses* for stage (1985) and screen (1988), rewarding him financially. Hampton's *The White Chameleon* (1990) draws both upon his own life and contemporary history, and I would call it a middle-scale play, which eludes his classification.

12. "Yugoslavia" rings today with grim irony; yet it reinforces Hampton's point about Horváth's cosmopolitanism, in contrast with the insularity of the Hollywood Germans.

13. Hampton's scenic directions require Horváth to speak with no accent when he addresses the audience directly, or converses with other émigrés, but with Americans he has an accent. There was, however, slippage, both in the London production and the 1992 TV adaptation (*American Playhouse*, October 19; BBC, *Performance Strand*, November 14). Nelson uses a similar strategy for his Czech refugees in *Between East and West* (1984). In Nelson's *Misha's Party* (1993), set in Moscow: "The characters in the play all speak the same language, regardless of what country they come from." Intellectuals all, the lexicons are similar, and impervious to accents.

14. In Nelson's familiar mode he signals these scene changes by projections.

15. One of the plays they see is *Les Liaisons Dangereuses*, Hampton's adaptation of the Laclos novel, which Nelson wittily mentions when we first learn that two faculty members (one married) have been sleeping together.

Bibliography

Chapter 1

Quotations from Simon's plays are taken from the three volumes of the Random House edition and the single volume of *Lost in Yonkers*. *Jake's Women* is published only in the Samuel French acting edition (1993).

Quotations from Ayckbourn's plays are taken from the individual Faber volumes.

CRITICISM OF AYCKBOURN

Billington, Michael, *Alan Ayckbourn*, London: Macmillan, 1990.
Dukore, Bernard, ed., *Alan Ayckbourn: A Casebook*, New York: Garland, 1991.
Joseph, Stephen, *Theatre in the Round*, London: Barrie & Rockliff, 1967.
Kalson, Albert E., "Alan Ayckbourn," pp. 15–32 in Stanley Weintraub, ed., *Dictionary of Literary Biography: British Dramatists Since World War II*, vol. 13, pt. 1, Detroit: Gale, 1982.
    Laughter in the Dark: The Plays of Alan Ayckbourn, London: Fairleigh Dickinson U. Press, 1993.
Page, Malcolm, *File on Ayckbourn*, London: Methuen, 1989.
Watson, Ian, *Conversations with Ayckbourn*, London: Macdonald, 1981.
White, Sydney, *Alan Ayckbourn*, Boston: G. K. Hall, 1984.

CRITICISM OF SIMON

Johnson, Robert K., *Neil Simon*, Boston: G. K. Hall, 1983.
McGovern, Edythe M., *Neil Simon: A Critical Study*, New York: Frederick Ungar, 1979.
Meryman, Richard, "When America's Funniest Writer Turned Serious," *Life* (May 7, 1971), 60B–83.
Simon, Neil, "Make 'em Laugh," interview with Clive Hirschhorn, *Plays and Players* 24(12) (September 1977), 12–15.

Chapter 2

Quotations from Bond's plays are taken from the three volumes of the Methuen edition.

Quotations from Shepard are taken from the following:

Melodrama Play, Cowboy Mouth, Angel City, and *Suicide in B-Flat* from *Fool for Love and other plays,* New York: Bantam, 1984;
Mad Dog Blues from *Unseen Hand and other plays,* New York: Bantam, 1986;
True Dylan from *Esquire* (July 1987), 59–67;
the remainder from *Sam Shepard: Seven Plays,* New York: Bantam, 1981.

CRITICISM OF BOND

Coult, Tony, *The Plays of Edward Bond,* 2d ed., London: Methuen, 1979.
Esslin, Martin, "Nor Yet a 'Fool' to Fame . . ." *Theatre Quarterly* 6(21) (Spring 1976), 39–44.
Hay, Malcolm, and Roberts, Philip, *Bond: A Study of His Plays,* London: Methuen, 1980.
Edward Bond: A Companion to the Plays, London: TQ Publications, 1978.
Hirst, David, *Edward Bond,* London: Macmillan, 1985.
Roberts, Philip, "The Search for Epic Drama: Edward Bond's Recent Work," *Modern Drama* 24(4) (December 1981), 458–78.
Bond on File, London: Methuen, 1985.
Scharine, Richard, *The Plays of Edward Bond,* Lewisburg, Pa.: Bucknell U. Press, 1976.
Spencer, Jenny S., *Dramatic Strategies in the Plays of Edward Bond,* Cambridge: Cambridge U. Press, 1992.
Wardle, Irving, "Interview with William Gaskill," *Gambit* 17 (1970), 38–42.

CRITICISM OF SHEPARD

Callens, Johan, "Between the Margin and the Center," Introduction to Brussels Shepard Symposium (May 1993), unpub.; available from author at Vreie Universitet of Brussels.
Chubb, Kenneth, "Fruitful Difficulties of Directing Shepard," *Theatre Quarterly* 4(15) (Aug.–Oct. 1974), 17–26.
DeRose, David, *Sam Shepard,* New York: Twayne, 1992.
Dugdale, John, *File on Shepard,* London: Methuen, 1989.
Hart, Lynda, *Shepard's Metaphorical Stage,* New York: Greenwood, 1987.
King, Kimball, ed., *Sam Shepard: A Casebook,* New York: Garland, 1989.
Kleb, William, "Sam Shepard," pp. 387–419 in Kolin, ed., *American Playwrights Since 1945.*
"Worse Than Being Homeless: *True West* and the Divided Self," pp. 117–25 in Marranca, ed., *American Dreams.*
Leverett, James, "Old Forms Enter the New American Theater," in Gerould, ed., *Melodrama.*

Bibliography

Marranca, Bonnie, ed., *American Dreams: The Imagination of Sam Shepard*, New York: Performing Arts Journal Publications, 1981.

Mottram, Ron, *Inner Landscapes: The Theater of Sam Shepard*, Columbia, Mo.: U. Missouri Press, 1984.

Oumano, Ellen, *Sam Shepard: The Life and Work of an American Dreamer*, New York: St. Martin's Press, 1986.

Shewey, Don, *Sam Shepard*, New York: Dell, 1985.

Tucker, Martin, *Sam Shepard*, New York: Ungar, 1992.

Wilcox, Leonard, "West's *The Day of the Locust* and Shepard's *Angel City*: Refiguring L.A. *Noir*," *Modern Drama* 36(1) (March 1993), 61–75.

   ed., *Rereading Shepard*, London: Macmillan, 1993.

Chapter 3

Quotations from Pinter's work are taken from the four-volume Methuen edition, except for the single-volume *Moonlight* (Faber).

Quotations from Mamet's work are taken from the Grove Press editions of his plays.

CRITICISM OF PINTER

The criticism on Pinter voluminously overtakes that on any living British playwright. My list is therefore selective.

Arden, John, "Telling a True Tale," *Encore* (May 1960); reprinted pp. 125–8 in Marowitz et al., eds., *The Encore Reader*.

Bensky, Lawrence, "Harold Pinter: An Interview," *Paris Review* (Fall 1960); reprinted pp. 19–33 in Ganz, ed., *Pinter*.

Ben-Zvi, Linda, "Harold Pinter's *Betrayal*: The Patterns of Banality," *Modern Drama* 23(3) (September 1980), 27–37.

Bold, Alan, ed., *Harold Pinter: You Never Heard Such Silence*, London: Vision Press, 1984.

Brown, John Russell, *Theatre Language: A Study of Arden, Osborne, Pinter, and Wesker*, London: Allen Lane, 1972.

Diamond, Elin, *Pinter's Comic Play*, Lewisburg, Pa.: Bucknell U. Press, 1985.

Dukore, Bernard, *Harold Pinter*, 2d ed., London: Macmillan, 1988.

Esslin, Martin, *Pinter: A Study of His Plays*, 3d ed., London: Eyre Methuen, 1977.

Gale, Steven H., *Butter's Going Up: A Critical Analysis of Harold Pinter's Work*, Durham, N.C.: Duke U. Press, 1977.

Ganz, Arthur, ed., *Pinter: A Collection of Critical Essays*, Englewood Cliffs, N.J.: Prentice–Hall, 1972.

Gordon, Lois, ed., *Harold Pinter: A Casebook*, London: Garland, 1990.

Kennedy, Andrew, *Dramatic Dialogue*, Cambridge: Cambridge U. Press, 1983.

Bibliography

Six Dramatists in Search of a Language, Cambridge: Cambridge U. Press, 1975.

Packard, William, "An Interview with Harold Pinter," *First Stage* (Summer 1967).

Page, Malcolm, *File on Pinter,* London: Methuen, 1992.

Quigley, Austin, *The Pinter Problem,* Princeton, N.J.: Princeton U. Press, 1975.

Wardle, Irving, "There's Music in That Room," *Encore* (July 1960); reprinted pp. 129–31 in Marowitz et al., *The Encore Reader.*

CRITICISM OF MAMET

Bigsby, C. W. E., "David Mamet," pp. 251–90 in *A Critical Introduction,* vol. 3.

Carroll, Dennis, *David Mamet,* London: Macmillan, 1987.

Dean, Anne, *David Mamet: Language as Dramatic Action,* Rutherford, N.J.: Fairleigh Dickinson U. Press, 1990.

"Musings on Mamet," *Drama* 3(169) (1988), 25–6.

Gussow, Mel, "The Daring Visions of Four New Young Playwrights," *New York Times* (13 February 1977) 2:1, 16.

Hubert-Leibler, Pascale, "Dominance and Anguish: The Teacher–Student Relationship in the Plays of David Mamet," *Modern Drama* 31(4) (December 1988), 557–70.

Jones, Nesta, and Dykes, Steven, *File on Mamet,* London: Methuen, 1991.

Kane, Leslie, "Time Passages," *Pinter Review* (1990), 30–49.

ed., *David Mamet: A Casebook,* New York: Garland, 1992.

Roudané, Matthew C., "An Interview with David Mamet," *Studies in American Drama 1945–Present* 1 (1986), 73–82.

Schlueter, June, and Forsyth, Elizabeth, "America as Junkshop: The Business Ethic in David Mamet's *American Buffalo,*" *Modern Drama* 26(4) (December 1983), 492–500.

Stafford, Tony J., "*Speed-the-Plow* and *Speed the Plough*: The Work of the Earth," *Modern Drama* 36(1) (March 1993), 38–47.

Van Leer, David, "Speed-the-Brow," *New Republic* (October 29, 1990), 32–8.

Wetzsteon, Ross, "New York Letter," *Plays and Players* 23(12) (September 1976), 37, 39.

Zinman, Toby Silverman, "Jewish Aporia: The Rhythm of Talking in Mamet," *Theatre Journal* 44(2) (May 1992), 207–15.

Chapter 4

Quotations from Caryl Churchill's work are taken from the two volumes of her plays published by Methuen; and from *Shorts,* London: Nick Hern Books, 1990 (*Schreber's Nervous Illness, The Hospital at the Time of the Revolution*).

Bibliography

Quotations from the work of Maria Irene Fornes are taken from:

Promenade and other plays, New York: Winter House, 1971 (*A Vietnamese Wedding, The Red Burning Light Or: Mission XQ3, Dr. Kheal, Molly's Dream, Tango Palace, The Successful Life of 3, Promenade*);

Plays, New York: Performing Arts Journal Publications, 1986 (*Mud, The Danube, The Conduct of Life, Sarita,* and an Introduction by Susan Sontag);

Fefu and Her Friends, first published in *Performing Arts Journal* 2(3) (Winter 1978), 112–40, republished in *Wordplays*, New York: Performing Arts Journal Publications, 1980;

Abingdon Square, in *American Theatre* (February 1988), sep. pag.;

Terra Incognita, in *Theater* 24(2) (1993), 99–111.

CRITICISM OF CHURCHILL

Cousin, Geraldine, *Churchill the Playwright*, London: Methuen, 1989.

Fitzsimmons, Linda, *File on Churchill*, London: Methuen, 1989.

" 'I won't turn back for you or anyone': Caryl Churchill's Socialist–Feminist Theatre," *Essays in Theatre* (November 1987), pp. 19–23.

Ignatieff, Michael, "A Punishing Routine," *Times Literary Supplement* (January 20, 1984), p. 62.

Kritzer, Amelia Howe, *The Plays of Caryl Churchill*, Basingstoke: Macmillan, 1991.

Randall, Phyllis R., ed., *Caryl Churchill: A Casebook*, New York: Garland, 1988.

Ritchie, Rob, ed., *The Joint Stock Book*, London: Methuen, 1987.

Watts, Janet, "Interview with Churchill," *Guardian* (February 3, 1977), p. 9.

Weintraub, Erica Beth, "Caryl Churchill," pp. 118–24 in Stanley Weintraub, ed., *Dictionary of Literary Biography: British Dramatists Since World War II*, vol. 13, pt. 1, Detroit: Gale, 1982.

CRITICISM OF FORNES

Austin, Gayle, "The Madwoman in the Spotlight," pp. 76–85 in Hart, ed., *Making a Spectacle*.

Betsko, Kathleen, and Koenig, Rachel, "María Irene Fornès," pp. 154–67 in *Interviews with Contemporary Women Playwrights*.

Cummings, Scott T., "Notes on Fornès, Fefu and the Play of Thought," *Ideas & Production* (8) (1988), 91–103.

Gruber, William, "Individuality and Communality in Maria Irene Fornes's *The Danube*," pp. 179–94 in Roudané, ed., *Public Issues, Private Tensions*.

Keyssar, Helene, "Drama and the Dialogic Imagination: *The Heidi Chronicles* and *Fefu and Her Friends*," *Modern Drama* 34(1) (March 1991), 90–106.

Marranca, Bonnie, "The State of Grace: Maria Irene Fornes at Sixty-Two," *Performing Arts Journal* 14(2) (May 1992), 24–31.

Bibliography

O'Malley, Lurana Donnels, "Pressing Clothes / Snapping Beans / Reading Books: Maria Irene Fornes's Women's Work," *Studies in American Drama 1945–Present* 4 (1989), 103–18.

Pevitts, Beverly, "*Fefu and Her Friends*," pp. 314–17 in Chinoy & Jenkins, eds., *Women in American Theatre*.

Wetzsteon, Ross, "Irene Fornès: The Elements of Style," *Village Voice* (29 April 1986), 42–5.

Wolf, Stacey, "Re/Presenting Gender, Re/Presenting Violence: Feminism, Form and the Plays of María Irene Fornès," *Theatre Studies* 37 (1992), 17–31.

Zinman, Toby, "Hen in a Foxhouse," pp. 203–20 in Enoch Brater and Ruby Cohn, eds., *Around the Absurd*, Ann Arbor: U. Michigan Press, 1990.

Chapter 5

Quotations from Rabe's plays are taken from the following editions:

The Basic Training of Pavlo Hummel and *Sticks and Bones*, New York: Viking, 1973;

In the Boom Boom Room, revised to the original two acts, New York: Grove, 1986;

The Orphan, New York: Samuel French, 1975;

Hurlyburly, New York: Samuel French, 1985;

Goose and Tomtom, New York: Grove, 1987.

Quotations from Hare's plays are taken from the Faber single-play editions, except *Knuckle*, *Licking Hitler*, and *Plenty*, which are grouped as *The History Plays*, London: Faber & Faber, 1984. I have also consulted his *Asking Around*, London: Faber & Faber, 1993.

CRITICISM OF RABE

Kellman, Barnet, "David Rabe's *The Orphan*," *Theatre Quarterly* 7(25) (1977), 72–93.

Kolin, Philip, *David Rabe: A Stage History and a Primary and Secondary Bibliography*, New York: Garland, 1988.

Zinman, Toby Silverman, ed., *David Rabe: A Casebook*, New York: Garland, 1991.

CRITICISM OF HARE

Dean, Joan FitzPatrick, *David Hare*, Boston: Twayne, 1990.

Gaston, Georg, "Interview: David Hare," *Theatre Journal* 45(2) (May 1993), 213–25.

Hare, David, *Asking Around*, London: Faber & Faber, 1993.
  "From Portable Theatre to Joint Stock ... via Shaftesbury Avenue," *Theatre Quarterly* 5(20) (December 1975–February 1976), 108–15.
  Interview in *Time Out* (April 7, 1978), 15.

Bibliography

Myerson, Jonathan, "David Hare: Fringe Graduate," *Drama* (149) (Autumn 1983), 26–8.

Nightingale, Benedict, "An Angry Young Man of the Eighties Brings His Play to New York," *New York Times* (October 17, 1982), 2:1.

Oliva, Judy Lee, *David Hare: Theatricalizing Politics*, Ann Arbor: UMI Research Press, 1990.

Page, Malcolm, *File on Hare*, London: Methuen, 1990.

Chapter 6

Quotations from Hampton's plays are taken from the Faber editions, except for *When Did You Last See My Mother?*, New York: Grove, 1967.

Quotations from Nelson's plays are taken from the Faber editions, except for *Bal*, published in *An American Comedy and Other Plays*, New York: Performing Arts Journal Publications, 1984.

CRITICISM OF HAMPTON

Hampton, Christopher (with Kidd, Robert, and Scofield, Paul), "Christopher Hampton's 'Savages' at the Royal Court Theatre," *Theatre Quarterly* 3(12) (October–December 1973), 60–78.

Bayley, Clare, "Profile," *Theatre* (4 July 1991).

Black, Sebastian, "Makers of Real Shapes: Christopher Hampton and His Story-Tellers," *Modern Drama* 25(2) (June 1982), 207–21.

Esslin, Martin, "In Search of 'Savages,'" *Theatre Quarterly* 3(12) (October–December 1973), 79–83.

Gross, Robert, ed., *Christopher Hampton: A Casebook*, New York: Garland, 1990.

CRITICISM OF NELSON

Jackson, Kevin, "Principles of the Faculty," *Independent* (12 July 1989), 15.

General bibliography

Abel, Elizabeth, ed., *Writing and Sexual Difference*, Brighton: Harvester, 1982.

Barnes, Philip. *A Companion to Post-war British Theatre*, London: Croom Helm, 1986.

Barr, Pat, *A Curious Life for a Lady: The Story of Isabella Bird*, London: Secker & Warburg, 1970.

Berkowitz, Gerald M., *American Drama of the Twentieth Century*, London: Longman, 1992.

Betsko, Kathleen, and Koenig, Rachel, *Interviews with Contemporary Women Playwrights*, New York: Beech Tree Books, 1987.

Bigsby, C. W. E., *A Critical Introduction to Twentieth-Century American Drama*, vol. 3, Cambridge: Cambridge U. Press, 1985.

ed., *Contemporary English Drama*, London: Edward Arnold, 1981.

Birch, David, *The Language of Drama*, London: Macmillan, 1991.

Bock, Hedwig, and Wertheim, Albert, eds., *Essays on Contemporary British Drama*, Munich: Max Hueber, 1981.

Brater, Enoch, ed., *Feminine Focus*, New York: Oxford, 1989.

Brazell, Karen, trans., *The Confessions of Lady Nijo*, London: Peter Owen, 1973.

Brown, John Russell, ed., *Modern British Dramatists*, Englewood Cliffs, N.J.: Prentice–Hall, 1984.

Bull, John, *New British Political Dramatists*, London: Macmillan, 1984.

Cave, Richard Allen, *New British Drama in Performance on the London Stage 1970–1985*, Gerrards Cross: Colin Smythe, 1987.

Chambers, Colin, and Prior, Mike, *Playwrights' Progress*, Oxford: Amber Lane, 1987.

Chinoy, Helen Krich, and Jenkins, Linda Walsh, eds., *Women in American Theatre*, New York: Theatre Communications Group, 1987.

Chothia, Jean, *Forging a Language: A Study of the Plays of Eugene O'Neill*, Cambridge: Cambridge U. Press, 1979.

Cohn, Ruby, *New American Dramatists 1960–1990*, Basingstoke: Macmillan, 1991.

Cornish, Roger, and Ketels, Violet, eds., *Landmarks of British Drama*, New York: Methuen, 1986.

Culler, Jonathan, *On Puns*, Oxford: Blackwell, 1988.

Davison, Peter, *Aspects of Drama and Theatre*, Sydney: Sydney U. Press, 1965.

Contemporary Drama and the Popular Dramatic Tradition in England, London: Macmillan, 1982.

Felski, Rita, *Beyond Feminist Aesthetics*, London: Hutchinson, 1989.

Figes, Eva, *Patriarchal Attitudes*, New York: Stein & Day, 1970.

Ganz, Margaret, "Schreber's *Memoirs of My Nervous Illness*: Art Proscribed," pp. 251–91 in *Humor, Irony, and the Realm of Madness*, New York: AMS Press, 1990.

Geis, Deborah R., *Postmodern Theatric[k]s*, Ann Arbor: U. Michigan Press, 1993.

Gerould, Daniel, ed., *Melodrama*, New York: New York Literary Forum, 1980.

Grossmann, Fritz, *Peter Breugel, Complete Edition of the Paintings*, London: Phaedon, 1973.

Hart, Lynda, ed., *Making a Spectacle*, Ann Arbor: U. Michigan Press, 1989.

Herman, William, *Understanding Contemporary American Drama*, Columbia, S.C.: U. South Carolina Press, 1987.

Hitchens, Christopher, *Blood, Class and Nostalgia: Anglo–American Ironies*, London: Chatto & Windus, 1990.

Hornby, Richard, *Drama, Metadrama and Perception*, Lewisburg, Pa.: Bucknell U. Press, 1986.

Innes, Christopher, *Modern British Drama 1890–1990*, Cambridge: Cambridge U. Press, 1992.

Itzin, Catherine, *Stages in the Revolution*, London: Methuen, 1980.

Kennedy, Andrew, *Dramatic Dialogue*, Cambridge: Cambridge U. Press, 1983.

Six Dramatists in Search of a Language, Cambridge: Cambridge U. Press, 1975.

Kerensky, Oleg, *The New British Drama*, New York: Taplinger, 1977.

Kolin, Philip C., ed., *American Playwrights Since 1945: A Guide to Scholarship, Criticism, and Performance*, Westport, Conn.: Garland, 1989.

Leech, Geoffrey N., *A Linguistic Guide to English Poetry*, London: Longman, 1969; 1991 ed.

McCrindle, Joseph F., ed., *Behind the Scenes: Theatre and Film Interviews from the Transatlantic Review*, New York: Viking, 1971.

Malkin, Jeanette R., *Verbal Violence in Contemporary Drama*, Cambridge: Cambridge U. Press, 1992.

Manheim, Ralph, and Willett, John, *Collected Plays of Bertolt Brecht*, vol. I, New York: Vintage, 1971.

Marowitz, Charles, Milne, Tom, and Hale, Owen, eds., *The Encore Reader*, London: Methuen, 1965.

Marranca, Bonnie, *Theatrewritings*, New York: Performing Arts Journal Publications, 1984.

Marranca, Bonnie, and Dasgupta, Gautam, *American Playwrights*, New York: Drama Book Specialists, 1981.

Maschler, Tom, ed., *Declaration*, London: MacGibbon & Kee, 1959.

Parker, Dorothy, ed., *Essays on Modern American Drama*, Toronto: U. Toronto Press, 1987.

Partridge, Eric, *Dictionary of Slang*, London: Routledge, 1984.

Quigley, Austin, *The Modern Stage and Other Worlds*, Methuen: New York, 1985.

Roberts, Peter, *Theatre in Britain*, London: Pitman, 1975.

Rogoff, Gordon, *Theatre Is Not Safe*, Evanston, Ill.: Northwestern U. Press, 1987.

Roudané, Matthew Charles, ed., *Public Issues, Private Tensions*, New York: AMS Press, 1992.

Rusinko, Susan, *British Drama 1950 to the Present*, Boston: Twayne, 1989.

Savran, David, *Communists, Cowboys, and Queers*, Minneapolis: U. Minnesota Press, 1992.

In Their Own Words, New York: Theatre Communications Group, 1988.

Schlueter, June, ed., *Feminist Rereadings of Modern American Drama*, Cranbury, N.J.: Associated University Presses, 1989.

Schreber, Daniel Paul, *Memoirs of My Nervous Illness*, trans. Ida Macalpine and Richard A. Hunter, London: Dawson, 1955.

Wandor, Michelene, *Look Back in Gender*, London: Methuen, 1987.

Winkler, Elizabeth Hale, *The Function of Song in Contemporary British Drama*, Newark: U. Delaware Press, 1990.

Worth, Katharine, *Revolutions in Modern English Drama*, London: G. Bell & Sons, 1973.

Zeifman, Hersh, and Zimmerman, Cynthia, eds., *Contemporary British Drama 1970–90*, Basingstoke: Macmillan, 1993.

Index of plays and playwrights

Plays

Playwrights